Management Lives

Management Lives

Power and Identity
in
Work Organizations

David Knights
and
Hugh Willmott

SAGE Publications
London • Thousand Oaks • New Delhi

SAGE Publications Ltd
6 Bonhill Street
London EC2A 4PU

SAGE Publications Inc.
2455 Teller Road
Thousand Oaks, California 91320

SAGE Publications India Pvt Ltd
32, M-Block Market
Greater Kailash – I
New Delhi 110 048

British Library Cataloguing in Publication data

A catalogue record for this book is available
from the British Library

ISBN 0 8039 8333 6
ISBN 0 8039 8334 4 (pbk)

Library of Congress catalog card number available

Typeset by Mayhew Typesetting, Rhayader, Powys
Printed in Great Britain by Redwood Books,
Trowbridge, Wiltshire

Contents

Preface

> The mind is primarily concerned, not with measures and locations, but with being and meaning.[1]

This book has been long in its genesis. The original idea to write such a text occurred several years, and almost as many draft manuscripts, ago. It is the product of a teaching collaboration on a course that we have developed over many years.

Background

The idea for the book was prompted initially by our understanding of managing as an everyday activity that involves interactions between people – interactions that are not unrelated or entirely dissimilar to other spheres of life, except perhaps in the rhetoric and hype that surround management. Since most management textbooks do not make the connection between managing and everyday life, and indeed envelop the activity of management within an academic and professional mystique, we have been drawn to alternative sources (e.g. novels) that might enable students to relate accounts of management to their own experience.

Approach

The title *Management Lives!* is intended to be ambiguous and a little controversial. It is concerned to illuminate the *lives* of people who, in different ways, are involved or affected by management. It includes those expressly identified as managers, but it extends to others who are managed, including the customers that are increasingly the targets of a competitive preoccupation with customer 'care' and service programmes. We refrain from treating management from the point of view of a set of theories and or a series of techniques that examine what are assumed to be effective yet diverse ways of managing (e.g. motivation, leadership, training, organizational structure). Instead, we seek to address *managing* as a vibrant, complex, challenging and even exciting human experience. Our approach is designed to counter the image of management as a branch of science or engineering, and to encourage an appreciation of managing as part and parcel of life and how it is *lived*.

This approach accords with a more general recognition among teachers that education is best facilitated where students identify with, and are actively involved in, the learning process. In order to 'make management live', we explore the lives of those who are touched by it, using the concepts of power, inequality, identity and insecurity to guide and enrich our analysis. In our view, these key concepts are central for understanding so many facets of human life – from work to the family, from business to leisure, from reproduction to sexuality and from the sacred to the profane.

Instead of organizing our course around established topics or focusing on the writings of authorities in management – such as Maslow, Fiedler or Mintzberg – we have encouraged our students to read more widely from a literature that would not conventionally be on a management syllabus. This has included the writings of Erich Fromm, Robert Pirsig and Harry Braverman, for example. We have also encouraged them to read a number of novels that offer a fictional exploration of central ideas in the course. A majority of students found the ideas explored in these texts more relevant to them personally and stimulating intellectually than the staple diet of management textbooks and associated readings. At the same time, they found a challenge in the invitation to read novels in a different, more reflexive and analytical way – as illustrative of ideas rather than just a good story. It could also be disturbing when, in contrast to management texts, students made connections between the ideas explored in the novels and their own lives and relationships. In sum, this book is less concerned with the specific and detailed, 'technical' functions of management, as described in most textbooks, than with the ways in which these technical activities affect the lives of managers. On the other hand, we are not concerned with the lives of management as a piece of voyeurism, as might be a journalist, so much as how the lives of managers, in the broadest sense, affect their work.

Students told us that the novels we recommended made what we were seeking to communicate more accessible and meaningful. Otherwise rather abstract ideas that previously had been perceived to have relevance only for passing exams suddenly came alive. The enthusiasm encouraged us to move further in this direction. Instead of simply providing an extensive list of novels that might be read by students as a supplement to more orthodox literature, we began integrating a small selection of these novels into the course. Gradually, they became primary rather than secondary reading and this book is a reflection of that evolutionary development in the course.

Usage

Since we began to use novels in the mid-1980s, we have discovered that their use in teaching management students is not as unique as we first thought. Colleagues elsewhere have told us how they also use novels to illuminate particular ideas or to leaven otherwise technical treatments of aspects of management. However, we believe this book is the first to integrate the use of novels within a conceptual framework for analysing the lived experience of management.

This highlights the limitations of, and offers an innovative alternative to, the use of textbooks for teaching students of management. Based on our experience of teaching final-year undergraduates who were consistently attracted to the course in above-average numbers, this book is perhaps even more relevant to postgraduate and MBA students who have completed a first degree and may have had some industrial experience. In order to champion a different approach, we have adopted a deliberately polemical tone and approach. We anticipate that this book will be used by a growing number of management academics that are critical of the conventional content of textbooks and experimental in their approach to pedagogic methods. Exceptionally, it may be adopted as an alternative to established textbooks. But we are not quite so arrogant as to deny the value of a good textbook in providing an introductory guide to a particular field of knowledge. More usually, this book will complement the continuing use of one or more textbooks to provide a different or fresh perspective. Encouraging students to read and debate both kinds of text can, we believe, facilitate the development of a more critical, questioning approach to the study of management.

Acknowledgements

In the preparation of this book we have been most indebted to our students who have helped shape its development and, in particular, those who taught on the course at different times. These are too many to mention but include: Frank Daniel, Jeff Simm, David Collinson, Deborah Kerfoot, John Roberts, Mike Shaoul, James Smith, Frank Worthington, Edward Wray-Bliss and Jo Brewis. This book is dedicated to them. We are also very grateful to Chris Grey, who taught on the course for a number of years and who has read and commented in detail on earlier drafts of the chapters. Irene Field and Philip Wooley also kindly commented on earlier draft chapters. We thank Sue Jones who originally encouraged us to undertake this project and Rosemary Nixon who has been patiently supportive in getting us to complete it. Finally, thanks go to Helen Dean, Mary O'Brien and Helen Ireson for their patience in retyping endless versions of the manuscript.

Note

1 Huxley, A. (1959) *The Doors of Perception and Heaven and Hell*. Harmondsworth: Penguin. p. 19.

1   Managing Knowledge

> The liberal arts teacher knows that Sophocles and Shakespeare (themselves great students of the art and science of management) will help in the 'real world', but their concrete application by any individual executive is unknown and may remain so.[1]

This book is the product of a series of tensions. Tensions, that is, between writing and teaching, between the calculations of our academic careers and our commitment to students, and between a fascination with the intellectual pursuit of theory and its marginalization in the immediacy of practice. Such tensions are doubtless heightened by moral and political leanings that do not always sit easily with working as management academics. One manifestation of this tension has been a frustration with the established form and content of books on management, including the most widely adopted texts that, in our view, rarely address or strive to understand management as *lived experience*.[a]

We argue that mainstream texts rarely 'capture' either the sense of managerial life at work or the imagination of students who have chosen to study business or management. We begin this chapter by expanding on our interest in developing a text that counteracts the neglect of managerial work as a lived experience. We highlight the limitations of more established genres – the textbook and the guru handbook – for writing about management and organization. A common limitation of the textbooks is that they strive to provide an exhaustive description of the methods and functions of management in a highly abstract manner. A shortcoming of guru handbooks is that their beguiling prescriptions are based on commonsense assumptions that are rarely subjected to close empirical or theoretical scrutiny.

Our view is that knowledge about management benefits from placing it within the broader context of human life and society, and that novels can be of assistance in illuminating the broader aspects of social life. We illustrate this view by drawing on *Nice Work*, a contemporary novel by David Lodge that features in all our chapters. *For convenience, we have included a brief synopsis of this and the other three novels used extensively in this text in Appendix A.* Our discussion of management is guided by a theoretical framework that comprises the central concepts of power,

---

a   A rare exception is Stephen Fineman and Yiannis Gabriel (1996) *Experiencing Organizations*, London: Sage.

inequality, identity and insecurity. These concepts inform our interpretation of the lived experience of managing and organizing in different areas of everyday life, but especially in the workplace. Like all such frameworks, the concepts comprise a set of selection devices that translate the infinity of meanings conceivably attributable to a text, whether it is a novel or a textbook, into a particular narrative. We discuss the elements of our framework towards the end of this chapter and again in Chapter 2.

In addition, Appendix B indicates the relevance of these concepts for the analysis of a wide range of social issues such as gender and ethnicity. We have tried to write a text that is not cluttered by the usual academic paraphernalia. We have therefore kept references to the absolute minimum and consigned them to endnotes. For convenience, more substantive points and comments have been placed in notes at the foot of the relevant page. At the end of each chapter we have indicated readings recommended for further study. Finally, each chapter contains a list of references cited in the footnotes.

The next couple of sections elaborate our concerns about the limitations of more established teaching media. If you are already disillusioned with textbooks and guru handbooks, and share our view that novels can illuminate lived experience, you may prefer to skim or skip these sections.

Against the text

Most established management texts treat their readers as if they – you, we – were comparatively ignorant, passive subjects. This is most apparent in the block-busting, door-stopping texts, some of which come complete with an instructor's manual, overhead transparencies and even a video. The producers of these texts make a Herculean effort to present a comprehensive summary of their subject. An equally Herculean effort is expected from readers in memorizing their contents. As one of our students put it, 'It's as if you're expected to get the model or technique, put it under your belt and say "right, I've got that" and then move immediately to the next bite of information'. Readers are presented with an endless stream of theories, typologies, bloodless descriptions and often patronizing prescriptions that they are expected to absorb in meticulous, mind-numbing detail. As Fineman and Gabriel[2] put it, the image of organizations and their employees emerging from these texts is 'square, solid, structured and imposing'. They continue:

> Rhetorically speaking, this tells the student that the organisational world is essentially like a jigsaw: fathomable, ultimately predictable, and can be assembled once they learn the 'how to' rules. . . . Conspicuously absent are amounts of, for example, chaos, uncertainty, work meanings, emotionality, humour, grief, sexuality, work/non-work interfaces.

Students who are required to slog through such textbooks might well wonder why their education is organized in this way. What possible purpose does this effort serve when, so often, their contents are memorized mindlessly for the purpose of passing exams, only to be forgotten within weeks, if not hours, of the examination?

An explanation, we believe, is to be found in the *symbolic*, not the practical, value of conventional textbooks. Management textbooks contrive to present management as a coherent, respectable body of knowledge, equivalent to the texts used by students of engineering or medicine. Symbolically, textbooks convey an impression of transmitting the specialist expertise that differentiates the knowledge acquired by students of management from other specialisms. In combination with other forms of assessment (e.g. examinations), management textbooks differentiate those who have read or sampled their contents from those who have not.

In his humorous account of his experience of studying for a Masters of Business Administration (MBA)[3] at a prestigious University, Robinson[4] records a fellow student saying, 'When, I start looking for a job, recommendations from Stanford Profs can't hurt'. Like other forms of judgement (e.g. the courts, job interviews and beauty competitions), MBAs form an integral part of dividing one section of the population off from one another. Individuals are divided into the worthy and the unworthy, the acceptable and the unacceptable, the competent and the incompetent – granting power, high earnings and prestige to the former at the expense of the latter. We may moan about the injustice of 'fat cat' salaries in industry or the limited educational opportunities available to those from disadvantaged backgrounds, but we rarely bother to give a moment's thought to inequality more generally. This is particularly so in management texts that promote the practices such as hierarchical and gender divisions that are central to the reproduction of such inequality. At the same time, the body of knowledge collected in textbooks is often found to be irrelevant and even counterproductive as a means of appreciating the contextual dynamics, complexities and diversity of management practice. It is perhaps an intuitive awareness of this 'unreality' that encourages a tendency for texts to be studied ritualistically. The process of memorizing their contents is sensed to be of limited relevance to the lived experience of students, managers and customers.[b]

---

b   Even when (a minority of) texts provide their readers with a critical review of academic scholarship on management and organization, they generally lack an appreciation of managing and organizing as a *lived*, *everyday practice*. With few exceptions (e.g. Sims, Fineman and Gabriel, 1993), most critical texts (e.g. Reed, 1985, 1989; Thompson and McHugh, 1995; Alvesson and Willmott, 1992, 1996) are readily accessible only to advanced or exceptionally diligent students. A number of in-depth ethnographic studies of management encourage a view of managing and organizing as involving continuous processes of 'making out' through processes of interaction and negotiation within complex relationships of power organization (e.g. Pettigrew, 1985; Jackall, 1988; Child, Rowlinson and Smith, 1990; Kunda, 1992; Collinson, 1992; Watson, 1994; Knights and Murray, 1994). However, the insights produced by these studies are rarely incorporated into textbooks.

There is a parallel to be drawn here between management textbooks and manuals written to provide information and instruction for other activities, such as motorcycle maintenance. As Pirsig[5] notes of instruction manuals, the knowledge contained within them is disembodied. It pays little or no attention to the lived experience of motorcycle maintenance:

> it occurred to me that there *is* no manual that deals with the *real* business of motorcycle maintenance, the most important aspect of all. Caring about what you are doing is considered either unimportant or taken for granted.

As Pirsig points out, there is always more to maintaining motorcycles than knowing the contents of the manual. There is, for example, the fostering of an awareness of how a bike runs and sounds. This awareness gives forewarnings of problems that may be developing. In manuals, the component parts of the bike are described but with scant regard for how the parts and systems mesh together. Manuals are unable to provide an awareness and understanding of how any particular bike is performing. The shortcomings of manuals are multiplied when it comes to the lived experience of human beings. Life at work, for example, tends to be far more complex and less predictable than the operation of machines.

Introducing the novel

In established texts, the lived reality of managing and organizing tends to be smothered beneath a jungle of competing models, theories and endless lists of 'key points'. In order to appreciate the living of management, we draw on a number of contemporary novels: principally *Nice Work* (David Lodge), *The Unbearable Lightness of Being* (Milan Kundera), *The Remains of the Day* (Kazuo Ishiguro) and *The Bonfire of the Vanities* (Tom Wolfe).[c] These novels are particularly effective in 'bringing to life' dimensions of human experience, at work and elsewhere, that are rarely acknowledged let

---

c   The potential to entertain and educate is perhaps greatest in novels and films. Even the ethnographer is restricted by the time and access permitted to conduct field research. It is therefore not surprising to find that a number of management academics have been attracted to the use of novels and films in recent years. Since we embarked on preparing this book in the early 1990s, we have been pleased to see the publication of a number of commentaries that resonate with our concerns. Most notable among these is Czarniawska-Joerges and Guillet de Montoux's (1994) edited collection of essays. Other contributions include Perry (1984), Wilkie (1989), Alvarez (1990), Roman (1994), Phillips (1995), Domagalski and Jermier (1995), Grey (1996) and Thompson and McGivern (1996). Nussbaum (1990) offers an extensive discussion of the relevance of novels for the exploration of the human condition in modernity. For a text that explores the relevance of film, see Hassard and Holliday (1998). However, it is relevant to note that, in contrast to the Czarniaswka–Joerges and Guillet de Montoux (1994) reader, our book is an integrated text rather than an edited collection.

alone explored within the established texts on management and organization.[d] This, quite literally, is one novelty of the book. It is fortuitous that *Nice Work* was serialized on BBC television and the other novels were made into films.

From textbook to novel

The novel provides us with a vehicle for bringing our subject matter to life in a way that can make it easier for students to explore the experience of managing and organizing. In place of the narrow, technical and disembodied representation of management evident in most textbooks, we use novels to appreciate how managerial work is no less human and 'troubled' than any other aspect of life, including that of studying for a university degree or teaching students. Of course, there is an obvious problem of credibility in using novels as an aid to understanding management and the organization of work. Classified as fiction, novels are commonsensically placed at the opposite end of the spectrum from management or business studies textbooks – even though much of the content of standard textbooks could be classified by a cynic as poor fiction. Outside the field of literary studies, novels are situated in the world of leisure and entertainment. The espoused purpose of textbooks, in contrast, is to 'educate'; or, more candidly, to enable students to gain qualifications. Even when a novel, such as David Lodge's *Nice Work*, is explicitly about the world of management (in the factory and the university), it is probable that, as readers, managers and academics assess this novel in terms of its capacity to be a 'good read'.

Certainly, when reading a novel it is easy to become engrossed in the narrative, fascinated by the characters, carried away by the story line and anxious to discover what happens next. Conversely there may be a feeling of frustration and disappointment when the novel(ist) is perceived to fail in this mission. Such a 'failure' can occur when the tension slackens or when the narrative is deliberately disrupted in an attempt to render the artifice of its constructed reality more transparent. Novelists want their readers to turn the next page and read their next book; and a variety of devices – 'postmodern' or deconstructive as well as classical – are more or less consciously deployed to permit particular patterns of consumption. But novelists also seek to communicate with, and indeed to 'educate', their readers. Through the medium of the novel, they want to convey their ideas and understandings, which, on occasion, can be in tension with the desire to establish or maintain an 'entertained' readership. We believe that our four chosen novels succeed more than most in being 'educational' as well as delivering a 'good read'.

---

d   Needless to say, there are many, many other novels that could serve our purposes equally well. We hope and anticipate that our framework will be relevant also for appreciating their contribution to the understanding of management as a lived practice.

Nice Work

Consider *Nice Work*.[e] Lodge's novel is an example of classic realism[f] (of a highly self-conscious kind), as exemplified in the work of Dickens, Zola and Sinclair Lewis. As readers, we are drawn by David Lodge into a world that appeals to our taken-for-granted sense of 'kitchen sink' drama that is heightened by elements of (surreal) farce – as, for example, when one evening the managing director finds his secretary 'having it off' with his marketing manager on the sofa in reception. The creation of believable, consistent characters that act 'in character' is perhaps the most important device for sustaining the illusion produced by the novelist. Paradoxically, however, the enticement to read further is often produced by placing the characters in situations where their sense of themselves is challenged and tested.

Characters are made to live dangerously, to face predicaments that, as readers, we experience as vicarious pleasure. We imagine, for example, how a particular character may react or, more importantly, what we would do in similar circumstances. In *Nice Work*, the conservative attitudes of Vic (the managing director) towards work and marriage are tested by a stranger (Robyn, an academic), who disrupts his taken-for-granted sense of reality. She does this by questioning the existence of what Vic has taken for granted, such as the display of soft pornographic posters on the walls of the factory and, more generally, Vic's place (as the dominant male) within a sexist industrial subculture. During the course of the novel, Vic's (experience of) life is transformed. For Lodge, the challenge is to persuade his readers that this change is 'realistic', in the sense of being consistent with the 'character' and circumstances of his hero. To anticipate an understanding that we elaborate in the next chapter, classic realism explores how we derive a sense of security from participation in familiar routines. But it also highlights how routines are made fragile by the dynamics of social change in modern societies.

---

e   For a different but not dissimilar interpretation of *Nice Work* that sets it in the context of other novels that explore British university life in the post-war years, see Carter (1990, esp. pp. 254 *et seq*). See also Grey (1996).

f   Until alternative forms of writing emerged – for example, in the works of D.H. Lawrence, Virginia Woolf, James Joyce, William Burroughs and, more recently, Thomas Pynchon, Don DeLillo or William Gibson – that challenged convention and were (eventually) received with critical acclaim, the novel was widely equated with classic realism. During the 1970s and 1980s, there was widespread experimentation, especially among young American authors, with alternative forms of writing. Classic realism was out of fashion. However, in recent years, there has been a return to the classic form, even by authors whose reputation was built on deviation from convention. Recently, in the introduction to *The Bonfire of the Vanities* (1988), Tom Wolfe has celebrated and defended the power of classic realism to communicate and address issues of contemporary relevance in an accessible way. We echo Wolfe's sentiments as we deploy *Nice Work* to affirm his argument that an important role of the novel is to demonstrate 'the influence of the society on even the most personal aspects of the life of the individual' (Wolfe, 1988, p. xviii).

It may still be objected, nonetheless, that the novel is purely fictional and therefore that it has, at best, a very marginal or supplementary role in the study of management. Certainly, our celebration of the novel as a source of insight into the practice of managing does not sit well with the pretensions of management to be a science, or at least a branch of engineering. One response to those who take 'science' or 'engineering' as a model for management is to point out that, when preparing to write *Nice Work*, Lodge undertook extensive research, visiting factories and interviewing executives. In fundamental respects, his fieldwork did not differ markedly from the methods of ethnographic researchers, especially the work of (industrial) anthropologists. The contention of ethnographers is that the kind of methods employed by Lodge enable the researcher to get closer to the 'reality' of managerial work than does research that relies on impersonal surveys or superficial, predetermined interview schedules. Without necessarily endorsing the strong claim that ethnographic methods give researchers direct access to 'reality', Lodge's informants may well have been less guarded when being interviewed by a novelist than by a management academic. Interviewees may be resistant to the academic researcher because of the possibility that their views and performance are being evaluated and reported to people more senior in the hierarchy. Even where standard assurances of anonymity and confidentiality and so on are accepted, interviewees may feel obliged to represent their work in impersonal or glowing terms in order to be taken seriously as competent 'professionals'. The novelist is less encumbered by the problems of mistrust and 'knowledge management'.

Lodge takes full advantage of his licence as a novelist to *condense* a variety of experiences, which he translates into a dramatic narrative. In contrast, social scientists routinely adopt the conventions of their discipline to present the data as a comparatively dry set of findings. To be clear, we are not asserting that the novel is inherently superior to organizational or management research as a means of making a statement about the social world. Nor are we implying that the novel is unconstrained by its own conventions, not least of which is its practice of bringing the story to a conclusion in a way that contrives a re-established harmony.[g] Instead, we are suggesting that the novel provides a highly accessible medium for exploring themes that are shared by the social scientist.

Accordingly, in this and subsequent chapters, we seek to draw out insights from a number of novels by stopping to reflect on the ideas and understandings that are contained within them. Of course, when we say that we are 'drawing out insights' that are 'contained' in the novels, we are speaking in a loose and rather commonsense manner. A moment's reflection reminds us that these insights arise from *our reading* of the novels – a

---

g   For example, in *Nice Work*, Vic's marriage is renewed as he 'comes to his senses' and Robyn receives a large inheritance that she invests in the new company established by Vic, both of which are devices for bringing the novel to an harmonious end.

reading that, through the medium of this book, we are inviting you to explore. How the author intended the novel to be read is impossible to say. Even authors' own *post hoc* rationalizations cannot be trusted. With the benefit of hindsight (or *post hoc* rationalization), novelists' accounts are likely to be coloured by anticipations of the kind of impression that will be conveyed by their seemingly 'author-itative' versions of a novel's motivation, meaning or central themes. In any event, why should the authority of the author be privileged when alternative interpretations are found to be equally plausible or more illuminating?

Once a book is published, what it means no longer remains the prerogative of the author, as the reader enters the enterprise as a collaborator in constructing the meaning of its narrative. In a 'postmodern' world, the irremediably 'open' and re-interpretable quality of texts, including novels, is being more widely accepted. Though rarely acknowledged, this 'openness' is also present in allegedly non-fiction writings, such as management texts. As we are seeking to emphasize, the distinction between 'fact' and 'fiction' is a constructed one, and therefore is open to deconstruction. A space, however marginal, may then be opened up for ways of making sense of work – for example through the novel – that were previously excluded because they were considered alien and therefore irrelevant for the study of management.

Relevance of the novel

By harnessing the powers of imagination and identification, the novelist enables us to appreciate and explore in greater depth the drama – the tragedy and the comedy – that is present, yet generally unnoticed, in the most mundane of encounters. We have found that practising managers as well as students tend to regard Lodge's fictional portrayal of the realities of managerial work as more telling, thought provoking and accessible than the contents of most established textbooks, guru guides or academic research studies. In part, this is because the novelist enjoys the literary licence to distil and dramatize issues that, at best, appear as brief, formulaic case studies in standard textbooks. Textbook writers, in contrast, are trapped in conventions that require them (to aspire) to be scientific, objective and comprehensive. As Lodge,[6] the author of *Nice Work*, has commented:

> novelistic techniques generate an excitement, intensity and emotive power that orthodox reporting or historiography do not aspire to. . . . The novel itself is a literary form evolved partly out of early journalism – broadsheets, pamphlets, criminals' confessions, accounts of disasters, battles and extraordinary happenings, which were circulated to an eagerly credulous readership as true stories, though they almost certainly contained an element of invention.

Novels, including *Nice Work*, *The Remains of the Day* and *The Bonfire of the Vanities* that pay particular attention to the world of work are especially valuable for our purposes. Yet because people working in organizations, including managers, are first and foremost human beings, insights into the experience and dynamics of life at work can also be derived from novels not ostensibly about work. For example, Kundera's *The Unbearable Lightness of Being* makes only brief references to the world of work, but is nonetheless insightful regarding the politics of working under a totalitarian communist regime. This is a novel about philosophical notions of what is 'really' of value in life, played out against a background of totalitarian repression in a post-Dubcek Czechoslovakia. Nonetheless, it has relevance for our discussion of management precisely because Kundera's exploration of other kinds of social practices can shed light on managing and organizing. Fundamentally, these practices involve interacting with other people in ways that cannot be reduced to the mechanical application of the formulaic models and prescriptions presented in the textbooks. Applying even the most mundane of techniques demands cooperation from people – people who are, in principle, capable of questioning their relevance and, in practice, frequently involved in resisting their intended uses. For this reason, managing and organizing are invariably precarious activities that require continuous practice and cannot avoid repeated failure and/or disruption. It is this precarious, processual and personally lived quality of managerial work that is so effectively and dramatically explored through the craft of the novelist.

It is to be hoped that by now, we have interested or annoyed you sufficiently that you will read on. If you are curious to see how novels might be used to generate insights into the practical experience of managing, you might move on to a later section, 'Managing as lived experience'. For those who remain sceptical but haven't yet returned this book to its shelf, it is worth noting that our analysis is guided by a number of core concepts – *power*, *identity*, *inequality* and *insecurity*. In addition to offering a more systematic way of analysing the practicalities of managing and organizing, these concepts provide a bridge to more familiar ideas and theories drawn from the literature on management and organization. In Chapter 2, we concentrate on introducing and illustrating the elements of this framework; then, in Chapters 3, 4 and 5, we make increasing links to a wider literature on social science and management.

Managing knowledge

There is a tendency, especially in Anglo-American society and in management or business studies courses more specifically, to reduce knowledge to information. Expressed in the form of numerous 'objective' facts, this tendency is evident in the popularity of quizzes that rely on contestants' capacity to memorize information about particular fields or topics. Earlier we alluded to the tendency of management textbooks to reduce knowledge to information, providing students with a seemingly exhaustive or encyclo-paedic set of partially related or unrelated 'facts'. These texts invite parrot-fashion learning of the kind that is directly comparable to cramming the night before an examination. The information presented and absorbed is rarely interesting intellectually or emotionally and is therefore discarded as soon as it has performed its immediate, instrumental function. We have also suggested that this information is rarely of direct relevance to the practice of management, its primary purpose being to lend an air of academic legitimacy to the study of management and to differentiate its contents from other disciplines and qualifications.

Information and understanding

When teaching and studying, and within society more generally, there is a tendency to conflate and confuse *information* and *understanding*. As noted earlier when we touched briefly on the example of motorcycle maintenance, knowing or parrot learning the information contained in a textbook, say, is not the same as understanding its contents. This difference is often (painfully) exposed in the oral examination of students. It can then become clear that a student who has absorbed information for the purpose of producing an examination answer is unable to engage in any sustained discussion of the course content. The difference, and the tendency to overlook its significance, is expressed in the contemporary cliché, coined originally by Oscar Wilde, that is contemptuous of the person who 'knows the cost of everything and the value of nothing'.

   Information tells us about the cost of a particular good or service and whether it is rising or falling in price. But only *understanding* can enable us to appreciate the significance of such information or to develop possible explanations of the processes and practices that result in price movements. Information can be readily accessed, rote learned and exchanged. Under-standing, in contrast, involves an active and creative engagement with the content of what is being learned. In order to develop an understanding, it is necessary to place information in a context or framework that gives it meaning and significance. Fitzgerald[7] makes a similar point when com-menting on the potentials and pitfalls of easy access to massive quantities of information through the Internet:

> We need to debate the relationships between information, knowledge and learn-ing. Accessing information is not the main purpose of the university. Creating knowledge and supporting learning is. The increasing easy access to huge quan-tities of information can as easily overwhelm and disable students as it can liberate and enable them.

The block-busting management textbook is the pre-electronic precursor to the information overload associated with easy access to the Internet.

Massive amounts of 'information' about theories and models of management and organization are stored in the established texts. And, of course, it is precisely for this reason that these texts are used to prepare course assignments or to cram for examinations. Information is readily retrieved and regurgitated before being appraised by teachers, who use the contents of the textbook as a benchmark when they evaluate the *completeness* of the student's knowledge. In contrast, 'understanding' is developed in the course of making *meaningful connections* between pieces of information and interpreting their relevance to a particular human endeavour. It is not a matter of having a complete or exhaustive command of some bits of information (as in the aptly named game *Trivial Pursuits*), but rather of having developed the ability to interpret the significance of such information within a *framework of understanding*. For example, it is one thing to be able to describe the main characters in a novel or outline the plot. It is quite another to develop some understanding of the *possible* significance of this information in terms of the ideas and issues that are explored through the narrative.

Recording and memorizing 'facts' involves the aggregation and acquisition of bits of information. Understanding involves reflection on new experiences or pieces of information, which are transformed into knowledge as they are incorporated within a framework of understanding. To paraphrase Karl Marx, such understanding is what distinguishes the worst of human beings from the 'best' of bees (or sponges, or computers).[h] Bees can generate and process information about sources of pollen. Computers can process information at superhuman speed. But neither is capable of translating information into insight and understanding. We now illustrate the relevance of this distinction between information and understanding by extending our earlier, brief reflections on the textbook and guru literatures.

Textbook syndrome   We suggest that (management) students are frequently treated like human sponges or computers rather than intelligent beings who are capable of *interpreting* the significance of information, not simply memorizing and regurgitating it. Established texts present the field of management in a way that is superficially comparable to the information about London streets that novice black cab drivers are required to assimilate. To obtain a licence they must 'do the knowledge' by, *inter alia*, knowing the names of all the streets, landmarks and quickest routes between them. Taxi drivers acquire their knowledge by connecting the abstract information about street locations and directions with the concrete experience of driving to different destinations. The knowledge of best

---

h   The allusion here is to a distinction made by Marx between the seemingly creative capacities of bees (who make hives) and human beings (who design and make buildings) in order to highlight the difference between instinctual and purposive forms of activity. We return to this in Chapter 3 where we address the differences between behaviourist and humanist theories of human conduct.

routes acquired by taxi drivers is complemented by a skill in interpreting the dynamics of traffic flows that change on a day-to-day, minute-to-minute basis. Much of what a taxi driver 'knows' and 'sees' is invisible and incomprehensible to the passengers. Only when diverse bits of information are placed and connected within a broader framework of understanding does this information begin to make sense and have meaning and value. By contrast, textbooks provide students with information about management and organization that aspires to be of general relevance but that is abstracted from any particular context.

The contents of textbooks are like a map, except that few specific street names or even roads are marked. Instead, and at best, the textbook can provide a series of ways in which the practices of managing and organizing are described and analysed. Most textbooks comprise an elaboration of the key to the symbols and conventions used by makers of maps. They give little indication of what is practically involved in navigating, as contrasted with the ability to recognize the symbols used by cartographers. The lived realities of managerial and organizational work are more dynamic, particularistic, political and productive of dilemmas and contradictions than the neat presentation of theories and models in textbooks ever allow or acknowledge.

Even so, when faced with a particular problem or dilemma, practising managers may (eventually) turn to textbooks for guidance. Unless they are searching for the details of a particular theory or technique, they immediately encounter a problem. Missing is any conceptual framework for analysing particular situations. The complexity and dynamics of organizational behaviour are reduced to a set of abstractions (e.g. different 'leadership styles') or variables (e.g. centralization) to which causal power is attributed. The resulting models presume that 'organizational behaviour' exists independently of the motives, beliefs, insecurities and power of organizational members. The texts portray and celebrate managers as super-rational agents who diagnose problems by using abstractions and applying techniques that are deemed to have been effective in some other context.

Textbooks present massive amounts of information about management and organization. But they provide little that may enable practising managers to make sense of their particular problem or dilemma. Their contents are comparable to the 'pulp novel' that transports readers into a reassuring fantasy world where romantic love exhausts reality, only to be occasionally disrupted by gratuitous sex and violence. However, despite their equally mythical nature, the abstract, rational and disembodied textbook 'take' on managerial decision making is a great deal duller than the sensually and erotically driven lives of the characters that populate pulp fiction novels.

Guru syndrome   The past decade has seen a mushrooming of management guru books in which consultants and businesses (e.g. Tom Peters, Michael

Hammer and John Harvey-Jones) offer recipes for improving corporate performance. These books, which have sold in their millions, are paraded in airport lounges and are laid to rest on the shelves of company executives. The massive growth of guru guides is symptomatic of the increasing irrelevance of management textbooks that, in comparison, are remote from managers' day-to-day experiences and worries. Racy in style and more accessible in presentation, they stimulate and fill a demand for guidance and reassurance about how to make sense of, and cope with, the practicalities and insecurities of managerial work in a world of accelerating change and unsettling uncertainty. Their more or less explicit message is that, for the discerning, courageous and innovative manager, a remedy – their remedy – is at hand. Whereas textbooks provide a tedious means of acquiring the information necessary to gain a lucrative qualification, the guru guides are the bibles, or at least sacraments, of executives anxious to signal their familiarity with the latest management fad or fashion. As has been noted:

> much of the current hysteria over labels such as 'the new organization' and 'empowerment' can be seen as an attempt to lend new energy to the collective enterprises that have recently found themselves in a period of doubt and realignment.[8]

When making their pitch, leading management gurus are invariably scathing about the inflexibility of corporate bureaucracies and their functionaries. But they never doubt the importance of management or the status of managers as an elite of expert problem solvers and change agents. In this Brave New World, where organizations are, or must urgently become, more adaptive, more effective and more efficient, there is a recurrent celebration of 'flexibility' that is often promoted through the 'empowerment' of staff:

> high involvement, minimal hierarchy, and increased rewards based upon new performance parameters (quality, responsiveness) are wholly consistent with the more freewheeling, fast-reacting organization. . . . Highly trained and thus more flexible workers, with a big stake in the action, are a must for constant adaptation to customer needs and constant innovation.[9]

A principal effect of this kind of guru commentary and prescription is to leave unexamined the value and efficacy of managerial work. The centrality and credibility of the manager as corporate hero and societal troubleshooter is taken for granted. Tom Peters, in particular, has been busily prescribing the identity of a new breed of corporate, and some would say postmodern, managers who are urged to *Thrive on Chaos*. Though flattering and superficially appealing, the visions and recipes emanating from consultants and gurus can appear no less idiosyncratic and idealistic than textbook theory and can seem mechanistic and mundane. To the more experienced or sceptical manager, both can appear naive or cynical in their failure to acknowledge, address and appreciate the perverse practicalities of managerial work, where local politics defy the logic of textbook wisdom and guru prescription. Common to both, we suggest, is a limited capacity to provide practitioners with a framework capable of analysing and understanding the richness, complexity and ambiguity of a world that is riven by competing and contradictory interpretations of meaning.

It should, by now, be obvious that this book departs from the established mission and content of both textbooks and guru guides. You may think that our reservations and criticisms about such books are excessive or misdirected. Perhaps they are, for in order to have any impact at all, the break with convention often has to be exaggerated, polemical or controversial. This much we have learned from the gurus! Even if you do not share our criticisms, you may still believe that developing alternative ways of making sense of management has some merit. However, we are not (quite) so arrogant as to suppose that this book could be a direct substitute for, as opposed to a complementary reading to, more established literatures on management. But our task is different from a majority of writers in the field. Our purpose is to stimulate an interest in management as a human endeavour with all the anxieties and excitements, accomplishments and failures that confront managers as people, individually and collectively. In departing from convention, we do not claim to have broken with more established approaches (after all, we are a product of them). Nor, relatedly, do we claim to have remedied their limitations. We seek only to make a small contribution to opening up and extending what seems to us to be an unhelpful, narrow and unduly sterile range of options currently available to management students and practitioners.

Managing as a lived experience

Without more ado, we now attempt to make good our earlier claims about the use of novels by illustrating their relevance for understanding the lived experience of managing and organising. We focus on Vic, the central character in Lodge's *Nice Work*. In this novel, Lodge explores how, despite its widespread representation as an impersonal and technical activity, the work of management remains predominantly a human experience, characterized by the pains and pleasures that are endemic to human existence.

Vic the manager

In the opening pages of *Nice Work*, David Lodge introduces Vic, the hero of his novel. Outwardly confident and successful, Vic Wilcox lies awake in the small hours of the morning, worrying about threats to his self-image as a competent, effective manager:

> Worries streak towards him like enemy spaceships in a video game . . . the
> assault is endless: the Avco account, the Rawlinson account, the price of pig-
> iron, the value of the pound, the competition from Foundrax, the incompetence
> of his Marketing Director . . . the vandalising of the toilets in the fettling shop,
> the pressure from his divisional boss, last month's accounts, the quarterly
> forecast . . .[10]

At work, Vic manages the appearance of being a 'macho' manager who
enthusiastically pursues a no-nonsense approach to business. Seeing him in
action, an observer would not imagine Vic lying awake worrying about the
price of pig iron. He would not admit to his colleagues, and probably not
even to himself, the extent to which he is burdened by such worries. This,
of course, does not mean that his staff are blind to his insecurities. Nor are
they completely ignorant of his life outside of work, including the
wretched, but perhaps not so unusual, state of his marriage. Vic is not
exceptional. On the contrary, Lodge deploys a number of literary devices
to encourage his readers to identify with Vic as a normal, ordinary human
being.

Vic's life is by no means all doom and gloom, worry and anxiety. He
derives considerable pleasure from his work. He enjoys the cut and thrust
of pulling off deals and beating the competition. But Vic is also reflective
enough to recognize that such gratification is short lived. He imagines the
process of competition as a relay race. Leading positions are temporary;
batons are dropped. Unlike a relay, however, there is no finishing line. This
means that there is always the opportunity, and associated pleasure, of
catching the competition, though tragically leading positions are rarely
maintained for long and there is no respite from competing in the race. It is
also possible for players – companies and employees – to be involuntarily
withdrawn from the race as they go bankrupt or are made redundant. Vic
has considerable control over the day-to-day operations of 'his' company,
Pringle's, but he does not own it. The buying, selling and restructuring of
companies, including Pringle's, are beyond Vic's influence – as he discovers
to his dismay and cost towards the end of the novel. Perhaps Vic's work is
a metaphor for life?

Nice play?

The workplace is also an arena for unexpected games and pleasures. In
Vic's case, he is volunteered by his boss to participate in a 'Shadow
Scheme', whose purpose is to forge closer links between industry and
universities (the scheme is further discussed in Chapters 2 and 5). This
public relations role, which Vic is reluctant to perform, unexpectedly
presents him with an opportunity to become romantically involved with
Robyn, a female university lecturer. No less meaningful and pleasurable
for Vic than pulling a stroke on the competition is the dream of extramarital sex (for the first time) with this attractive, younger woman.

Vic's business schedule is organized to indulge his sexual fantasies, though with no conscious or serious intention of making them a reality. In the (comic) event, Vic is completely unprepared for the moment of their fulfilment. Finding himself in a hotel on a business trip with Robyn, the object of his desire, Vic:

> regards himself with wonderment led by the hand by this handsome young woman towards her bedroom, as if his soul is stumbling along out of step with his body . . . [Once in the bedroom], he pushes her against the door and begins to kiss her violently, his hands clutching and groping all over her. Only passion, he feels, will carry him across the threshold of adultery, and this is what he supposes passion is like.[11]

Explorations of managers' sexual escapades, or consideration of sexual and other (e.g. heroic) fantasies in guiding their decisions and behaviour, would certainly make textbooks livelier. They would also make them more true to life.[i] Fantasies (e.g. business plans) as well as gossip about their meaning and prospects of fulfilment are an endemic feature of working life in organizations. But they are rarely recognized in textbook accounts of business and management, or even in academic journal articles.

However, we digress. To return to our central theme, a parallel can be drawn between Vic's lack of sexual experience and his fantasies about it and the gap between accounts of management presented in textbooks and the lived realities of managerial work. Is it too fanciful to suggest that Vic's suppositions about passion are comparable to accounts of management and organization found in textbooks? Each is detached from the lived and embodied experience with which it is confronted; and the direct or naive application of its understandings, we suggest, is likely to produce similarly perverse and perhaps comical effects. We have the benefit of hindsight in Vic's case as Lodge describes how, in feeling sorry for him, the object of Vic's fantasies – Robyn – takes command of the sexual encounter and salvages what could otherwise have been a humiliating episode. No such parallel rescue is likely to befall those who naively apply the prescriptions of management textbooks, supposing them to portray or prescribe what 'real' management is like. That is why, once the principal function of textbooks in enabling students to pass examinations and gain qualifications has been fulfilled, they are rarely disturbed from their place 'on the shelf'.

The personal and the political

Important aspects of human existence, though not officially part of management theory and practice, nonetheless condition what managers and other employees do and how their work is conducted. Taking Vic as

---

i   These issues are beginning to receive more attention from researchers. See, for example, Burrell, 1984; Hearn *et al.*, 1989, Sinclair, 1995; Collinson and Hearn, 1996.

an example, it would seem that his compulsion to compete aggressively at work is not unrelated to a lack of self-esteem derived from other relationships (e.g. his wife and children). What is 'cause' and what is 'effect' in Vic's life is difficult, and perhaps impossible, to discern. As is so typical of human existence, there is an interaction of effects. The demands of Vic's job drain him of energy so that he becomes preoccupied with work problems, to the neglect of his family. But, equally, Vic's absence from home, psychologically and physically, means that his marital relationship amounts to little more than an exchange of grunts over the breakfast table.

Textbooks and guru guides tend to take for granted what may loosely be termed the *personal* and the *political* (small p) dimensions of managerial and organizational work, or these dimensions are (dis)regarded as an irrelevance for getting the job of management done. In lived experience, however, the personal and the political are inextricably intertwined. Many of Vic's 'private' problems and worries, we suggest, are directly related to his 'public' position of power and responsibility as a managing director. His hang-ups and juvenile fantasies can be connected to his highly traditional (patriarchal) marriage. In this marriage, his (submissive) wife feels unable to confront Vic's masculine preoccupations with work and its claimed legitimacy within the conventional domestic division of labour where the male assumes breadwinner status and responsibilities. It may be speculated that an unreflective masculinity led Vic to invest himself in the business of breadwinning through career advancement, to the comparative neglect of all other relationships.

As discussed earlier, when it comes to *interpreting* and *understanding* what managers are doing and thinking, textbooks and guru guides provide precious little indication or illumination of the complex personal and political dynamics of managerial and organizational work. In such texts, the pattern of behaviour exemplified by Vic might be identified as that of a dedicated, hard-nosed, professional manager. Rarely would he be understood as a production-centred manager who has yet to grasp the realities of contemporary capitalism where companies are the pawns or predators of corporate acquisition and divestment. Devoid of a direct discussion of the personal and political dimensions of working life, textbooks and guru guides represent managers as robotic, sexless functionaries, and not as human beings who do what they can to 'get by', 'get on' and 'get off' – in all kinds of ways.

Of course, *Nice Work* could be read without paying much attention to the details of what Vic does for a living, let alone how he organizes and manages (and is managed and organized by) his employees. That the leading characters – Vic and Robyn – are both employees of large, bureaucratic organizations where most of the action of the novel occurs could be disregarded, as attention is focused on their relationship. Their interactions could be interpreted simply as the behaviour of two distinctive types of individual – the traditional, self-made chauvinist (Vic) and the progressive, middle-class feminist (Robyn). However, to detach the personalities, values and prejudices of these characters from the social and organizational contexts of their interactions is to overlook the formation and development of the personal in the political. For example, Vic's changing feelings towards Robyn, and Robyn's changing feelings towards Vic, are products of the politics of everyday (working) life. Their initial expectations and prejudices are challenged by an emergent mutual respect born out of the attraction and exploration of Vic and Robyn's differences.

In the following chapters, the 'personal in the political' is explored by using a conceptual framework that comprises four interlinked concepts: power, identity, inequality and insecurity. Our final task in this chapter is to sketch how we define and use these concepts.

Interpreting everyday life

We noted earlier how the facility of reading a novel as something more than a story or narrative involving a number of characters and a plot requires a *framework* with which to develop *an* interpretation of its broader *meaning and significance*. We now seek to expand our understanding of our central concepts first by reference to *Nice Work* and then by considering the lecturing approach favoured by an ex-colleague of ours.

Interpreting the factory

As managing director of Pringle's, Vic exercises considerable *power*. When, for example, one of his managers attributes excessive 'down-time' on a machine to an incompetent operative, Vic's response is: 'Let's get rid of him'.[12] Vic is then reminded that there is no basis to fire this employee since he has not received the relevant training. In response, Vic tells the manager to: 'train him, even if he can't grasp it. Are you with me?' Once a series of warnings has been given, the worker can 'legitimately' be fired: 'Shouldn't take more than a fortnight. All right?' End of story. Except that the effective exercise of power is dependent on a workforce whose willingness to cooperate may be weakened by such manipulations and calculations, should they become known.

The limits of the power invested in Vic's position as managing director, and especially his dependence on others, becomes clear when the shopfloor workers proceed to withdraw their labour following a tip-off from Robyn about Vic's plans to remove the incompetent operative (see above). These workers were able to resist what they regarded as an abuse of managerial power. Such resistance has its history in the experience of exploitation and domination at work that stimulated the formation of unions and associated discourses that have challenged (the universal exercise of) managerial prerogative.

Power cannot sensibly be conceptualized as something that is located in individuals as a personal possession. The exercise of managerial power is relational: it is dependent on ensuring the continued consent or compliance of the workforce. It resides in the relationships that may facilitate or impede the exercise of power. In *Nice Work*, the power exercised by Vic depends on his employees – his fellow managers (e.g. the marketing manager) as well as the foundry workers. Conversely, albeit weakly organized, the workers exercise power by virtue of their productive performance on which Vic's own reputation and value in the marketplace depends. Also employees exercise power in diverse forms of active or passive resistance, such as allowing machines to break down, vandalizing the toilets or, ultimately, withdrawing their labour.

Just as the exercise of power invariably depends, at least minimally, on the (cooperative) agency of others, the *identity* of an individual (or a group) is dependent on how s/he is regarded and represented by others. In Vic's case, evaluations made by his wife, his children and, above all, his divisional boss are of critical importance for his sense of self-identity. This dependency acts to influence or soothe Vic's insecurities, which 'zap' him in the early hours. But his worries are contained by his sense of identity as a hard-nosed manager. This serves to justify the making of tough, business decisions so that he does not worry about the consequences of his actions for individual employees on the factory floor. Employees are viewed as commodities: 'Let's get rid of him, then.' There is no thought for the effects of such decisions on other members of the workforce (perhaps Vic assumes that they will be pleased to have lost an incompetent operator), let alone the dependants of the man whom Vic contrives to sack.

Inequality in society ensures that Vic's chances in life are markedly different from those of his employees, and that there is little sense of their sharing a common humanity or fate. As individuals, employees are vulnerable to the operation of labour markets, where they are readily dismissed and replaced by others willing to work more compliantly or for lower wages. By organizing and campaigning collectively to place legal constraints on the operation of markets, workers have increased the dependence of employers on labour. Here they have partially redressed the consequences of labour's treatment as a commodity to be bought and sold, hired and fired.

Insecurity stems not just from a recognition of the scarcity of material goods and symbolic statuses. It arises also from the impossibility of controlling the conditions that support a stable sense of identity. For identity necessarily relies on our interdependence with others whose views and actions escape our control. Indeed, it is often argued that those who successfully pursue the accumulation of money, power or status are often among the most insecure of people. This is because they have the most to lose from its loss – that is, their very sense of purpose and self-identity. The late Howard Hughes was one of the richest men in the world, but so insecure that he lived a reclusive life. His apartment was regularly doused with disinfectant and he only ate food that had been clinically prepared so as to avoid any threatening contamination. His wealth and power did nothing to assuage his paranoid psychosomatic insecurity.

Vic loses sleep about things that could reflect poorly on his own performance and identity as a manager – such as the competition from Foundrax or the breakdown of machinery. His perceived ability to control these things, he knows, will affect how his divisional boss assesses him. A positive evaluation will boost his self-esteem. Conversely, a poor rating threatens to violate his self-image – a threat that keeps Vic awake at night. Yet he also partially senses that so much of what happens to him, such as Robyn's appearance as his 'shadow' and her key role in negotiating a favourable deal on an expensive piece of equipment, is a result of good fortune, which he is powerless to influence or control. For all his status and influence, Vic finds himself in a quandary. If he claims the credit for what is good fortune, then he reinforces the idea that he is an exceptionally capable manager and thereby raises the stakes. If, on the other hand, he regards his position as managing director as the outcome of a series of lucky breaks, he undermines his preferred sense of identity as an effective manager.

Interpreting the lecture

To illustrate further the relevance of our conceptual framework, we now consider an example drawn from our own workplace. This concerns the approach to teaching taken by one of our ex-colleagues. Though based on 'fact', this example is in many ways more fantastic than the fictions to be found in novels.

Our colleague's introductory lecture began by amassing a pile of texts on the lecture bench. In a spectacular gesture, he then swept the books to the floor, declaring: 'That's all rubbish, all you need to know about business is how to make a profit.'[13] In our colleague's case, the credibility of this claim was supported by a dual career. In addition to holding a professorial appointment at the university, he enjoyed a high-profile reputation as a successful (part-time) senior executive and corporate fixer. Through his dramatic rejection of textbook knowledge, our colleague cleared a space – symbolically and physically – for advancing an alternative approach to teaching. This approach, which relied heavily on 'war stories' and personal anecdotes, was a kind of precursor to the many 'how I did it' books published by leading business people in recent years.

The dramatic 'rubbishing' of textbook knowledge can be interpreted in a number of ways. It can be viewed as a theatrical shock tactic for grabbing students' attention – the equivalent of the explosive experiments conducted by professors of chemistry. It can also be interpreted through the central concepts of our framework. By elevating street-wise experience and practice over dust-dry textbook wisdom, the decisive importance of our colleague's *identity* (and status) as a senior executive and businessman was at once assumed and asserted. The *inequalities* between teacher and student were dramatically manifested in the gesture of sweeping the books to the floor. Student awareness of our colleague's high-profile successes in the world of business was effectively mobilized to convey the potency of practical example and the impotency of dry academic and theoretical learning. Our colleague could, of course, well afford to be cavalier and scathing about academic knowledge, precisely because his success as businessman meant that he was no longer dependent materially or symbolically on a university career.

More positively, the dismissal of academic knowledge challenges the reluctance of teachers to demystify their disciplines. The dramatic rejection of textbook knowledge demonstrates how close business is to everyday commonsense reality. At the same time, this act scorned and devalued ivory tower 'expertise' and the distinctive scholarly identity associated with it. But does the direct substitution of 'business wisdom' for 'academic knowledge' make any pedagogical difference? Probably not. For the certainty with which anecdotal business commonsense is dispensed generally provides little space for students either to think through issues for themselves or to participate in an 'open' learning experience.

It is thus possible to interpret our colleague's 'rubbishing' of textbook wisdom as a self-indulgent act, full of sound and fury but signifying little of substance. Instead of regarding it, at face value, as an act of *power* and self-confidence, it could be seen as an expression of *insecurity*, marked by the felt need to make a conspicuous display of a distinctive set of business credentials. For those students in his audience who had developed, or were seeking to acquire, a less business-centred *identity*, our colleague's behaviour would probably have appeared more disturbing or farcical than reassuring or impressive. His displacement of all other sources of knowledge by anecdotal accounts of 'proven' ways of how to make a profit could be seen as a weak and intellectually bankrupt way of avoiding critical engagement with the 'rubbish'. When viewed in this more sceptical light, our colleague's gestures are seen to diminish, rather than enhance, his credibility as a university teacher.

The politics of teaching and the struggle to learn

Turning to students, we suggest that they are not mere passive victims of teaching. They are also willing accomplices of lecturers in maintaining the dependency relationships of the educational status quo. This is not least because students who stray from the conventional path of acquiring qualifications may put at risk a promising career and prestigious social identity. The authority of a textbook or a charismatic teacher may be seized on as an equivalent to the comfort blanket.[j] Clasping the blanket,

---

j It is paradoxical that the more they become aware of this dependency, the greater the likelihood that, even as they snuggle up to the blanket, students will feel somewhat sceptical, if not dismissive, of the practical relevance of textbook wisdom. This scepticism can be kept beneath the surface when textbook material is conveyed by a lecturer with communicative skill and humour. Alas, a majority of lecturers do not exhibit the skills of a good entertainer; nor do they have the relevant experience to litter their lectures with anecdotal experiences.

the audience participates or colludes in reproducing particular relations of power and identity. These relations are exemplified in the deference accorded to senior figures by those who aspire to join their ranks.

Not infrequently, lecturers and students collude in the understanding that textbooks and lecture notes provide 'the right answers' – if not in any ultimate sense, then at least for the purpose of passing examinations. Earlier we emphasized the open and indeterminate quality of human interactions in organizations and society. The meaning of events, such as our colleague's dramatic gesture of sweeping the books from the desk at the start of his lecture, is inescapably a matter of interpretation and negotiation. In this sense, the world is like a text. The possibilities for interpretation are, in principle, boundless. But, in practice, the sense that we can make is limited by whatever frameworks of interpretation are culturally available and plausible to us. What makes the textbook and/or lecture notes especially seductive is a belief that they contain 'the right answer', as Chris Evans'[k] catchphrase would have it. This combines with anticipation that they will minimize the level of effort and risk required, securing the desired outcome of examination success.

Insecure in their encounters with each new generation of youth who seem even more hedonistic and instrumental than the last, lecturers are inclined to pump out masses of information to their students. Often this is presented with the assistance of numerous transparencies or slides at a speed sufficient to preclude reflection or fidgeting as students strive to copy the materials into their notes. A banking concept of knowledge[14] is routinely employed where information is transmitted from the lecturer's overheads to the student's notebook without passing through the mind of either, to be stored like items in a credit balance that are faithfully reproduced in the examination.[1] For lecturers, the workload and anxiety are diminished when the same lecture notes and overheads are delivered each year. Exemplifying the comatose nature of such teaching, another of our colleagues recently related how he thought he was awakening from a dream in which he was giving a lecture to his third-year students, only to find that he was!

We confess that our own teaching has often slipped into a more conventional mode. Educators, like everyone else, are caught up in a world where inequalities prevail and individuals seek to exercise power in order to ensure that they enjoy some of the material and symbolic privileges that are

---

k   A British television and radio show host and media entrepreneur.

l   The banking concept assumes that there is a 'fixed' and necessary amount of knowledge to be disseminated before a student can claim to be proficient in a particular subject. A credit balance, in the form of a set of notes, is identified as the means of acquiring the desired qualification. It is for this reason that academics guard with extreme defensiveness the length of their courses and the time devoted to them. Yet one could readily argue that, if the quality of learning were taken into account, an hour where students are genuinely involved in the learning process may be worth more than a whole semester of being 'lectured at' as passive recipients of information.

unequally distributed or secured. Collecting degree certificates and/or generating research publications is as much a part of that process as building up financial capital. They are simply different ways of accumulating resources that can be deployed in the exercise of power. The banking concept of education is difficult to dislodge from the minds and practices of both teachers and students. A passive approach to learning requires less effort and involvement. It also makes it easier for energies to be directed elsewhere – usually into part-time employment and increased leisure for students, and consultancy or research for academics.

Dynamics of power and insecurity lead academics to treat knowledge as a commodity that they possess and students 'want'. Students quickly understand that it is 'best' or least risky to regurgitate views that do not conflict with or challenge those held by the lecturer. Consequently, the creative aspect of student work becomes restricted to finding accessible ways of re-articulating the lecturer's own views. Conventional textbooks help to sustain or reproduce the fiction of knowledge as a 'fixed' and objective entity. By default, students seek to minimize the effort and pain involved in obtaining a degree. Fearing a loss of control, lecturers also tend to shy away from the uncertainties and demands of developing a more open and active engagement with students. This fear, we believe, is rooted in a desire to protect an authoritative academic identity from potential challenge by students who may voice their doubts and criticisms about the choice of course content as well as its mode of delivery. More frequently, however, students have become accustomed to a more passive form of learning and reinforce this approach. Students may have high and anxiety-arousing expectations of what university education will demand of them. By default, nevertheless, they also tend to expect and even prefer a familiar, standardized approach to teaching that can be more readily and predictably absorbed and regurgitated. Both teachers and students are drawn to a low risk, 'banking' pedagogy that is safe but dull, dispassionate but also disappointing.

However, it should not be assumed that the capacity of students to contain their boredom and frustration is inexhaustible. The 'banking' process may be disrupted, either through physical or mental absenteeism. Most lecturers have had the experience at one time or another of their voice being drowned by the chatter of students, demonstrating that their instrumentalism has its limits. Even when they remain attentive, copying down the lecturer's every word, students are often disdainful of the method and quality of such teaching. When given a voice to say what they think is 'good' or 'bad' about their experience of education,[m] the latter may well outweigh the former.[n]

---

m This evidence has been collected from students every year for more than a decade at the beginning of a third-year course and used to contrast the attempt of this course to break the vicious circle of instrumentalism and indifference (see Grey, Knights and Willmott, 1996).

n Complaints include bored and indifferent lecturers, the use of often dog-eared overheads signalling their perennial usage without updating, and an over impersonal if not depersonalized approach to staff–student relations.

The authority of lecturers who rely on the regimes of truth ensconced in textbooks, or who substitute anecdote and exhortation for analysis, is precarious. As the final days of Ceauşescu, the ex-president of Romania, clearly demonstrated, relations of power can be challenged or become inverted. The potential collective resistance of students is constrained by their perceptions of being in competition with one another for scarce qualifications and by an instrumental preoccupation with securing the best possible credentials on leaving university. But students cannot help themselves from disrupting the more tedious lectures. Precisely because power is relational and identities are precarious, even virtuoso lecturing performances can rebound on the lecturer.[o] Likewise, even the most autocratic of managers is obliged to solicit and secure minimal acquiescence from colleagues, subordinates and superiors – if s/he is not to become isolated, resisted, sidelined or eventually rendered redundant.

An overview

Our intention in this book is to develop an understanding of management at work that departs in style and content from accounts provided by existing textbooks. We do not seek to be comprehensive in our coverage of issues ordinarily regarded as central to the study of management. We also attempt to avoid treating its subject matter in an overly abstract manner where the tasks or 'functions' of management are privileged over the people who carry them out. In developing a more embodied understanding of managing, we treat managers as human beings who grapple with a panoply of personal as well as professional issues. Personal experiences are part and parcel of managerial work. They are no less relevant for an understanding of management practice than the activities they undertake. Yet the dynamic, experiential dimension of work is largely ignored in the established literature. To analyse the lived experience of managing, we focus on four interrelated concepts – power, inequality, identity and insecurity – that are no less relevant for understanding everyday life. A number of well-known novels are used to illustrate our analysis in a way that is intended to be entertaining as well as instructive.

It is our intention that this book will facilitate an approach to the teaching of management that understands it as a lived and embodied activity – management lives and how management lives. By reading and discussing this book, we anticipate (without fully expecting!) that students of management may find their subject matter more interesting and challenging, both intellectually and professionally. Our hope is that this book will serve as a primer for students who could, with the insights

---

o   This is so unless, of course, the teacher has the presence, sharp wit and verbal (or material) dexterity to accomplish a restoration of the (hierarchical) social order – for example, by successfully mocking, and thereby deflating, the disruptive element.

gleaned from it, go on to read other, more traditional texts with new inspiration and critical vision.

In Chapter 2 we draw extensively on *Nice Work* to introduce issues dealt with in the book as a whole. By exploring the contrasting lives of a postmodern feminist academic and a managing director of an engineering company, Lodge's novel explores and questions (their) conventional understandings and taken-for-granted assumptions about management and work. Not only does *Nice Work* challenge some deeply embedded managerial assumptions in a way that many academic texts fail to do; it does so in a highly entertaining manner. In the other chapters of this book, we return repeatedly to *Nice Work* to illustrate its central themes and concepts.

In Chapters 3 and 4, we focus in depth on aspects of everyday life and managing that are illuminated through the concepts of identity/insecurity and power/inequality respectively. Each chapter draws on a different novel as the primary resource for developing a meaningful illustration of, and complement to, academic treatments of these issues. They share a concern to move beyond a commonsense interpretation of work by developing a more reflective and critical understanding of its contemporary management and organization. In Chapter 3 we explore two common but opposing perspectives on human nature – behaviourism and symbolic interactionism – before drawing on elements from each to develop an alternative under-standing of individuals' preoccupation with self-image and social standing. Milan Kundera's novel *The Unbearable Lightness of Being* is used exten-sively to illustrate our analysis.

Chapter 4 considers the operation of power and inequality in the context of the aristocratic household portrayed in Kazuo Ishiguro's *The Remains of the Day*, which we contrast with the fast-moving world of 1980s New York that is the subject of Tom Wolfe's *The Bonfire of the Vanities*. *The Remains of the Day* describes how the fine distributions of hierarchical power and status reproduce themselves at both ends of the system of stratification, such that the servant class replicates within its own ranks a parallel hierarchical ordering of status. Connecting issues of power and inequality with those of identity and insecurity, this novel also explores how a sense of security may also be accompanied by a (paranoid) fear of its precariousness and immanent loss. The comparison with Wolfe's *The Bonfire of the Vanities* usefully marks out the distinction between deference, in the form of devotion to the aristocratic master, and the status differ-entials generated by the competitive, success-seeking preoccupations of New York society. Our concern in this chapter is to conceptualize power and inequality as the medium and outcome of management practice in a way that appreciates their precarious and dynamic character.

Chapter 5 explores the continuities and differences between managing as an everyday practice and as a specialist activity. It also examines the historical development of the modern organization and, in particular, the connections and tensions between instrumental and moral relations as these are played out in efforts to 'humanize' workplaces. It concludes by returning to *Nice Work* to provide a detailed application of our theoretical framework to a tense exchange between two senior managers. In this interaction, we argue, power is exercised within a hierarchical relationship of inequality that is plagued by insecurities about performance and promotion and is therefore consequential for identity.

Summary

We have argued that management textbooks and guru guides tend to invite, endorse and reproduce a detached, instrumental and closed attitude towards studying and working. They appeal to students, teachers and practising managers as a way of managing through minimalist techniques or use of effort, brainpower and time. But they can also be counterproductive. Managers can become fixated on particular formulae for success or rendered bewildered and cynical by the array of conflicting prescriptions on offer. Staff–student relations can become locked in a vicious spiral of instrumentalism and indifference that makes the learning process a war of attrition. Studying becomes at best an unpleasant chore and at worst a pain to avoid until the very last minute – when a deadline for a continuous assessment essay is looming or an exam is to be taken the next day.

When working within the confines of educational institutions, the pursuit of personally meaningful knowledge is widely tempered by an obligation to prepare students for examinations. Examinations may invite an instrumental and superficial banking (cramming) of information for purposes of demonstrating the candidate's knowledge of the subject. Nonetheless, it is possible to set questions that, in addition to demanding a knowledge of the subject, encourage answers that yield more than a recycling of 'facts' or theories. It is possible to teach in ways that, in addition to encouraging examinees to incorporate a critical appreciation of the relevance of pertinent literature, are attentive to its relevance to personal and social, as well as management and organizational, life.

We want to encourage our readers to value and develop their own interpretive and critical resources, so that they are able to engage more personally and meaningfully with management as a lived practice that is continuous with everyday experiences rather than remote from them. Our attraction to novels as a vehicle for teaching revolves around a belief that they offer a means of bringing to life the central themes of the book. They do so, we anticipate, in ways that are interesting for practitioners of management as well as for management students. In the remaining chapters, we attempt to make good our claim that novels illuminate practices of organizing and managing – activities that involve all kinds of challenges, tensions and pleasures.

Recommended further reading

The following are relevant for exploring further issues of *management education*:

Burgoyne, J. and Reynolds, M. (1997) *Management Learning*. London: Sage.
French, R. and Grey, C. (1996) *Rethinking Management Education*. London: Sage.
Willmott, H. (1994) 'Management education: provocations to a debate', *Management Learning*, 25 (1): 105–36.

The tensions, complexities and dilemmas of managerial work are examined in the following:

Collinson, D. (1992) *Managing the Shopfloor*. Berlin: de Gruyter.
Collinson, D. and Hearn, J. (eds) (1996) *Men as Managers, Managers as Men*. London: Sage.
Kunda, G. (1992) *Engineering Culture: Control and Commitment in a High-Tech Corporation*. Philadephia: Temple University Press.
Watson, T. (1994) *In Search of Management: Culture, Chaos and Control in Managerial Work*. London: Routledge.
Willmott, H. (1997) 'Rethinking management and managerial work: capitalism, control and subjectivity', *Human Relations*, 50 (11): 1329–60.

The following explore the *relevance of novels for the study of management*:

Czaniaswka-Joerges, B. and Guillet de Montoux, P. (eds) (1994) *Good Novels, Better Management: Reading Organizational Realities*. London: Harwood Academic Publishers.
Cohen, C. (1998) 'Using narrative fiction within management education', *Management Learning*, 29 (2): 165–81.

The following are congruent with the *conceptual framework* used in this and the following chapters:

Knights, D. and Willmott, H.C. (1989) 'Power and subjectivity at work: from degradation to subjugation in social relations', *Sociology*, 23 (4): 535–58.
Kondo, D. (1992) *Crafting Selves: Power, Gender and Discourses of Identity in a Japanese Workplace*. Chicago: University of Chicago Press.

Notes

1 Vargish, T. (1994) 'The value of humanities in executive development' in H. Tsoukas (ed.), *New Thinking in Organizational Behaviour*, Oxford: Butterworth-Heinemann, pp. 221–234.

2 Fineman, S. and Gabriel, Y. (1994) 'Paradigms of organisations: an exploration in textbook rhetorics', *Organisation*, 1 (2): 375–99, pp. 376–7.

3 The MBA is the most prestigious of business degrees.

4 Robinson, P. (1994) *Snapshots from Hell: the Making of an MBA*, New York: Warner Books, p. 145.

5 Pirsig, R. (1974) *Zen and the Art of Motorcycle Maintenance*, London: Bodley Head, p. 27.

6 Lodge, D. (1992) *The Art of Fiction*, Penguin: Harmondsworth, p. 203.
7 Fitzgerald, M. (1996) 'Polar bores miss multimedia point', *Times Higher Education Supplement*, July 5, p. 12.
8 Eccles, R.G. and Nohria, N. (1992) *Beyond the Hype: Rediscovering the Essence of Management*, Cambridge, MA: Harvard University Press, p. 29. See also Cleverley, G. (1971) *Managers and Magic*, London: Longman.
9 Peters, T. (1989) *Thriving on Chaos*, London: Macmillan, p. 39.
10 Lodge, D. (1989) *Nice Work*, Harmondsworth: Penguin, p. 13.
11 *Nice Work*, p. 290.
12 *Nice Work*, p. 143.
13 Reported in *UMIST Times* (details withheld to protect anonymity).
14 See Freire, P. (1970) *The Pedagogy of the Oppressed*, Harmondsworth: Penguin.

References

Alvarez, J.L. (1990) 'Narrative fiction as a pedagogical tool in management teaching', Working Paper, IESE, Barcelona.
Alvesson, M. and Willmott, H. (1992) *Critical Management Studies*, London: Sage.
Alvesson, M. and Willmott, H. (1996) *Making Sense of Management: a Critical Introduction*, London: Sage.
Burrell, G. (1984) 'Sex and organizational analysis', *Organization Studies*, 5 (2): 97–118.
Carter, I. (1990) *Ancient Cultures of Concept: British University Fiction in the Post-War Years*, London: Routledge.
Child, J., Rowlinson, M. and Smith, C. (1990) *Reshaping Work: the Cadbury Experience*, Cambridge: Cambridge University Press.
Collinson, D. (1992) *Managing the Shopfloor: Masculinity, Subjectivity and Workplace Culture*, London: Routledge.
Collinson, D. and Hearn, J. (eds) (1996) *Masculinity and Management*, London: Sage.
Czarniaswka-Joerges, B. and Guillet de Montoux, P. (eds) (1994) *Good Novels, Better Management*, London: Harwood Academic Publishers.
Domagalski, T.A. and Jermier, J.M. (1995) '"I would prefer not to": class dynamics and deep subjectivity in Herman Melville's "Bartleby the Scrivener – A Story of Wall Street"', paper presented to the 12th Colloquium of the European Group for Organization Studies, Istanbul.
Eccles, R.G. and Nohria, N. (1992) *Beyond the Hype: Rediscovering the Essence of Management*, Cambridge, MA: Harvard University Press.
Freire, P. (1970) *The Pedagogy of the Oppressed*, Harmondsworth: Penguin.
Grey, C. (1996) 'C.P. Snow's fictional sociology of management and organizations', *Organization*, 3 (1): 61–84.
Grey, C., Knights, D. and Willmott, H.C. (1996) 'Is a critical pedagogy of management possible' in R. French and C. Grey, *Rethinking Management Education*, London: Sage.
Hassard, J. and Holliday, R. (eds) (1998) *Organization – Representation: Work Organization in Popular Culture*, London: Sage.
Hearn, J., Sheppard, D., Tancred-Sheriff, P. and Burrell, G. (eds) (1989) *The Sexuality of Organization*, London: Sage.
Jackall, R. (1988) *Moral Mazes: the World of Corporate Managers*, Oxford: Oxford University Press.
Knights, D. and Murray, F. (1994) *Managers Divided: Organization, Politics and IT Management*, London: Wiley.

Kunda, G. (1992) *Engineering Culture Control and Commitment in a High-Tech Corporation*, Philadephia: Temple University Press.

Lodge, D. (1989) *Nice Work*, Harmondsworth: Penguin.

Lodge, D. (1992) *The Art of Fiction*, Harmondsworth: Penguin.

Nussbaum, M.C. (1990) *Love's Knowledge: Essays in Philosophy and Literature*, Oxford: Oxford University Press.

Perry, N. (1984) 'Catch, class and bureaucracy: the meaning of Joseph Heller's *Catch 22*', *Sociological Review*, 32 (4): 719–41.

Peters, T. (1989) *Thriving on Chaos*, London: Macmillan.

Pettigrew, A. (1985) *The Awakening Giant*, Oxford: Blackwell.

Phillips, N. (1995) 'Telling organizational tales: on the role of narrative fiction in the study of organizations', *Organization Studies*, 16 (4): 625–49.

Pirsig, R. (1974) *Zen and the Art of Motorcycle Maintenance*, London: Bodley Head.

Reed, M. (1985) *Redirections in Organizational Analysis*, Tavistock: London.

Reed, M. (1989) *The Sociology of Management*, Brighton: Wheatsheaf/Harvester.

Robinson, P. (1994) *Snapshots from Hell: the Making of an MBA*, New York: Warner Books.

Roman, L. (1994) 'Love and organization', *Scandinavian Journal of Management*, 10 (2): 207–22.

Sims, D., Fineman, S. and Gabriel, Y. (1993) *Organising and Organisations*, London: Sage.

Sinclair, A. (1995) 'Sex and the MBA', *Organization*, 2 (2): 295–317.

Thompson, J. and McGivern, J. (1996) 'Parody, process and practice: perspectives for management education', *Management Learning*, 26 (3): 379–93.

Thompson, P. and McHugh, D. (1995) *Work Organizations: a Critical Introduction*, London: Macmillan.

Vargish, T. (1994) 'The value of humanities in executive development' in H. Tsoukas (ed.), *New Thinking in Organizational Behaviour*, Oxford: Butterworth-Heinemann, p. 222.

Watson, T.J. (1994) *In Search of Management: Culture, Chaos and Control in Managerial Work*, London: Routledge.

Wilkie, R. (1989) 'Values and decisions', paper presented at the Third Conference of the British Academy of Management, Manchester Business School, September.

Wolfe, T. (1988) *The Bonfire of the Vanities*, London: Picador.

2 Organizing Work

In this chapter we illustrate how different kinds of work are meaningful to some people and not to others. We also explore how the nature and organization of work change in the context of complex and variable power relations. We draw on David Lodge's novel *Nice Work* to 'bring to life' and illuminate issues that may otherwise seem rather abstract and remote. This we do by deploying an interpretive framework founded on four central and interrelated concepts – power, identity, inequality and insecurity.

As we noted in the previous chapter, novels could shed light on the everyday lived experiences of men and women at work. They can counter-act textbook accounts of management in which managers are represented as disembodied subjects, narrowly confined to the instrumental and technical content of their function in the division of labour. On their own, however, novels are easily read as an entertaining story devoid of any wider significance. An absorbing and entertaining narrative may, paradoxically, act to limit reflection on its illumination of the world of everyday life, including the realms of work and management. To counter this pedagogical limitation, we select from and, in effect, disrupt the seductive power of the narrative as we direct attention towards wider issues that are illuminated through the use of our four key concepts.

The chapter comprises three main sections. The first presents the elements of our conceptual framework for interpreting the experience of working in modern organizations. In the second section, we draw on this framework to examine the working lives of Vic, a middle-aged male managing director of a factory, and Robyn, a young female academic – the two main characters in *Nice Work*. This leads into a discussion of work from a historical and then an existential perspective. This section concludes with a discussion of contrasting and shifting orientations to work illustrated by reference to characters in Lodge's novel. In the third section, we examine various conceptions of meaning and its problematic character in paid employment. We focus initially on employees at Vic's workplace before addressing the work of staff and students at universities. Our aim is to counter the tendency of textbook accounts of management to gloss over the lived experience of managers and the personal and social relevance of organizing work. We also seek to show how broader social issues relating to inequalities of ownership and control are intertwined with personal worries and dilemmas arising from insecurities about identity and the exercise of power.

Conceptualizing (working) life

Our four interrelated concepts – power, inequality, identity and insecurity – in combination provide a framework for interpreting the social world, including the fictional worlds portrayed in novels. Clearly, this way of reading reality/texts is analytical in orientation. We are concerned less with the details of the main characters and their lives than with themes and issues – 'the messages' – that we detect through the use of our interpretive framework. We begin by sketching briefly our four key concepts before moving immediately to an examination of various aspects of working life illustrated through *Nice Work*. Readers may wish to consult this conceptual sketch as they work through the remaining sections of the chapter.

Power, inequality, identity and insecurity

Power is often associated with the coercive and repressive features of social life. It is the means through which a ruling class, political elite or managerial group controls subordinate strata within a society or an organization. More recently, power has been associated with the very existence of social relations.[1] From this newer perspective, power is not simply or exhaustively negative, coercive and zero sum (i.e. *A* has power over *B*). It is also productive and positive (i.e. *A* and *B* are each enabled as well as constrained within relations of power). Power is understood to transform human beings into subjects that identify with the ideas and practices through which power is exercised.

When understood in this way, power is seen to constitute subjects – whether members of the ruling class/elite or members of a subordinate group. At the same time, there is no suggestion or presumption that individuals necessarily defer, succumb or subjugate themselves to forms of power. On the contrary, subjects often exercise their own power in the form of resistance. In *Nice Work*, both Vic (the businessman) and Robyn (the academic) may be seen as products of the exercise of power around particular models or knowledge of the organization of work – one based primarily on market principles, the other on collegial relations. In turn, they exercise power respectively over employees and students. Vic draws on his knowledge of the market for labour and how to work it to his advantage as a hard-nosed businessman. Robyn's knowledge of poststructuralist theory enables her to construct and affirm her identity as a leading-edge literary theorist.[a] Vic

---

a   While it is not essential to know what poststructuralist literary theory is in order to understand our or Lodge's text, some kind of working definition may be helpful. Following a lengthy tradition of thought that presumes there to be structures of reality (e.g. class, capitalism etc.) that determine life in society, poststructuralism has sought to deconstruct such universal grand narratives or theories. In their place, it is suggested that meaning is contingent on the local conditions of its construction. Poststructuralist analysis deconstructs the basis of positions that appear to be firm and authoritative by demonstrating how they are constructed, not given or fundamentally centred (see Willmott, 1998).

relates to his staff in accordance with a view that they have little opportunity to resist his commands. In contrast, Robyn invites her students to challenge the conventional wisdom in everyday life as part of their developing a poststructuralist sensitivity.

Inequality describes differences in wealth and status, such as the inequalities of income and privilege between managers and employees and between men and women. These inequalities are institutionalized in so far as they are embedded in, and reproduced by, working relations (e.g. hierarchy and job segregation by gender or ethnicity), employment practices (e.g. recruitment and promotion) and other social formations (e.g. markets or the family).

In *Nice Work*, the social distance between Vic and the shopfloor workers make it easier for him to contrive the dismissal of one of his workers, which we described in Chapter 1. However, he is then shown to be dependent on the workforce who, collectively, withdraw their labour when they find out about his plan. The existence of interdependencies through which inequalities are routinely maintained and periodically challenged means that those who occupy more senior, privileged positions depend on others with whom they are obliged to negotiate or conciliate when in dispute.

Identity describes the status that is widely ascribed to a person. For example, 'manager' or 'academic' is an identity, as certain cultural understandings are conveyed about the person who is so identified. Associated with these understandings are expectations about how such a person will, and should, behave. Often but not invariably, many of these common understandings are adopted and shared by that person. In such a case there is a degree of consistency between the individual's self-identity and the social identity ascribed to him or her.

In *Nice Work*, we see the dynamics of the connection between social identity and self-identity. Vic begins to see discrepancies or inconsistencies in his social identity as a tough, 'macho' manager who is nonetheless offended, when he comes to think about it, by the soft pornography that decorates the factory shopfloor. Ordinarily, such a person would not find 'girlie' pictures offensive, nor would they normally develop a keen appreciation of literature and poetry. This alternative sense of self-identity has been aroused as a consequence of Vic's association with Robyn, the academic feminist, in whom he begins to develop a more than professional interest.

Insecurity arises when people are unable to interpret a situation in a way that confirms their own sense of themselves – for example, as a 'bright student' or as a 'caring person'. Social situations are especially difficult in this respect, since we can never be fully sure of, let alone control, how others view us. Yet it is through our sense of how others view us that we develop and evaluate self-identity. 'Knowing' the other person reduces the stress or tension of this uncertainty in social encounters. However, this uncertainty cannot be entirely eliminated, as people are continually changing as a result of new circumstances, experiences and relationships.

One way of attempting to limit or remove insecurity is to reduce and displace the complexity and idiosyncrasy of individual experience by attaching oneself to a typical social identity. Social identities are institutionalized or regularized in socially established sets of values/ideologies (e.g. 'feminist', 'socialist', 'Christian') or roles such as family position (e.g. 'wife', 'father'), occupation (e.g. 'manager', 'teacher') or leisure activity (e.g. 'football supporter', 'rock fan'). Even so, these identities remain precarious because individuals are unable to control the conditions that give rise to their formation and reproduction.

In *Nice Work*, Vic lies awake in the early hours worrying whether he will succeed in holding his job down. His fear is that he will not be confirmed in his self-identity as an effective, no-nonsense manager. Robyn experiences some insecurity when she moves outside of her established sphere of university life into a managerial territory where her identity as a feminist (and an academic) is viewed negatively.

Working lives

The lives of Vic Wilcox and Robyn Penrose collide when she agrees to participate in a joint industry–university scheme. This requires her to spend a day a week 'shadowing' Vic. Vic had recently been appointed as managing director of a medium-sized engineering firm called Pringle's, which had just been acquired by a bigger industrial holding company, Midland Amalgamated.

When Vic first meets Robyn, he is filled with rage and horror. He recognizes Robyn as the same woman who had been picketing outside the university the previous week when this industrial action had held up the traffic. His secretary had told him verbally that his shadow was 'Robin' and it had never occurred to Vic that this might be 'Robyn', i.e. female. Flustered, but determined not to show it, Vic retreats to the toilets for a few moments to think about how to deal with this unexpected development. As he relieves himself, he thinks:

> Jesus wept! Not just a lecturer in English Literature, not just a woman lecturer in English Literature, but a trendy, leftist feminist lecturer in English Literature! A tall trendy, leftist feminist lecturer in English Literature. . . . What the hell was he going to do with this woman every Wednesday for the next two months?[2]

Little did Vic imagine that within a few weeks he would become infatuated with Robyn, and arrange for her to accompany him on a business trip to Germany where she would 'allow herself' to have sex with him.

Robyn is portrayed as a 'politically correct' feminist. She is seen to encounter considerable difficulty in applying her principles when these collide with the complexities and ambiguities of her personal and professional life. To her partner, she professes a distaste for 'penetrative sex', especially of the missionary variety. Nonetheless, she makes herself available to Vic, a decision that could be interpreted in many different ways. It could be seen as an exercise of power over Vic, and certainly it left him besotted by her. Alternatively, it might be viewed as a feminist project to liberate a man from his masculinist perception of women as passive and submissive objects of sex. Lodge writes that 'she sees herself not as seducing Vic but as putting him out of his misery'.[3] But is this the misery of Vic's sexuality that she perceives to be trapped within one dimension – sexual conquest and 'penetrative sex'? Or is it a misery born of not having experienced the pleasure of sex? Is Robyn behaving humanely (i.e. with empathy and consideration) to offer Vic a taste of what he has missed? Or is she cultivating a desire that she will decline to fulfil as she escapes Vic's unwanted attentions by pursuing her academic work?

Either way, Robyn's actions have the effect of increasing the power that she exercises in the relationship. Initially, she was dependent on Vic to make her weekly visits to Pringle's tolerable. Following the trip to Germany, the tables are turned. Vic's understanding of Robyn's consent to sex leads him to assume an intimacy with Robyn to which she is, at best, indifferent. This is not just a power reversal but a reversal of how sexuality has been traditionally and stereotypically (and patriarchally) viewed – that is, as male conquest with minimal commitments and as female submission with the expectation of a permanent emotional relationship.[4] It is also possible to interpret Robyn's apparent indifference as a rationalization of a tension between, on the one hand, her self-identity as a feminist who is resistant to male conquests and, on the other, the flattery of her femininity by the ardour of Vic's desire.

Vic makes sense of his feelings towards Robyn in terms of romantic love. As he kisses her throat and strokes her breasts, he tells her: 'I love you.' Later, when Robyn tells him that 'there's no such thing' as love, and that 'it's a bourgeois fallacy', he insists that 'I love your silk cunt with my whole self for ever and ever'. The allusion here is to an earlier conversation in which Robyn applies her knowledge of semiotics to analyse the meaning of an advertisement for Silk Cut cigarettes. For Vic, the advert is simply a piece of silk with a slit in it. For Robyn, in contrast, the silk has 'voluptuous curves and sensuous texture', which clearly is a metaphor for the female body, complete with an elliptical slit.

Despite her refusal to regard 'the self' as anything more than a construction of language – 'a rhetorical device' – Robyn finds that she is 'not unmoved' by Vic's declaration of love. Intellectually, she believes in poststructuralism, which tells her that 'we aren't unique individual essences existing prior to language. There is only language.' Yet when Vic conveys his feelings by using the language of romantic love (and when his feelings are intensified by its use), she discovers that emotionally she is touched by Vic's feelings for her.

What has this got to do with organizing work? What it illustrates is how the organization of everyday life, including working life, is managed through interpretive frameworks that enable us to place and position others within our world. When they first meet, Vic and Robyn engage in such organizing work. They each apply (stereotypical) ideas about academics (Vic assumes that they are male) and industrialists (Robyn assumes that they are philistines), to identify and make sense of one another. Their meeting is also a product of organizing work – by their superiors within the organizational hierarchy who have hatched up the idea of a shadow scheme. Positioned in a game of others' design, both Vic and Robyn are more interested in making their Wednesday meetings bearable than participating in the scheme. They render this arrangement productive for themselves by becoming intimately, rather than just professionally, involved with each other. By getting to know each other through a relationship that is physical as well as intellectual, the adequacy and coherence of their respective ways of making sense of the world are challenged as each discovers a good deal about the boundaries of their self-identities. Their prejudices and inhibitions are exposed to a process of critical examination. The irony is that a level of mutual understanding is accomplished that far exceeds the limited instrumental or PR objectives of the shadow scheme.

The historical meaning of work

What counts as work, and how it is valued, differ across time and space. Consequently, the sphere of work cannot be said to have any absolute boundaries or incontrovertible intrinsic meaning. The most inclusive definitions of work encompass everything that human beings do to maintain their material and symbolic existence. In many cultures, what counts as work are activities associated with coercion, in the form of physical threat or material inducement. Rarely in history has a positive value been placed on work. The ancient Greeks regarded it as demeaning (a curse) and avoided it by using slaves. The Hebrews, by contrast, viewed hard work simply as a way of expiating sin.

In western Europe, the Protestant ethic was innovative in valuing 'hard work' as an indicator of spiritual salvation. One consequence of this ethic was the promotion and legitimation of the accumulation of personal wealth through disciplined, productive activity. Over time, industriousness and productivity have become decoupled from sacred meanings. The pursuit of material possessions has largely displaced the significance of work as a means of salvation. This development is also reflected in an emphasis on leisure and especially consumption, in addition to work, as a source of identity.

As long as employed work is the source of income that permits consumption, it is likely to remain a central element of identity. In modern societies, the sphere defined as 'work' tends to be arbitrarily restricted to activities that are rewarded by wages or in kind. Virtually every kind of activity becomes commodified as something that is exchanged for a wage – from corporate transactions (e.g. management consultancy) to personal services (e.g. sexual consultations). However, the boundaries are often blurred – as in the case of the unpaid 'work' of 'homeworkers', mainly

women, who perform low status, unpaid labour (e.g. childminding, cleaning, cooking, washing, and often caring for disabled and/or frail relatives).
Indeed, the status of this activity is so low that it is rarely graced with the
term 'work.' People 'go out' to work – that is, their activity must be sold to
an employer as a commodity before it deserves to be valued as 'work'. Men
have not generally been inclined to participate actively in forms of unpaid
work, thus leaving women who pursue paid employment as a source of
status or meaning with a 'double burden'. It is not surprising that the
feminist movement, to which Robyn in *Nice Work* is committed, has been
preoccupied with advancing the position of women in the workplace rather
than valuing the activity of child rearing and other aspects of unpaid
labour.

In pre-industrial cottage industry, work and home were closely integrated and family members exercised control over the production process.
In advanced capitalist societies, by contrast, work has come to be equated
with paid employment and is assumed to occur outside of the home.
Factory work divides the spheres of employed work and home, as labour is
hired by a separate class of owners and organized by management. In *Nice
Work*, Vic had overall responsibility for the day-to-day running of Pringle's
factory. He was assisted by a number of senior managers who had
responsibility for different 'functions', such as production and marketing.
Junior managers and supervisors were responsible for the direction of
shopfloor and office staff. As work is located in the factory or the office,
employees experience a gradual loss of control over when and how they
work. Managers and overseers are employed by factory owners to organize
and supervise their labour and production.

Industrial work

Current forms of management and workplace organization, as typified by
Pringle's, are the product of socioeconomic transitions from feudal to
industrial societies. This transformation of work has been theorized in
different ways by three of social science's founding theorists – Durkheim,
Marx and Weber. *Durkheim* (1858–1917) believed that the workplace
provides a basis of social integration so long as people are not forced to do
jobs and acquire skills that are meaningless to them. He contended that
mutual interdependence and reciprocal exchange could fill the vacuum
consequent on the erosion of solidarity and stability that accompanied the
process of industrialization. Economic interdependence, he believed, could
provide a new basis for social and moral integration.

When examining capitalism as a particular mode of production, *Marx*
(1818–83) argued that the specialization of activity, vertical as well as
horizontal, enables production to be organized in a way that yields a
surplus appropriated by owners from the productive work of employees.
Marx regarded capitalism as a highly efficient but politically unstable
system of production, which must eventually give way to socialism. Only

following a socialist revolution could the full productive potential of labour be realized, as it would no longer depend on human (worker) degradation. For Marx, this transformation was inevitable, because labour as the source of productive power would recognize its exploitation and capital would reach a limit to its productive growth. Yet capitalism continues, and indeed has no rival since the demise of the Soviet Union and the liberalization of the Chinese economy. However, the contradictions and crises of capitalism continue unabated. Its productively destructive logic is exposed when, at the end of *Nice Work*, Vic's factory is taken over, resulting in mass redundancy. Profitability takes precedence over people's jobs and lives.

Hierarchical control at Pringle's would have been seen by *Weber* (1864–1920) as a comparatively rational form of organization where authority is vested in expertise. Vic occupies his position as managing director by virtue of his qualification as an engineer (he took an MI Mech. Eng. from the local college of advanced technology), combined with many years' managerial experience. Vic's demands on other Pringle's employees, both managers and workers, may have been formally or instrumentally rational as a means of raising productivity. But these demands were not necessarily substantially rational for Vic or for other Pringle's employees. The demands on Vic generated a great deal of stress and several sleepless nights. For his fellow employees, Vic's calculations undermined their individual job security, and ultimately contributed to the closure of the factory with its attendant job losses. So, although formally rational, Vic's management of Pringle's had numerous effects that could be described as 'irrational' in the sense that neither he nor his employees enjoyed any lasting benefits from them.

The existential meaning of work

We now reflect further on the existential meaning of work – the meaning that the experience of work has for those engaged in it. This meaning is illustrated when, well into the novel but before they become sexually intimate, Vic offers to take Robyn for a pub lunch. When Robyn asks for a draught bitter, Vic remarks that he has never bought that for a woman before. Robyn comments, in a good-humoured way, that his experience of life must have been 'very limited'.[5] Vic concedes that this is true, and then confides that he sometimes lies awake in the small hours counting the things that he has never done – such as playing an instrument, pitching a tent, speaking a foreign language, visiting the pyramids.

Vic is about to say 'sleeping with a woman other than my wife' when he says resignedly: 'All I'm good for is work. It's the only thing I'm any good at.' Robyn seeks to console him by saying: 'Well, that's something. To have a job you like and be good at it.' 'Yes,' Vic agrees, 'it's something.' But, without saying it, he thinks that 'in the small hours it didn't seem enough'.[6]

This exchange between Vic, the successful businessman, and Robyn, the struggling academic, illustrates the importance of work to most people. It also hints at the feelings of frustration and meaninglessness associated with many kinds of work. How often does one hear people say: 'It's a pity we have to work for a living'? But *Nice Work* also draws our attention to how work that is meaningful can become so absorbing or consuming as to displace or destroy other sources of meaning and pleasure, such as family, marriage, leisure etc.

A sense of 'is that all there is?' leads Vic to count the things he has never done. The void in his experience of life is powerfully conveyed when, as he makes a visit to his office late one evening, he spies his secretary and his marketing manager copulating with great ardour on the reception lobby sofa. Vic did not approve of this 'hanky-panky between married folk, especially when it was mixed up with work.'[7] For Vic, work was a sphere of impersonal but preferably cordial relations into which personal desires and pleasures should not intrude – which makes his subsequent liaison with Robyn particularly ironic. Still, instead of applying his moral principles to avert his gaze and subsequently condemn and punish their immorality, Vic experiences 'a sense of being on the edge of depths and mysteries of human behaviour that he had never plumbed himself'.[8] Vic's sight of 'the full-blooded fucking of a passionate woman' was tinged with envy as he sensed it as 'a kind of defeat'.[9] It conveyed an intensity of feeling that Vic had perhaps never felt, and certainly had never shared with his wife. It was an experience, and one that perhaps connected subconsciously to feelings of emptiness in the early hours, that he could not remove from his mind.

A suppressed feeling that he had become trapped by a tunnel-visioned devotion to work came increasingly to the surface as Vic's relationship with Robyn developed. Having dedicated his life to little else, work for Vic had become the sole source of meaning and self-esteem – 'it's the only thing I'm any good at'. Vic accepts that having a job that he enjoys is indeed 'something'. But, equally, when he is not absorbed in the competitive pleasures of the 'rat race', as he later describes it, he feels that it is 'not enough'. Through Robyn, he is introduced to literature and to poetry whose (romantic) contents resonate with the feelings aroused by a growing sexual attraction to his shadow. His liaison and subsequent friendship with Robyn arouse Vic from the slumber of being habitually, obsessively engrossed in his work. It would be a mistake, however, to regard Vic's workaholism as a purely individual pathology. Instead, it is symptomatic of the contemporary emphasis on the importance of employment (especially for men) and the status as well as material rewards associated with 'top' jobs, such as Vic's.

How work is experienced, and what it means for individuals, are closely related to their positioning within hierarchies. For those occupying career jobs, work is more likely to be an important source of status and identity. At the bottom of hierarchies, where individuals exercise comparatively little control over the design and direction of their work, there is a tendency to regard work instrumentally – more as a source of income than of identity. Still, even here, the loss of employment can be devastating psychologically as well as materially. For it is not necessarily the activity of work itself that is important for identity. Equally important are the familiar routines and social relations through which individuals sustain a sense of structure and meaning in their (working) lives.

Consider Shirley, Vic's secretary who, it might be said, is in a comparatively servile and probably dead-end job. She nonetheless derives a sense of pleasure, meaning and self-esteem from playing sexual politics with Vic to deflate his position as MD. Vic expected employees to respect his status. He is clearly unsettled by the familiar way in which Shirley, a mature woman with piled hair of 'an improbable yellow hue' and a 'voluptuous bosom',[10] interacts with him:

> It was not with any encouragement from himself that she began to address him as Vic, but he was obliged to concede the point. She had worked for Pringle's for years, and Vic was heavily dependent on her know-how while he eased himself into the job.[11]

The relationship between Shirley and Vic illustrates the precariousness of social status. As noted earlier, we depend on others to recognize and confirm our (symbolic) reality, and they may be disinclined to do this. Eventually, Vic could be in a position to replace Shirley whom he had inherited from his predecessor – once he has appropriated her fund of local knowledge. But, until then, Vic needs her at least as much as Shirley needs him. Despite occupying the uppermost position in the formal hierarchy, Vic is obliged to accommodate Shirley's familiarity, which undercuts a social distance that he would prefer to maintain.

There is also a more ticklish, but no less troublesome, sexual dimension to their relationship. Despite his position of authority, Vic's sexual inexperience and puritanical morality put him on the defensive, as he is intimidated by Shirley's brash sexuality over which he, as her employer, could exercise very little control. Vic's status as Shirley's boss could not be challenged directly. So, more or less consciously, Shirley mobilized other resources – her local knowledge as well as her sexuality – to exercise power over Vic. She successfully played on Vic's (sexual) insecurities and exploited his dependence on her goodwill.

Lodge's depiction of Shirley, which may be criticized for being male chauvinist in its reliance on a popular stereotype of working-class femininity (Bet Lynch[b]), illustrates how a sense of status and identity may be derived less from working as a secretary than from her social skills in commanding the terrain of sexuality at the workplace. However, in the very exercise of this power, Shirley simultaneously reproduces her social identity as an object of libidinal desire and conquest. As a consequence, her interaction with men is restricted to communications that pass through this

---

b   A character who used to be in *Coronation Street*, a popular British soap opera.

channel where all messages are infused with sexual innuendo and banter. It is an irony that these social skills enabled her to derive considerable pleasure and excitement from her work. They also allowed her to develop an extended network of contacts and relationships, which would make it easier for her to find another job than it would be for her boss. Later, when Vic was trying to come to terms with the loss of his job, he 'wondered whether the three women would survive the merger. Probably they would – there always seemed to be a need for secretaries and telephonists.'[12]

The unease that Vic feels at Shirley's sexuality and directness – for example, when she shows him her daughter's portfolio of topless photos – is juxtaposed with his relationship to Robyn, who poses the opposite kind of threat to Vic's apparently secure, but actually precarious, masculinity. Robyn is no less direct than Shirley when it comes to sex. Indeed, she is in many ways more direct and disarmingly matter of fact about it, speaking about sex openly as if it were simply another topic of her research. Robyn also seems to have an ability to switch her desire for sex on and off as if it were just like any other activity that was seemingly unconnected or, at least, capable of being separated from her emotional life. Vic is caught between being embarrassed by Shirley's crude flaunting of her sexuality and being perplexed by Robyn's cerebral treatment of it as a need to be fulfilled, irrespective of the emotional context in which it may take place.

Orientations to work

Vic is of a generation and social background where gaining a place at grammar school, getting a steady job and, if possible, progressing up the career hierarchy were 'the done thing'. Other interests would be willingly, and almost unnoticeably, set aside. The high status attaching to his work is, for Vic, a vital source of self-esteem. More generally, Vic assumes that being in work is a necessary condition of self-respect. This loss of respect for his seemingly work-shy son, Raymond, who in Vic's eyes is not a 'real man', reflects his belief that self-esteem is derived from employment. In response to Robyn's suggestion that people should be prepared for 'creative leisure' (by studying English at university, for example), Vic muses:

> Men like to work. It's a funny thing, but they do. They may moan about it every Monday morning, they may agitate for shorter hours and longer holidays, but they need work for their self-respect.[13]

Vic assumes that the desire to work is natural, something that is intrinsic to self-respect. He also regards work as something separate from his life. He would not accept that his work is his life, yet he is obliged to concede that work does indeed seem to consume his entire life. It simply does not occur to Vic that the association of work and self-respect is historically and culturally relative – that is, something in which people are taught to believe.

The consumerism of the post-war years, with its emphasis on hedonism and easy credit, has posed a challenge to established priorities and expectations – a challenge that has been reinforced by higher levels of unemployment and more casual, short-term forms of employment. Raymond, Vic's teenage son, expects work to be immediately and intrinsically pleasurable. Likewise, Raymond's sister, Sandra, is more interested in becoming a hairdresser than in gaining entrance to university. To Vic, his children lack self-discipline: they are indifferent to their school work and are uninterested in getting a job. He feels his blood pressure rising when, as he prepares to make his regular, early start for work, he thinks of his son. Having dropped out of university four months ago, Raymond lies asleep 'swaddled in a duvet upstairs, naked except for a single gold earring, sleeping off last night's booze'.[14]

Vic's children's attitude to work can be interpreted in many ways. Perhaps they are laid back about work because they have had a materially privileged upbringing. Or perhaps it is because Vic and his wife have neglected the 'moral' development of their children. Or, just maybe, it is because Raymond and Sandra observe the pressures, frustrations and restrictions that work places on their father. It may be speculated that they see little point in struggling to put their feet on the bottom rungs of a respectable career ladder that seems to promise much but, in a world of restructuring, downsizing and intensification, delivers less and less.

Raymond's ambition is to do work that is personally meaningful. A similar sentiment is expressed by Robyn when she corrects Vic for suggesting that reading is the opposite of work, something you do to relax. She acknowledges no boundary between work, leisure and life. Responding to a question about when she starts work, she retorts: 'I never stop working. If I'm not working here [in the University], I'm working at home. This isn't a factory you know. We don't clock in and out.'[15] Raymond's dream is realized when, to Vic's amazement, the 'electronic know-how' acquired from his leisure pursuits results in his being offered a job. Without applying for it, Raymond takes up a position as an assistant producer in a recording studio.

Raymond's employment in the music business is symbolic of a shift in 'postindustrial' societies from manufacturing industry, where Vic has always worked, to service and leisure industries. Employed within a declining industrial sector, Vic loses his job when Pringle's is sold. Shocked by the ruthless and impersonal manner of his dismissal, which makes him feel reduced to the status of a worker who is given his cards (even though he accepts a golden handshake and takes his company car), he declares: 'I'm not sure that I want to work for a company again. I'm fed up with flogging my guts out for companies.' He resolves to start his own business.

On reflection, Vic considers how, since he was a child, he has been caught up in the taken-for-granted world of aspiring members of the working class. He had simply assumed the normality and inevitability of seeking to 'improve' himself, materially and symbolically, by gaining qualifications and a secure job. Working his way up the educational and corporate hierarchy seemed to be the obvious, sensible and worthwhile thing to do. In the small hours, Vic now wonders about the wisdom of his choices, if indeed he really did exercise any meaningful choice. He has been a productive, well-disciplined employee. He has made a good living. But he has also enabled others to make much more money – others who probably had the time and money to do many of the things that he wishes he had done, such as visiting the pyramids; others who have decided that he is to be made redundant.

Vic wonders whether the benefits gained from conventional ambition and predictable conformity outweigh the costs. Perhaps the Greeks were right: perhaps he is just a modern slave. Still, there it is: work, Vic reflects, is the only thing that he is good at – not least because he has passed up opportunities to try anything else. As a consequence of such reflections, Vic's response to redundancy is not to seek another comparable job but, rather, to work for himself. This decision does not directly address the frustrations that he experiences in the small hours. But it does offer him a possible way of continuing to provide for his dependants without the prospect of being treated by his employer 'with as much feeling as a load of pig-iron'.

Despite his elevation, via grammar school and the local college of advanced technology, to the respectable middle class, Vic had worked hard all his life to benefit those in a different class who, in the end, treated him with no more respect than an unskilled foundry worker. Vic is as much distressed about the manner of his departure from Pringle's as the actual loss of his job. As a successful manager, Vic well understood that Midland Amalgamated, the conglomerate that owned Pringle's, could 'get rid of me whenever they like'.[16] However, despite this knowledge, his dismissal came as a shock. He had assumed that his hard work and diligence would save him from this fate. Since his appointment as MD at Pringle's, Vic had energetically met and overcome considerable resistance to making the production process more capital intensive.[17] These changes involved significant job losses. He had also pushed through a sweeping reduction in Pringle's product range, thereby gaining economies of scale through standardization and the deskilling of jobs. Despite much resistance to his plans, Vic had been successful: he made the company profitable within a year, which is precisely what he had been hired to do.[18]

Little did Vic imagine that, just as the turnaround had been achieved, the company would be acquired by a competitor that, in his assessment, was 'on its fucking knees'.[19] The explanation for this decision, given by the Chairman of Midland Amalgamated, was that Pringle's did not fit into the conglomerate's long-term strategy. But Vic challenged this explanation. 'What you mean', he retorted, 'is that by selling off Pringle's now, you can show a profit on this year's accounts at the next AGM.'[20] What Vic could now grasp more clearly was how Pringle's and its employees, including himself, were just pawns in the game of capitalism. The efforts and sacrifices of himself and other Pringle's employees in making the company more productive and competitive were not to be rewarded. Or, rather, the rewards were to be enjoyed by the shareholders of Midland Amalgamated, not by the workforce that had 'made the company profitable within a year'.

It was claimed by the chairman of Midland Amalgamated that he had recommended Vic as the future managing director of the merged company. However, stories were circulating in the industry of 'eccentric' actions that Vic had taken. The chairman alleged that Vic's instruction to remove all the pin-ups from the factory had set the buyers of Pringle's against him (this move had been triggered by objections raised by the 'righteous' Robyn, Vic's 'guardian angel', as the cynical marketing manager described her). The significance attributed to this action suggested to the buyers of Pringle's that Vic had lost touch with business values.[c] Vic had intervened to deprive workers of pleasures and distractions that cost the company nothing and perhaps reduced the likelihood of industrial unrest by fostering and elevating a macho and individualist self-identity over a (working) self-identity.[d]

Robyn's contact with Vic also leads her to review her attitude to her work. As a consequence of her conversations with Vic, it dawns on her that there are millions of people 'who haven't the slightest interest' in what she does. Even if they knew what she did, they would question why anyone should pay her to do it. Robyn is disturbed by the thought that most people simply 'don't give a damn' about what matters to her most. Charles, her partner, responds to her feelings of self-doubt by saying that they are a product of the weight that she is giving to common-sense thinking, as exemplified by Vic's initial, dismissive reaction to her account of her work. Robyn concedes that Charles is right intellectually. She, too, believes that there is no rational basis for privileging the authority of common sense. Yet she is unconvinced by his argument that students must learn about poststructuralism – her specialist area of expertise – because what it reveals is 'true'.[e] She sees this as a bizarre defence of poststructuralism, as it contradicts its own distinctive claim to be arguing that there is no central 'truth' or meaning to which everything must defer.

For Robyn, the tensions surrounding her ambivalence to poststructuralism remain unresolved. She derives considerable satisfaction from

---

c When contemplating Vic's eccentric removal of the 'girlie' pictures, it is also relevant to note his puritanism that verges on prudishness. In developing his character, Lodge emphasizes Vic's unreflective investment in 'solid moral values', his dogged marital fidelity despite a breakdown in sexual relations, and the sublimation of his sexual energies in (hard) work. It is only when Vic is confronted and challenged, intellectually as well as sexually, by Robyn's self-assured but unflaunted femininity that his sexual interest is aroused, and his eyes are opened to the presence of the pin-ups that offend his moral self-identity.

d This is not to deny the connection between these two identities (see Knights and Collinson, 1987; Collinson, 1992).

e See footnote a, p. 31.

communicating these ideas to students and writing her books, even if she has no way of rationally justifying her advocacy of poststructuralist analysis. In this, she is encouraged by Vic who, despite his initial doubts about her analyses of even the most mundane artefacts like advertisements, identifies her as 'a natural teacher' whose work has enriched his appreciation of the everyday world: 'That stuff about metaphor and metonymy, for instance. I see them all over the shop now. TV commercials, colour supplements, the way people talk.'

What makes work meaningful?

For both Robyn and Raymond, work only makes sense if it involves them in doing something that they find deeply meaningful – an activity that absorbs them, and with which they identify completely. 'It would be worth doing even if one wasn't paid anything at all,'[21] as Robyn puts it. This view of work contradicts that of many people who regard much of what they do as drudgery. It is therefore worth reflecting on what makes Robyn's work different.

It is often assumed that the type of work determines whether or not it is meaningful. Routine, repetitive work is deemed to be inherently monotonous and boring and thus is devoid of meaning. In contrast, work that is varied and challenging offers scope for personal involvement that makes it more meaningful. We accept that repetitive jobs are generally experienced as boring, but we believe that there is a danger of implying that there could be a technical means of making work more meaningful – for example, by simply making tasks more varied.

What makes the work of both Robyn and Raymond meaningful is not its intrinsic content but their relationship to its purpose and organization. They work broadly to a programme and timetable of their own design and, as a result, do not draw a great distinction between work and non-work. As Vic says pointedly of Robyn's work, and would no doubt say of Raymond's job as an assistant record producer, 'it's nice work if you can get it'.[22] His point is that only the privileged few have jobs with which they strongly identify and would willingly do even if they were not paid to do so. The remainder, Vic rationalizes, either have the wit to get their feet on to a career ladder, as he did, and accept that they will be handsomely paid for it; or end up in dead-end jobs that are neither interesting nor well paid. That there is increasingly a division between comparatively secure, well-paid, full-time jobs and part-time, casual, insecure jobs is difficult to deny. At the beginning of the novel, Vic assumes this to be inevitable. Later, his understanding shifts to one that would lead him to view the erosion of job security as an outcome of a particular, capitalist logic of organizing resources. This is one that seeks to minimize labour costs as a way of securing a competitive advantage for purposes of generating profits for shareholders.

Industry and society

Dead-end jobs are plentiful in Pringle's, where Robyn is shown semi-skilled work the like of which she has never seen before. On her first visit to the foundry, she is shocked to find so many dirty, repetitive jobs. She asks whether the work couldn't be done by machines or at least organized to allow workers to move about to break up the monotony. Vic's response is that replacing workers with machines would be worth while only if machinery were cheaper. The quantities produced were too small to make automation a profitable proposition. The organization of work, Vic authoritatively tells Robyn, comes down to the bottom line – as does everything else, in his experience. In any event, he claims, the work is not so bad. This is because: 'They switch off, they daydream. If they were smart enough to get bored, they wouldn't be doing a job like this in the first place.'[23] Countering Robyn's description of factory work as brutalizing and oppressive, Vic tells her that he receives hundreds of applicants for each job advertised. As for rotating people around jobs, he says that factory work is monotonous, and that 'the operatives like it that way' – they don't like being 'shunted about'. What's more, they would then demand more pay and waste time moving from job to job.

Vic accounts for the monotonous organization of work in terms of the low intelligence of employees who, supposedly, are incapable of working in any other way and who like to daydream. Vic perceives his employees' daydreaming and their knee-jerk demands for higher pay as symptomatic of their inferior intelligence. He also suggests that if there were anything seriously unsatisfactory about the conditions of work in the foundry, there would not be hundreds of people applying for each vacancy. What Vic overlooks, whether knowingly or out of ignorance, is how this (highly fragmented) way of working has been historically imposed on labour by the logic of capital in its competitive and unceasing search for more profitable forms of production.

Here, it is worth noting how so-called 'new-wave' manufacturing methods, often influenced by Japanese practice, require operatives to exercise their native intelligence (albeit in highly circumscribed and self-exploiting ways). This gives the lie to Vic's rationalization of the organization of work in terms of the natural barriers of low employee intelligence. Likewise, his reference to the hundreds of applicants for every job advertised completely overlooks the high levels of unemployment during the period in which the book is set. It also ignores the desperation and sacrifice of people who are willing to risk their health and be treated as disposable commodities in order to support themselves and their dependants.

Vic refuses to acknowledge the connections between 'industry' and 'society'. For example, in response to Robyn's observation that all the managers at Pringle's appear to be white while the shopfloor workers are predominantly black, Vic fumbles with a cigarette and retorts: 'Don't ask me to solve society's problems.'[24] What he doesn't say is that solving society's problems would create problems for him, because no one would be 'willing' to do dirty factory work. As things stand, he need not worry about this: UK immigration policy during a period of full employment in the 1950s and 1960s ensured a continuous supply of cheap labour that offered an economic justification for the lack of capital investment. Vic is blind to how his willingness to trade on the effects of race discrimination in wider society does not simply reflect 'society's problems' but actually reproduces them. Ethnic segregation in the community is paralleled by job segregation at work.

More generally, Vic's answer to industrial problems is neither to analyse nor to find ways of solving them but, rather, to 'give management more muscle'[25] so that actions can be taken that suppress any kind of workplace resistance or struggle. In the 1980s labour legislation in the UK was developed to diminish the power of organized labour to mount effective resistance against employers. Since then, there has been massive corporate restructuring involving large-scale redundancies in the name of efficiency and competitiveness. This has facilitated the reassertion of managerial prerogative, but has also posed a threat to managers' own job security. The costs of a leaner, more competitive economy are borne by society as a transfer of wealth is made from taxpayer to corporations. The latter increase their profits and the former pick up the social security tab to pay for the social effects of rationalization and redundancy programmes.

Workers' responses to such developments and pressures can be seen as a rational way of managing their situation of subordination and dependence. Workers, like those at Vic's factory, retain a sense of dignity by distancing themselves from their work. Work is then treated merely as a means to other more meaningful ends and, wherever possible, pleasure is derived from informal interactions with others or by playing the system, as illustrated by Shirley, Vic's secretary, and Brian Everthorp, the marketing manager who Vic had seen, having been on the sofa at work.

Meaning is not something that can be injected into work through programmes of job rotation or enrichment, through increasing worker involvement or even through attempts to change company cultures. Of course, such measures may be welcomed or at least tolerated, to the extent that they offer some relief from existing sources of frustration or when they are accompanied by improvements in pay and conditions. What these schemes do not address directly – because their purpose is to boost productivity, not to foster more meaningful work – is the limited control that workers can exercise over the acquisition of knowledge and skill and the organization of productive activity within workplaces. Workers' control over the institutions within which knowledge and skill is defined, acquired and applied is very limited. Others decide which skills and knowledge are to be valued, how they are to be acquired and where they are to be applied. Even Vic, when looking back on his own education and working life, saw how he had been processed by a system designed (by others) to churn out products like himself – that is, engineers and managers sufficiently skilled and disciplined to generate profits by keeping the wheels of industry turning.

Having explored some of the connections between industry and society, we now turn to the relationship between society and academia.

Academia and society

Robyn's relationship with Vic is contrasted to her experience with her colleagues in the English department of her university. Lodge – himself a professor of English when he wrote *Nice Work* – shows how a precarious and inferior status attaches to the temporary nature of Robyn's employment. In principle, an ethic of collegiality spares her from autocratic control by a 'boss', in the form of her head of department. In practice, this ethic makes her post highly vulnerable to cuts in funding. Moreover, Robyn's (unreflective) commitment to a collegial ethic results in her campaigning most actively to resist redundancies. Yet the removal of some 'dead wood' would actually enhance her chances of securing a full-time appointment. Her non-instrumental orientation to work renders her vulnerable to exploitation by colleagues who are more concerned with preserving their own employment than with practising a collegial ethic. Her immersion in work seems to render her oblivious to these contradictions. It is therefore unclear whether Robyn's attitude is governed by a principled resistance to cuts in the funding of universities or a blindness to their consequences for her own future employment.

Lodge contrasts Robyn's orientation to that of her ex-live-in lover, Charles, a fellow academic. Disillusioned with working in universities among people 'who are depressed, demoralized, fatalistic',[26] Charles takes up a well-paid job with a merchant bank. This offers a more attractive alternative to being stuck in a dead-end lecturing job where 'the prospects are bleak: bigger classes, heavier workloads, scant chances of promotion or moving to a new job'. At the same time, Charles has some misgivings about his career change, not least because of how he anticipates it will be viewed by others, including Robyn. To justify his decision, he appeals to poststructuralist thinking. His change of job, Charles suggests, amounts to no more than an exchange of one system of meaning for another – a change from 'a game with high philosophical stakes for a game with high monetary stakes'.[27] Indeed, he claims that working in the City will give him more scope to pursue an interest in poststructuralism as a 'hobby' (just as other men play with model railways), without 'the anxiety of integrating it into one's work'.

Robyn is unprepared to accept such a relativist application of post-structuralist thinking. Charles's inclination to deconstruct everything (e.g. academia), except deconstruction theory of course, leads Robyn to be indignant about what she regards as his desertion of academia. In her mind, the importance of poststructuralist theory lies in its questioning of conventional wisdom. Robyn's work is rendered meaningful to her by the power of poststructuralist analysis to disrupt common-sense understandings – such as the idea that each person/author has a 'self' that regulates their behaviour. A seemingly unshakeable belief in the value of the power of poststructuralism to challenge received wisdom lends purpose and passion to Robyn's teaching and scholarship. It is ironic, then, that when she rows with Charles over his move to the City, she appeals to the common-sense view of individual choice that poststructuralism discounts. When responding to his explanation of his departure from academia, she uses the phrase 'You shit', which implies that his actions are motivated by intentions that Robyn ascribes to Charles's self. Her anger is provoked not only by Charles turning his back on academic life, but also because he deployed poststructuralism, a supposedly critical theory, to justify what she considers to be his (reactionary) pursuit of money making.

Calling Charles a 'shit' may also be interpreted as a reactive defence to an anxiety stemming from Robyn's own half-buried misgivings about the practical relevance of poststructuralist theory. When pressed by Vic to justify what she teaches, she finds herself appealing to established, liberal values concerned with 'maintaining cultural tradition' and 'improving students' communication skills'.[28] She does not argue that the value of poststructuralism lies in its capacity to debunk or question whether anything, including work, has an absolute meaning. In contrast to Vic who feels in his guts the limited meaning of his work in the early, witching hours, Robyn's awareness of the precariousness of her own faith in poststructuralism is purely cerebral and unconnected with feelings, emotions or values. Vic's 'naive' questioning of the value of poststructuralism is unnerving for Robyn. She spares herself from a more passionate, penetrating encounter concerning its limits by appealing to precisely those liberal rights and values about cultural tradition, knowledge and education that poststructuralist perspectives have exposed as disciplinary, technologies of power.[29] Not surprisingly, Robyn finds herself floundering as she struggles to provide a satisfactory answer to the question posed earlier by Vic: 'Why should society pay to be told that people don't mean what they say or say what they mean?'[30]

Robyn was at some loss to answer Vic's question about why 'society should pay' to be told that 'people don't mean what they say'. This question is no less relevant for a book like this. Why, it may be asked, should students have to 'pay' to take a critical look at management? Why not simply teach them to be better managers? Our answer is that what counts as being a 'better manager' is by no means self-evident. Instead, it is a product of particular power–knowledge relations. It is often assumed that 'better' means 'more efficient' or 'more effective'. Vic, for example, can be seen as a 'better' manager in so far as he organizes his workforce in a way that makes them more productive or more profitable. If this meaning of 'better' is adopted, then the study of management is expected to address essentially technical questions about which set of techniques is most productive or profitable. For example, can investment in an automatic machine for Vic's foundry be justified in terms of its contribution to increased productivity, quality and/or flexibility? From the perspective of a capitalist logic, no doubt it can. However, an approach to management education that focuses on the techniques for addressing and resolving such problems takes for granted the political and economic framework in which it currently exists. It also assumes without question that the purpose of management is to organize production and distribution in the most efficient and profitable manner.

An alternative approach, favoured by Robyn when lecturing and adopted in this text, is to concentrate on how the meaning of work – whether the work of managers or the work of novelists – is negotiated, culturally and historically. The value of this approach is that (i) it recognizes that techniques are themselves cultural artefacts whose content and plausibility rests on assumptions that are always open to challenge – as the changing fashions of management theory testify; and (ii) it appreciates how techniques or recipes for management action are mediated by the social and organizational contexts of their use. The most intractable problems of management, it may be suggested, are not those involved in the development and refinement of techniques (as the standard textbooks presume) but, rather, arise from their practical interpretation, evaluation and application.

This is something that Vic intuitively recognizes in his dealings with employees at Pringle's and that arouses Robyn's interest. The cut and thrust of Pringle's are viewed by Robyn as a universe apart from her familiar university world. Yet she also identifies a parallel between her relationship with her students and Vic's way of managing the foundry and 'teaching' his staff. She notes that Vic did not shower his managerial colleagues with information or directives. Instead, wherever possible, he encouraged them to develop their own solutions, albeit that these had to be consistent with his agenda for 'turning round' the company. Within the constraints of making Pringle's profitable, Vic believed in enabling his employees to work out for themselves what needed to be done, rather than imposing his solutions on them and demanding compliance with them:

> [Robyn] could see that he was trying to teach the other men, to coax and persuade them to look at the factory's operations in a new way. He would have been surprised to be told it, but he used the Socratic method. . . .[31]

In a comparable way, we have been 'coaxing' and 'persuading' you to look at management and organization in a new way. Unlike Socrates and Vic, however, we are unable to enter a direct dialogue. Were this possible, we could frame our understanding in relation to your reading of, and comments on, our text. The challenge we face is one of adapting and converting an emergent critical approach to the study of management and organization into teaching practices that are consistent with this approach.[f]

Summary

In this chapter, we have explored the terrain of 'work meanings, emotionality . . . sexuality, work/non-work interfaces'[32] that are generally unrecognized in conventional (and in many critical) textbooks on organization and management. Instead of taking the established body of knowledge of management and organization as our point of departure, we have sought to highlight the human dimensions of managing and organizing. We began by outlining a conceptual framework, comprising the linked concepts of power, identity, insecurity and inequality, to interpret the social realities of work organization. We combined the use of this framework with illustrations drawn from a novel to illustrate and 'bring to life' the lived reality of managing and organizing. First, we explored the changing meaning of work and orientations towards it. Then, we considered the issue of what makes work meaningful by focusing on the distinctive contexts of industry and academia.

Notes

1 Foucault, M. (1980) *Power/Knowledge: Selected Interviews and Writings 1972–1977*, edited by Colin Gordon. London: Tavistock. Foucault, M. (1982) 'The subject and power', in H. Dreyfus and P. Rabinow, *Michel Foucault: Beyond Structuralism and Hermeneutics*. Brighton: Harvester Press.
2 David Lodge (1989) *Nice Work*. Harmondsworth: Penguin. p. 116.
3 *Nice Work*, p. 289.
4 Hollway, W. (1984) 'Gender difference and the production of subjectivity', in J. Henriques, W. Hollway, C. Urwin, C. Venn and V. Walkerdine (eds) *Changing the Subject*. London: Methuen.

---

f   The impact of quality assessment of teaching in higher education in the UK has not been extensively researched. Nonetheless, there is anecdotal evidence that the demand for learning objectives for each lecture/seminar tends to assume and reinforce a traditional 'banking' model of knowledge and teaching (see Chapter 1). We are by no means certain that this tendency can be effectively resisted, though a growing emphasis on student interaction and participation in, and assessment of, lectures and seminars (in the UK at least) can be supportive of a less pedantic and prescriptive approach to teaching when it is not constrained by the expectation that lectures will comply with their pre-planned content and delivery. The obvious difficulty is that quality teaching of this kind is resource intensive and it is far from clear that the cost constraints and productivity pressures will not render it inoperable. Information technology and the Internet may offer a less labour-intensive alternative, but this requires a major injection of capital that is not readily available in UK universities. In terms of stimulating a genuine critical dialogue, it is also untested. Moreover, there are some indications that such depersonalized forms of communication are less than ideal for encouraging open, intellectual discourse, as opposed to merely passing on information. See Grey et al., 1996.

5 *Nice Work*, p. 255.
6 *Nice Work*, p. 255.
7 *Nice Work*, p. 230.
8 *Nice Work*, p. 230.
9 *Nice Work*, p. 231.
10 *Nice Work*, p. 35.
11 *Nice Work*, p. 35.
12 *Nice Work*, p. 367.
13 *Nice Work*, p. 126.
14 *Nice Work*, p. 19.
15 *Nice Work*, p. 334.
16 *Nice Work*, p. 135.
17 *Nice Work*, pp. 124–5.
18 *Nice Work*, p. 364.
19 *Nice Work*, p. 364.
20 *Nice Work*, p. 365.
21 *Nice Work*, p. 126.
22 *Nice Work*, p. 346.
23 *Nice Work*, p. 124.
24 *Nice Work*, p. 134.
25 *Nice Work*, p. 345.
26 *Nice Work*, p. 311.
27 *Nice Work*, p. 313.
28 *Nice Work*, p. 218.
29 *Power/Knowledge*; Hunter, I. (1993) 'Personality as vocation: the political rationalities of the humanities', in M. Gane and T. Johnson (eds), *Foucault's New Domains*. London: Routledge.
30 *Power/Knowledge*, p. 218.
31 *Nice Work*, p. 219.
32 Fineman, S. and Gabriel, Y. (1996) *Experiencing Organisations*. London: Sage.

Recommended further reading

The conceptual framework – power, inequality, identity and insecurity

For an application of this framework to the analysis of work, see:

Knights, D. and Willmott, H. (1989) 'Power and subjectivity at work: from degradation to subjugation in social relations', *Sociology*, 23 (4): 538–58.

The meaning of work

The following offer challenging accounts of the changing meaning and contemporary significance of work:

Anthony, P. (1977) *The Ideology of Work*. London: Tavistock.
Giddens, A. (1973) *Capitalism and Modern Social Theory: an Analysis of the Writings of Marx, Durkheim and Weber*. Cambridge: Cambridge University Press.
Grint, K. (1991) *The Sociology of Work*. Cambridge: Polity Press.

Meakin, D. (1976) *Man and Work: Literature and Culture in Industrial Society*. London: Methuen.

Industry, academia and society

Studies that illustrate the relationship between industry and society, and society and academia, respectively, are:

Knights, D. and Murray, F. (1994) *Managers Divided*. London: Wiley.
Prichard, C. and Willmott, H. (1997) 'Just how managed is the McUniversity?', *Organization Studies*, 18 (2): 287–31.
Slaughter, S. and Leslie, L. (1997) *Academic Capitalism*. Baltimore: Johns Hopkins University Press.
Watson, T. (1994) *In Search of Management*. London: Routledge.

References

Collinson, D. (1992) *Managing the Shopfloor*. Berlin: de Gruyter.
Fineman, S. and Gabriel, Y. (1996) *Experiencing Organisations*. London: Sage.
Foucault, M (1980) *Power/Knowledge: Selected Interviews and Writings 1972–1977*, edited by Colin Gordon. London: Tavistock.
Foucault, M. (1982) 'The subject and power', in H. Dreyfus and P. Rabinow, *Michel Foucault: Beyond Structuralism and Hermeneutics*. Brighton: Harvester Press.
Grey, C., Knights, D. and Willmott, H. (1996) 'Is a critical pedagogy of management possible', in R. French and C. Grey, *New Perspectives on Management Education*. London: Sage.
Hollway, W (1984) 'Gender difference and the production of subjectivity', in J. Henriques, W. Hollway, C. Urwin, C. Venn and V. Walkerdine (eds), *Changing the Subject*. London: Methuen.
Hunter, I. (1993) 'Personality as vocation: the political rationalities of the humanities', in M. Gane and T. Johnson (eds), *Foucault's New Domains*. London: Routledge.
Knights, D. and Collinson, D. (1987) 'Disciplining the shopfloor: a comparison of the disciplinary effects of managerial psychology and financial accounting', *Accounting, Organization and Society*, 12 (5): 457–77.
Willmott, H.C. (1998) 'Towards a new ethics? The contributions of posthumanism and poststructuralism', in M. Parker (ed.), *Ethics and Organisation*. London: Sage.

3   Identity and Insecurity at Work

In Chapter 2 we explored aspects of the lives and associated worldviews of two types of people. Vic Wilcox is a 'hard-headed' businessman whose faith in market principles is put to the test by becoming one of their victims in a humiliating redundancy. Robyn Penrose is a committed feminist intellectual who is incensed by her ex-partner's self-serving (mis)use of fashionable intellectual ideas to justify his desertion of academia for a highly paid job in the City. Both are largely unaware of the strength of their attachments to the values of business and feminism respectively. Vic and Robyn are completely absorbed in their work and the identities they have acquired through it. They therefore find it difficult to recognize the tensions and contradictions suffusing their lives – until, that is, the encounter with each other unsettles their taken-for-granted sense of themselves.

In this chapter we focus on Milan Kundera's novel *The Unbearable Lightness of Being*. We explore and illustrate perspectives on humanity that can shed light on the formation of subjectivity and identity. Under particular consideration is how we all have to 'work at' identity in contemporary work organizations and society. By comparing and contrasting two influential theories – behaviourism and symbolic interactionism – we examine competing understandings of human nature that either deny or affirm a belief in human autonomy or 'free will'. Classical behaviourism leaves no space for a self or sense of identity that mediates between stimuli in the environment and responses to them. Symbolic interactionism, in contrast, takes identity as the central focus for its analysis of human behaviour.[a]

---

a   It would, of course, be possible to focus on other theories or perspectives. Indeed, our colleague Chris Grey, offering some helpful comments on an earlier draft, suggested that a more appropriate way to frame the debate on human nature might be to contrast genetic theory and psychoanalysis. Not only do these pose similar questions of a polarity between determinism and 'free will', or more strictly between biological and social conditioning, he argues, but also they may be seen as closer than behaviourist theories to the common-sense assumptions held by students. However, we believe that our choice is appropriate to the subject matter of this book – management. Some version of behaviourism almost always underlies the accounts, descriptions or prescriptions of management and organization. Indeed, it is partly because classical behaviourist assumptions about human nature remain implicit features of management practice that they are self-fulfilling. By believing that it is human nature to respond favourably to positive and unfavourably to negative rewards, for example, managers induce in their employees precisely the kind of behaviour that sustains the belief. Symbolic interactionism highlights another implicit, yet contrasting, feature of both the theory and practice of management and organizations, as it addresses the less visible sense of consciousness that it claims to be a medium and outcome of behaviour. In particular, it seeks to theorize the identity that is a reflection of, and yet serves to sustain or threaten, specific behaviour or social interactions.

The chapter is structured as follows. We begin with a brief outline of the features of Kundera's novel that are of significance for the succeeding discussion. The chapter proceeds to an analysis in which we consider how, in everyday life and in academic texts, assumptions about human nature prevail that are rarely made explicit. We next consider two opposing theoretical approaches to studying human behaviour – behaviourism and symbolic interactionism – which respectively reflect the division between deterministic and voluntaristic conceptions of human nature. This incorporates a critical analysis that highlights both the strengths and the weaknesses of behaviourism, after which the same attention and procedure are applied to symbolic interactionism. In both cases, there is a specific focus on the significance of these approaches not only for the study of human nature but also for the analysis of identity and debates about freedom or human autonomy. Finally, we develop the perspective on social behaviourism to discuss problems of freedom, insecurity and identity from both an existential and a sociopolitical point of view. This provides the opening for an alternative, posthumanist theory of identity. In the conclusion, there is a return to the problems of the unbearable lightness (or the burdensome heaviness) of being that is the dominant theme of Kundera's novel.

The burden of identity

In this section we provide a synopsis of Kundera's novel, attending particularly to processes of identity formation and development. *The Unbearable Lightness of Being* (*ULB*) falls somewhere between the comparatively conventional narrative of *Nice Work* and the genre of 'magical realism' found in the writings of, say, Angela Carter or Gabriel Garcia Marquez. In *ULB*, Kundera is concerned to explore a series of metaphorical and conceptual separations in modern life, such as those between freedom and constraint, pleasure and pain, and love and sex. Its narrative is interspersed with political, philosophical and ethical commentaries on a number of issues. Among these, deliberations on identity and chance are of special interest to us.

Kundera's novel offers a comparatively accessible, yet sustained and insightful, commentary on the dynamics and tensions of identity formation and development. Our interpretation of the central themes of *The Unbearable Lightness of Being* necessarily departs from other possible readings. However, as elsewhere in this book, our concern is not to provide a 'better' or 'more definitive' reading. Rather, we draw selectively on our chosen texts to illustrate and discuss features of organizational life that are largely excluded from textbook accounts of management or organization. At the heart of Kundera's novel is the struggle of the main character, Tomas, to derive meaning from his existence without becoming trapped or weighed down by its burdens.

ULB explores a central dilemma in life between desire for a secure identity, on the one hand, and escape from the responsibilities that such a desire brings, on the other. Managers (or feminists and students) are no different from others in experiencing this dilemma; nor are the authors of textbooks on management. Yet they/we tend to avoid discussing these matters. This means that a number of complexities and uncertainties about management are disregarded. Certain taken-for-granted assumptions about human nature and existence are made without reflecting on their implications. Kundera's novel helps us in our task of appreciating the significance of what is missing from, or taken for granted in, management texts.

Tomas is a hospital surgeon who lives in Prague in the late 1960s. This was a turbulent period in Czechoslovakia when the Soviet army intervened directly to suppress the liberal reform of communism led by Alexander Dubcek. Tomas is too preoccupied with his work and a seemingly insatiable desire for sex to become actively involved in the struggle against Soviet domination. He is also largely estranged from family and community. Divorced seven years ago, and choosing never to see his son again because of the difficulties of transforming court access into an everyday practical reality, Tomas has also been disowned by his parents:

> In practically no time [Tomas] managed to rid himself of wife, son, mother, and father. The only thing they bequeathed to him was a fear of women. Tomas desired but feared them. Needing to create a compromise between fear and desire, he devised what he called 'erotic friendship'.[1]

Tomas's fear of the power of women (e.g. a mother's power to deny love to her child) leads him to prefer relations with women in which there are no mutual obligations other than the requirement to fulfil the desire for sexual pleasure. However, a series of coincidences lead Tomas to find himself in a relationship where expectations and obligations extend beyond the bounds of 'erotic friendship'. Despite himself, he becomes drawn into a romantic friendship that ends in marriage. Yet his compulsive desire for 'erotic friendship' remains. There is, then, a fundamental conflict between the lightness of (adulterous) promiscuity and the weight of marital obligations. This, and much else in the novel, suggests that Tomas is trapped in a life of sexual conquests. This is a life that temporarily makes him feel 'free' from the demands of emotional commitment, the weight of responsibility of marriage, and the unending duties of his profession.

At first, Tomas rationalizes his infidelities by telling himself that sex and love need not be synonymous – the implication being that his promiscuity in no way diminishes his love for his wife, Teresa. Later, he develops a more sophisticated justification for his promiscuity. The uniqueness of each person, he contends, is accessible only through knowledge of their most intimate expressions where social conventions are momentarily suspended. Tomas understands sexual intercourse as a search for the unique 'I', that one-millionth 'part dissimilarity' which 'only in sexuality . . . becomes precious because not accessible in public'.[2] It is the small part in another human being that is unimaginable 'that is, what cannot be guessed at or calculated, what must be unveiled, uncovered, *conquered*'.[3]

Kundera's novel develops on two levels simultaneously: the philosophical and the mundane. Some fundamental questions of human existence are explored through the everyday experiences of work, marriage, sex and politics. As the title of the novel suggests, one important question is the significance of the metaphorical contrast between 'lightness' and 'weight', and the question of which is to be seen as the more important and positive.[4] Kundera tells us that the ancient Greek philosopher Parmenides had no difficulty in deciding that lightness was positive and weight negative, whereas Beethoven concluded exactly the opposite. In a quotation that serves as a springboard for his reflections, Kundera writes, citing Beethoven:

> The weighty resolution is at one with the voice of Fate ('Es muss sein!' – it has to be); necessity, weight, and value are three concepts inextricably bound: only necessity is heavy, and only what is heavy has value.[5]

One way to sum up a central theme of Kundera's novel would be to say that because the lightness of being (i.e. its arbitrariness and futility) is unbearable, we struggle to give our lives some weight. Without weight, our lives lack meaning or significance. It is only by identifying (with) seeming certainties ('Es muss sein') – in the form of a professional mission, sexual conquest, marriage, political commitment – that the problem of meaning is temporarily resolved. However, this 'resolution' is imperfect as we become burdened by the weight of responsibility associated with such commitments. We then desire to return to the anonymity and lightness of 'just being'. At the centre of human existence, then, are an ambivalence and alternation between the poles of lightness and weight.

We enter the world untrammelled by responsibilities. However, we soon become unsure of what and who we are as the comparatively uncomplicated, but not necessarily secure or happy, experience of infancy is left behind. Our lives are repeatedly filled with a desire for security that is pursued by acquiring, more or less consciously, a sense of identity as 'this' or 'that' kind of person. However, any such identity (e.g. 'girl', 'daughter', 'musician') carries with it responsibilities – at the very least to behave in ways that ensure its confirmation. These responsibilities can then be experienced as a weighty burden from which it is difficult, if not impossible, to escape.

The progressive accumulation of weight – in the form of identity and associated responsibilities – is rarely fully conscious or intentional, Kundera suggests. Rather, it is more often the result of accidental, coincidental, contingent events, or is simply an unintended consequence of other pursuits. Try as we may to plan and control what happens to us, much is a matter of chance. There may be some (life) planning but, despite this, efforts to design and control the shape of events are often blown off course by wholly unanticipated developments.

Kundera's meditations on human existence circle around this paradox of how arbitrary, accidental and coincidental events and relationships (the lightness of being) are productive of the weight of responsibility, from which a release is often then sought. In Tomas's life, a series of unplanned events results in him following a professional career as a surgeon, supporting the struggle against a repressive regime, and becoming 'trapped' into, and within, his marriage to Teresa. Such seemingly fragmented events appear as determinations of 'being', from which the only escape is another series of unplanned events and accidents. And indeed this is precisely how the novel unfolds.

For example, as a result of quite arbitrary political action on the part of the secret police following Tomas's publication of an article that was critical of the Communist regime, he is dismissed from his position at the hospital. After his release from one of his major commitments as a surgeon, Teresa seeks to pull him away from his other preoccupation – his pursuit of extramarital sex and mistresses who make no extrasexual demands on him. But before this happens, Tomas takes up a job as a window cleaner, an occupation that presents even more opportunities for promiscuous liaisons with women who are at home while their husbands or partners are at work. Only when Teresa persuades him to move out of the city into a rural backwater is Tomas released from what he had himself begun to perceive as a weighty compulsion to pursue his sexual adventures. One reading of this development is that, when freed from the burden of professional and political commitments, Tomas no longer needs the escape into a world of 'pure pleasure' – of sex without responsibility. At the very least, he may be seen to realize that a sense of (masculine) identity attained through sexual conquest is no less inherently oppressive than pursuing a professional career, mobilizing political resistance or 'working at' a marriage.

In a later section of this chapter, we return to Kundera's novel to extend our discussion of identity. For now, we continue by considering a series of competing conceptualizations of human nature and the formation of identity. This prepares the ground for a critical review of two prominent theories of human nature – behaviourism and symbolic interactionism. One or other of these generally underpins most common-sense, as well as many scientific, understandings of human behaviour.

The battle for human nature

Besides being a central, if implicit, feature of most novels, the concept of identity plays a similarly tacit role in most management and organizational texts. In these texts, repeated reference is made to managers, employees, customers, diverse stakeholders etc., without any sustained discussion of the formation, negotiation and representation of individual's identities or their significance for management and organizational practice.[b] Although an explicit consideration of identity is exceptional, social scientists and management writers invariably subscribe to assumptions about human nature that either deny or presuppose its significance.

A common presumption is that it is 'human nature' to be individualistic and purely self-interested. This is despite disagreements about the 'needs' of individuals, including those of identity, which such self-interest allegedly seeks to satisfy. Common-sense ideas about individual, rational self-interest have been uncritically assumed in economics, biology and psychology[6] throughout their history. Notably, utilitarian theory and neoclassical economics are based on an assumption of individual self-interest. Modern biology has constructed and celebrated the notion of the 'selfish gene'.[7] This, in association with social evolutionism and with its 'survival of the fittest' ideology, reinforces individualistic assumptions about human nature. Likewise psychology, whether in its behaviourist or cognitive forms, reduces the complexities of social life to the individuals whose impulses and perceptions become the unit of analysis. We now challenge these assumptions and, by working through their logic, discover certain tensions and contradictions that provide 'good' reasons for abandoning them.

The selfish gene?

Consider the study carried out by Colin Turnbull[8] of a tribe called the Ik. In the pursuit of food, members of this tribe would injure and even kill their fellow tribe members. Brothers and sisters regularly stole food or sexual partners from one another. Parents would eat while their offspring were crying of hunger. A conclusion from this might be to argue: 'It's human nature to look after yourself first.' Or consider the dealers or fund managers in London, New York or Tokyo or 'yuppies' in the City and other financial centres.[c] They can acquire an income in one week that exceeds what some earn in a lifetime. Like Sherman McCoy in Tom Wolfe's novel *The Bonfire of the Vanities*, Ivan Boesky worked in Wall Street. He made millions of dollars acting as an arbitrageur, fixing mergers through the use of junk bonds, before he was arrested for fraud.[d] Indeed,

---

b For important exceptions to this rule among textbook authors, see Thompson, P. and McHugh, D. (1995) *Work Organizations: a Critical Introduction*, 2nd edn. London: Macmillan; and Clark, H., Chandler, J. and Barry, J. (1994) *Organization and Identities*. London: Chapman and Hall.

c For an entertaining, insider account of the financial house Salomon Brothers, on which Tom Wolfe's *The Bonfire of the Vanities* (see especially Chapters 4 and 5 below) is allegedly modelled, see Lewis, M. (1989) *Liar's Poker*. London: Hodder and Stoughton.

d In the UK, Barlow Clowes used and lost their clients' money in speculative business ventures while promising them a 'gilt-edged' security on their investments. In the Guinness affair, some very rich men, including Gerald Ronson, the boss of the Heron Corporation, were jailed for illegal financial dealings. Being rich does not seem to be a constraint on breaking the law to become even richer.

the avarice and greed that fuel the pursuit of wealth are often a consequence of becoming wealthy. Despite his fall from grace, Boesky has gone on record to say that greed is 'natural' and 'good' – a statement that is legitimized by 'free' market economics.

To give a more mundane example, it is not unusual for students to discover that many copies of books on reading lists have been loaned from their library or are missing from the shelves. So, when a copy of an important reference book or journal is located, there is a strong temptation to act individualistically by tearing out the desired pages or by 'hiding' the book in a place other than its correct classification. Then it is possible to use that book on another occasion without fear of it being used (or stolen) by another reader.

The conclusion that might be drawn from each of these examples is that it is human nature to be selfish; and therefore that purely self-interested behaviour is what dominates human life. Examples in everyday life abound, rendering this view seemingly incontrovertible. Even so, we wish to challenge the idea that selfishness is a self-evident fact of human nature. Despite its dominance, the view that human beings are inherently selfish can be challenged on the grounds that such assumptions are the product of a distinctive, narcissistic culture rather than an essential quality of human nature.

In the absence of critical self-reflection, or institutions that routinely challenge rather than reinforce this understanding of human nature, the dominant, seemingly self-evident view of human nature readily becomes self-fulfilling. In part, this is because those exercising power treat assumptions about individual self-interest as self-evident 'facts'. Such 'power/ knowledge' can have the effect of transforming individuals into subjects who secure their meaning and identity through confirming its demands. In other words, what we are arguing here is that individual self-interest is as much, and probably more, a consequence of a particular kind of culture and the exercise of power within it than it is a manifestation of human genes.

Contextualizing human nature

In *The Battle for Human Nature*, Barry Schwartz suggests some alternative ways of looking at 'self-interest'. Instead of mounting a direct challenge to assumptions of self-interest, he draws attention to their conditions and consequences. In particular, he emphasizes the *self-fulfilling* character of self-interest theories (e.g. neoclassical economics, 'need' theory) that attract widespread (common-sense) support. Schwartz also highlights the unintended consequences associated with calculations based on a self-interest theory of human nature.

For example, when it is assumed that employees are only motivated by extrinsic rewards (e.g. money) and jobs are then (re)designed principally around such economic incentives, there is a displacement of other or prior bases of work motivation (e.g. creative problem solving). There is considerable evidence to support this argument. Lepper and Greene[9] discovered that students lost interest in solving problems once economic rewards were introduced. In a motor vehicle factory, the introduction of a bonus system resulted in workers being prepared to work only on condition that the bonus could be achieved. When the scheme was withdrawn, labour cooperation and productivity declined. It is what Schwartz[10] terms the '"I used to do this because it was fun; then they started paying me, and now it just seems like hard work" effect'.

Schwartz observes that social scientists are obliged to derive their assumptions about 'human nature' from what is observable in the behaviour of human beings. Yet this behaviour, and how it is interpreted, is itself inescapably a product of particular institutions and power relations. Modern western governments have supported a market-based paradigm of economic behaviour founded on the assumption that the most fundamental characteristic of human nature is self-interest. This assumption then becomes a widely accepted 'fact' about human nature. The 'openness' and plasticity of human nature, which are evident in the diversity of moral values and social norms within and between cultures, are disregarded. Despite the undecidability of human nature, the 'battleground' within the mainstream of social science (e.g. economics, psychology, sociology) is restricted to competitive claims over how the shared assumption of self-interest is to be represented.

Despite this, within the social sciences there is a further battleground where each discipline competes to give 'weight' to its own conception of human nature. More or less consciously, social scientists vie with each other to produce a plausible or useful account of their subject matter. In doing so, the connection between knowledge production and the power that renders certain propositions more credible than others is frequently overlooked; or mystified by the idea that scientific research is impartial, neutral or value free.

Claims about human nature

We have noted how universal attributes, such as self-interest and opportunism, are routinely ascribed to human nature. But Schwartz invites us to reflect on how these attributes are culturally and historically derived. They are produced in particular societies or social contexts at specific times. There are, Schwartz argues, at least three possible ways to speak about whatever universal qualities are attributed to human nature. It may be claimed that:

1 Individual self-interest is natural – it is the way all people are, have always been and *must necessarily be*. A human being without self-interest would be like a dog without a bark.

2 People are self-interested, always have been and will continue to be, *under certain 'natural' conditions*. As in the example of the Ik tribe above, people are selfish when their lives are directly at risk from starvation etc.
3 People's 'behaviour' depends on the particular *social*, *economic* and *cultural conditions* under which they live, and through which their identities are formed; and they would be different were these conditions otherwise.

If one subscribes to the first of these interpretations, then there is nothing that can be done about self-interest, for it is deemed to be synonymous with what it is to be human. Subscribing to the second interpretation would allow for the possibility of the behaviour of individuals to be guided by motives other than self-interest in situations where their life is not directly threatened by natural forces. In societies where welfare policies provide a basic level of subsistence, for example, few lives are in immediate threat from the uncertainties of nature. In such conditions, forms of altruism occur but are subject to erosion where material insecurity re-emerges.

The third interpretation suggests that it is not simply material or physical insecurity but insecurities of identity that impel individuals to be self-interested. It is because human beings seek to survive symbolically as well as materially that they can become self-interested even when their biological survival is not threatened. For example, in circumstances where the citizens of a country are physically threatened by a hostile power, it is likely that any already established sense of national identity will be strengthened in a way that attenuates the unbridled pursuit of individual self-interest. War has traditionally integrated nation states and inspired individuals, often drawn from the least privileged sections of society, to sacrifice everything for the collective good of 'King and country'.

Of these three interpretations, we find the third most persuasive because it acknowledges the 'openness' or 'undecidability' of human nature and thereby provides a more compelling account of the diversity of human behaviour within and across cultural and historical contexts. Where 'altruistic' behaviour is comparatively rare, it is because economic inequality and hierarchical power generate insecurities. In turn, these insecurities tend to give credibility or weight to the belief that their resolution is to be found only in a competitive and individualistic pursuit of scarce material goods and 'secure', socially valued identities.

Of course, any behaviour can ultimately be attributed to individual self-interest. Even when behaving in ways that are conventionally seen as altruistic, charitable or other-regarding, individuals can still be viewed as self-interested. Altruistic acts can simply be understood as the way such individuals secure for themselves a sense of purpose, meaning and identity. Quite clearly, then, the concept of self-interest is not a useful way of discriminating one set of behaviours from another, since it can be applied, albeit tautologically, to every situation of human life. When the attribution of selfishness is made, we are saying no more than that those individuals are interested in doing what they are interested in.

Having said this, and acknowledging that no one can escape the attribution of self-interest, not all behaviour is commonly perceived to be equally morally attractive or reprehensible. Morally attractive behaviours are usually given encouragement by labelling them as altruistic, charitable, caring or selfless. Their encouragement is usually greater when the assumption of individual self-interest is challenged. This can occur not just through interpersonal evaluations and judgements, which have a limited effect, but also by social institutions (e.g. work, family and politics) that foster communal, yet pluralistic, rather than competitive and individualistic values.

Even if it is accepted, or believed, that Schwartz's third interpretation of self-interest is the most persuasive, there are competing explanations of how human behaviour is 'conditioned' by its context. We now examine behaviourism and symbolic interaction theory, as both are based on the understanding that human action is contextually conditioned. Behaviourism understands the formation of identity to be a response to the pattern of stimuli received from the environment. Symbolic interactionism, in contrast, assumes that identity is the outcome of a process of interpretation in which individuals develop and exercise a measure of 'free will' and choice.

Behaviourism: stimulus and response

> Give me a dozen healthy infants, well-formed, and my own specified world to bring them up in and I'll guarantee to take any one at random and train him to become any type of specialist I might select – doctor, lawyer, artist, merchant-chief and yes, even beggarman and thief, regardless of his talents, penchants, tendencies, abilities, vocations, and race of his ancestors.[11]

Popularized by Skinner,[12] Watson's behaviourist thinking conceptualizes human behaviour as the product of arbitrary events or 'stimuli'. These elicit responses that are dependent on the individual's past conditioning. Absent from behaviourism is any sense of human beings as interpreters of the conditions of their existence. Whatever response is triggered by environmental stimuli, this response is understood to be a product of previous conditioning.

Behaviourism has its inspiration in the work of Pavlov, famous for his salivating dogs. Watson first applied Pavlov's ideas to human beings. He believed that, by constructing a given environment, it would be possible to predict the development of a child into an adult, for example, and thereby to determine their behaviour. Crucially, this approach rejects the common-sense view that the actions of human beings are directed by consciousness or 'free will'. Such a belief is regarded as a pre-scientific illusion, for science

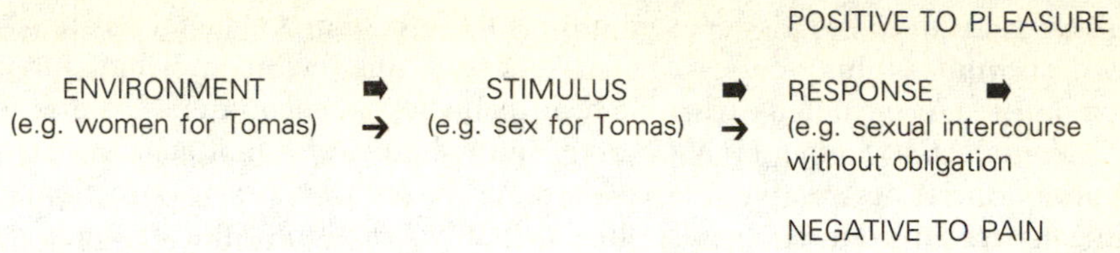

POSITIVE TO PLEASURE

ENVIRONMENT		STIMULUS		RESPONSE	
(e.g. women for Tomas)	➡	(e.g. sex for Tomas)	➡	(e.g. sexual intercourse	➡
	➜		➜	without obligation	

NEGATIVE TO PAIN

FIGURE 3.1 *Behaviourist model*

has to treat human behaviour just like any other object that simply reacts to forces outside itself:

> A scientific analysis of behaviour dispossesses autonomous man and turns the control he has been said to exert over to the environment.[13]

Terms that imply some degree of human autonomy – such as 'thinking', 'willing', 'perceiving', 'sensing' – are dismissed as unobservable 'mentalistic' concepts.

A basic message of behaviourism is that, as human beings, we are deluded by a belief that we are in control of our own lives. The sense of being 'in control' or of being autonomous agents who possess 'free will' is illusory, behaviourists argue, because, in reality, what human beings do is simply an outcome of prior material and psychological conditioning. The common-sense understanding that individuals make choices, are responsible for these choices and are rewarded or punished accordingly is contrasted with a scientific view of human behaviour in which:

> a person is a member of a species shaped by evolutionary contingencies of survival, displaying behavioural processes which bring him under the control of the environment in which he lives, and largely under the control of the social environment. . . . The direction of the controlling relation is reversed: a person does not act upon the world, the world acts upon him.[14]

In sum, behaviourists claim to demonstrate that all human activity is a product of stimuli, which trigger responses in accordance with the past pattern of stimulus–response behaviour. There is a positive or receptive response when the stimulus–response chain has previously resulted in pleasurable experiences and a negative or hostile response when pain has been experienced. Behaviourist theory is thus founded on a philosophy of hedonism (see Figure 3.1).

Consider Tomas's persistent promiscuity in *The Unbearable Lightness of Being*. He appears to be programmed and trapped by his own hedonistic sexual desires and anticipated pleasures. From a behaviourist perspective, Tomas's sexual exploits are a response to a series of positive associations linked to new partners and the pleasures of sex without obligation or guilt. Likewise, his 'reform' is triggered by the accumulation of pain, emanating primarily from his wife's repeated efforts to force him to change. Tomas's own account of his actions can also be explained from a behaviourist perspective. As we noted earlier, he regards his sexual encounters as a means of gaining access to the 'Holy Grail' of individuality and uniqueness. From a behaviourist perspective, Tomas's account would be seen as a rationalization derived from a humanist illusion that bestows on us the idea that we possess 'free will'.

The illusion of free will

Human beings, behaviourists contend, are compelled to respond in predictable ways to given stimuli once particular stimulus–response patterns – such as Tomas's habitual sexual conquests – are established. However, what if the predicted response patterns are not manifested? In other words, how do behaviourists account for deviations from the behaviours that their stimulus–response models predict? Such deviations are not taken as evidence of the exercise of 'free' will or the limits of behaviourism. Instead, they are attributed to the influence of stimuli on behaviour that has yet to be identified.

How, then, do behaviourists explain the illusion of 'free will' or autonomy? According to Skinner, the idea that we are autonomous beings is widely accepted and defended for two reasons; first, because discretion and choice appear to be exercised and confirmed as we control, subdue or manage the forces of nature and society. In the process of acting on the world, we (mistakenly) attribute to our lives and human nature a sense of autonomy and freedom. Second, and relatedly, the idea of autonomy is flattering. Or, as Skinner puts it, 'it confers reinforcing privileges'.[15] It provides us with a comforting belief in our own wilful capacity to determine our own fate when, according to behaviourists, that fate is sealed by the conditioning of the environment: 'a person does not act upon the world, the world acts upon him'.[16]

Behaviourists also contend that our (mistaken) belief in autonomy has perverse and damaging consequences. When we labour under the assumption that we exercise 'free will', punishments – including self-chastisment in the form of guilt and remorse – are administered when we fail to exercise our autonomy, or will-power, to comply with others' expectations. The more rational course of action, behaviourists argue, is to remove the stimuli that produce the deviant behaviour; or, more positively, to introduce stimuli that reinforce acceptable forms of behaviour. What behaviourism makes possible, Skinner argues, is a dispassionate, rational approach to the (re)design of the human environment, an approach that is uncluttered by traditional wishful thinking about the autonomy of human beings:

> Were it not for the unwarranted generalization that all control is wrong, we should deal with the social environment as simply as we deal with the non-social. . . . We accept that we depend upon the world around us, and we simply change

the nature of the dependency. In the same way, to make the social environment as free as possible of aversive stimuli we do not need to destroy that environment or escape from it; we need to redesign it.[17]

For behaviourists, the challenge is to set in motion a rational programme of social and organizational change. This would provide positive reinforcements for desired forms of behaviour, and thereby progressively eliminate the need for negative (punitive) measures to punish unacceptable behaviour.

Some idea of what he has in mind can be gained from reading Skinner's novel, *Walden Two*, in which the technology of behaviourism is systematically applied. In this commune, all work is shared, everyone's behaviour is controlled by the principles of behaviourism, and everyone is happy. Moreover, everyone is made to feel free because this feeling is strongly desired. For the planners of the Skinnerian utopia, however, this feeling is scientifically understood to be an illusion conjured out of the principles of behavioural engineering. From a behaviourist perspective, Tomas's move to the idyll of the countryside, for example, is not a product of a freely willed decision to determine his own fate. Rather, it is an outcome of the complex stimulus–response chains that play on him. These eventually induce him to change his lifestyle and abandon previously established patterns of interaction. The scarcity of 'freely available' women in this rural 'backwater' removed the stimuli that had previously aroused his sexual appetites. An alternative account, as we shall see later, might understand Tomas's behaviour to be less motivated by the pleasures of sex *per se* than by a socially constructed masculine preoccupation with sexual conquest as a means of affirming his virility and power as a man.

Critical reflections on behaviourism

The key assumptions underpinning behaviourism can be summarized as follows:

- Behaviour is lawful. Its laws are amenable to the same methods of investigation used by natural scientists. They are discovered through establishing a correlation between environmental stimuli and behavioural responses.
- Behaviour is determined by environmental as well as genetic factors. Of these, the environmental factors can be observed and changed to ensure that behaviour corresponds with that which is desirable.
- When applying a scientific approach, it is misleading to identify 'feelings' or other inner states of mind as causes of behaviour.

A number of criticisms can be levelled at behaviourism. Consider first its claim to be scientific. According to Popper,[18] a major criterion of a scientific theory is that it is capable of refutation or being falsified. As Chomsky[19] has pointed out, within behaviourism the stimulus (cause) of behaviour is not independent of the response (effect), since we define the stimulus in terms of the response. Take the example of a baby crying. When the baby stops crying it is possible to say that the response (effect) is a result of a stimulus (cause), such as the return of the parent. But this can only be asserted after, and only if, the baby stops crying. Suppose that the baby continues to cry. This behaviour is then attributed to stimulus–response patterns that have yet to be fully identified. Such attributions can always be made to explain (away) behaviour that seems not to fit the model: the theory is shown to be irrefutable or incapable of disproof. As Chomsky argues, behaviourism is then understood to amount to no more than an uninteresting truism – people respond favourably to what they find pleasurable and unfavourably to what they find painful. The problem is that we do not know what people find pleasurable and painful in advance of a response; and even after observing people responding in particular ways, we cannot guarantee that their pleasure/pain priorities will remain stable over time and context.

We noted in the previous chapter how Vic, the central character of David Lodge's novel *Nice Work*, believed that his factory operatives preferred work to be routinized and monotonous because they then 'switch off' and 'daydream'. It is not difficult to find academic studies that lend support to such an interpretation. Goldthorpe et al.[20] found that car workers at Vauxhall were preoccupied with the size of their wage packet, as opposed to job satisfaction or employee participation. This finding would seem to support the assumption of numerous managers, including Vic, that a majority of employees have no interest in work except for the money they are paid in wages.

Yet, as we argue at greater length in Chapter 4, assumptions about the economic motives of workers are based on observations of particular employment conditions where labour is treated as a disposable commodity. Assembly-line work in particular leaves employees little choice but to become economically instrumental and 'switched off'. When reorganized into cells and individualized assembly-line work zones (e.g. at Volvo's Gothenberg plant), a sense of identity may potentially be derived from the collective team responsibility for managing production. It is then more possible for other, non-pecuniary aspects of the job to become increasingly valued and meaningful.[21] However, even when there are job security and better conditions of work, there is no guarantee that employees will comply with changes in working practices. Behaviourism ignores how responses to stimuli (e.g. 'enrichments' in job content) are mediated by interpretive work, which is resistant to programming. The stimulus–response formula completely disregards how the meaning and appeal of stimuli are conditional on the symbolic value that is ascribed to them. In summary, there are at least four reasons for questioning behaviourism.

First, behaviourism simplifies the environment and human behaviour almost to the point of absurdity. This becomes clear when we consider how we gain access to the 'environment'. For it is only through our conceptualizations of that 'environment' that we come to 'know' what it is. Moreover, these conceptualizations are not independent of how we perceive ourselves as 'this' or 'that' kind of person. So, for example, an 'environmentalist' has a completely different vision of the environment from someone who is ecologically illiterate or indifferent to the environmental effects of their actions. Our behaviour is routinely mediated by the way in which we represent ourselves through processes of 'reflexive monitoring'[22] that cannot be reduced to the operation of stimulus–response chains.

Second, if we lack freedom of choice, as Skinner argues, how can we 'decide' to accept his ideas, including his recommendations for the redesign of our environment? The only answer consistent with his thinking is that prior conditioning leads us, in stimulus–response fashion, to accept his authority. However, this claim seems to be contradicted by Skinner's opinion that most (if not all of us) are labouring under the illusion of human autonomy. Notwithstanding his claim to be able to simulate autonomy and thereby 'flatter' the sense of human freedom and self-determination, we remain highly sceptical. If, as Skinner contends, human beings are fooled by the illusion of autonomy, then we will surely be resistant (aversive) to a programme that, from our (deluded) viewpoint, will be perceived to deprive us of our freedom.

Third, when we ask who is to take control of the redesign of the environment, we encounter a contradiction. Skinner's answer is that 'we' are going to take control. But who, exactly, is this 'we'? How is the redesign process to be accomplished prior to the introduction of the behavioural technology that, presumably, claims to guarantee the rationality of choice necessary to perfect the design? Chomsky[23] suggests that an effect of Skinner's thinking is to provide scientific respectability for technocratic programmes of control. These, he argues, are designed to reinforce the status quo, not to change it, even though some behaviourist programmes (e.g. behaviourist sex therapy) may have a reformist impact.

Fourth, and most fundamentally, we may ask whether an exaggerated sense of individual autonomy (convincingly associated by Skinner with flattery) is necessarily equivalent to the idea that autonomy is completely illusory. While the plasticity of human nature requires us to learn from our environment (or be shaped by it, as Skinner would put it), the complexity of influences casts doubt on a simple view of the environment determining behaviour. Even without admitting such non-behaviourist concepts as consciousness, the multiplicity and complexity of environmental stimuli would make it difficult to predict an individual's behaviour. Once consciousness enters into the equation, prediction becomes virtually impossible. As we argue in the following section, many social scientists believe that an understanding of the self-indicative capacities of human consciousness is of critical importance. Symbolic interactionism, in particular, builds its theory around a perception of the role played by human consciousness in the development of a sense of self that always mediates between the organism and that which is external to it.

That said, there are aspects of behaviourism that we find instructive. As Skinner has argued, the way in which freedom is regarded by so many social thinkers as an 'absence of constraints' on the individual, thereby inflating the possibilities for self-determination, is indefensible. We also agree that individual autonomy is much exaggerated in western societies where humanistic ideas and 'human rights' philosophies have been uncritically embraced. Behaviourism encourages us to question widely held assumptions about the autonomy of human beings. It asks us whether we are deluding ourselves about the degree of control that we can exercise. In this respect, the paradoxical effect of behaviourist philosophy may be to enhance our sense of freedom rather than to convince us that our behaviour is totally determined by contingencies.

Even if autonomy is an illusion, it is a necessary one, as it permits those who violate certain fundamental norms and rules to be held responsible for their acts. For this reason, autonomy is a defining characteristic of what it is to be human and it thereby becomes a non-negotiable aspect of identity. Human autonomy, as Foucault[24] continually reminds us, is both liberating and disciplining. Finally, we accept Skinner's point when he criticizes the philosophers of freedom for neglecting the ways in which individuals can value, as envisaged in his novel *Walden Two*, being turned into 'happy robots' through the use of positive rewards. As students often remark when they are challenged to think more deeply: 'Why bother if it only makes you more discontented?' It was this robotic condition of work that Vic Wilcox in *Nice Work* took for granted and sought to preserve in his factory, but to which Robyn, voicing a liberal humanist view, objected. Skinner's critique of humanistic thinking is worth keeping in mind when considering the opposing ideas about human nature represented by symbolic interactionism.

Symbolic interactionism: meaning and self

The foundations of 'symbolic interactionism' were laid by Mead,[25] who stressed the role of meaning in the process of organizing human behaviour. Human conduct, Mead argued, is mediated by symbols in the form of language that represent and communicate a shared reality. In this way, symbols are used to render the world meaningful as we communicate to ourselves as well as to others. Consider the case of Tomas in *The Unbearable Lightness of Being*. He constructed the symbolic universe of 'erotic friendship', which he faithfully lived out, from available ideas about (male) sex and power.[e] The meaning ascribed to his sexual liaisons enabled him

---

e   Kundera suggests that Tomas's pursuit of 'erotic friendship' was motivated by 'a desire not for pleasure (the pleasure came as an extra bonus) but for possession of the world (slitting open the outstretched body of the world with his scalpel)'; Kundera, M. (1989) *The Unbearable Lightness of Being*. London: Faber and Faber. p. 200.

to account for, order and legitimize relationships with women where no demands other than sexual ones were permitted.

For symbolic interactionists, communication is accomplished through a process of self-reflection and interpretation:

> The actor selects, checks, suspends, regroups, and transforms the meanings in the light of the situation in which he is placed and the direction of his action. Accordingly, interpretations should not be regarded as a mere automatic application of established meanings but as a formative process in which meanings are used and revised as instruments for the guidance and formation of action. It is necessary to see that meanings play their part in action through processes of self-interaction.[26]

Symbolic interactionists challenge the belief that meanings either reside in the things themselves or are an expression of internal psychological states of mind (e.g. attitudes, needs, perceptions). Rather, meaning emerges through a process of continuous *negotiation* and also in internal conversations, through which meanings are continuously generated and/or reformulated.

Much social science, including behaviourism, is criticized by symbolic interactionists for disregarding or minimizing the fundamental importance of meaning. Signs and symbols mediate the interactions between human beings as well as between people and the world surrounding them that they endow with meaning:

> Meaning is either taken for granted or played down in practically all of the thought and work in contemporary social science and psychological science. . . . If one declares that the given kinds of behaviour are the result of the particular factors producing them, there is no need to concern oneself with the meaning of the things towards which human beings act.[27]

From a symbolic interactionist perspective, the role of meaning and self-consciousness in guiding action and interaction is central. Self-consciousness arises when, as infants, humans learn, through their interactions with parents, siblings etc., to identify themselves as discrete and responsible beings in the world. As this consciousness develops, the world becomes 'heavy' as others' expectations of who we are and how we should behave are internalized. In *The Unbearable Lightness of Being*, it is precisely the weight of others' expectations that Tomas, in his relationships with women especially, strives to avoid. By restricting his relationships with other women to that of 'erotic friendship', the influence of the other on him, especially romantic meanings associated with sexually intimate relations, is minimized. As Tomas expresses it:

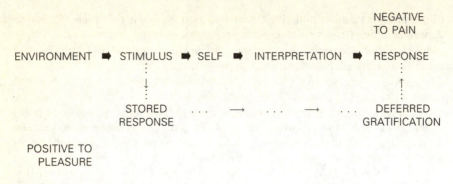

FIGURE 3.2 *Symbolic interactionism*

> The only relationship that can make both partners happy is one in which sentimentality has no place and neither partner makes any claim on the life and freedom of the other.[28]

An initial, rather limited, way of representing symbolic interactionism is to understand it as a modified version of the behaviourist model. A concept of 'self' now mediates between stimuli and responses, as in Figure 3.2.

In this model, the adult self incorporates a whole range of understandings about how human beings interpret stimuli, such as those associated with seduction. These understandings are learned through interactions with numerous 'significant others' who, in addition to parents and siblings and peers and friends, include work colleagues and mere acquaintances. By drawing on these understandings, the adult self interprets the meaning and significance of situations. In the process, they intervene in the production of meanings, defer responses by storing them up for consideration at a later time, ignore meanings, dissemble or resist them etc. The model incorporates an appreciation of how individual behaviour is conditioned by an assessment of interpretation by others. For example, behaviour may be motivated by a desire to gain the recognition or approval of others as a means of maintaining or boosting one's sense of self. Each of Tomas's sexual encounters enabled him to confirm his sense of himself as free and self-determining in the face of the many domestic, professional and political pressures to surrender this freedom.

The process of self-formation

Mead[29] uses three concepts – the 'I', the 'Me' and the 'Generalized Other' – to articulate his understanding of the process of self-formation. Consider an example drawn from *Nice Work*, which we discussed in Chapter 2. When Robyn, a feminist academic, is ushered into Vic Wilcox's office for the first time, she expects to meet a man who fits a 'generalized other' concept or stereotype of 'managing director' – 'grand and gross, with plump flushed cheeks and wings of silver hair'.[30] Such concepts, or stereo-types, are developed to negotiate our way around the world.[f] Robyn 'almost smiled with relief' to discover that Vic was much less imposing and remote than her generalized stereotype of 'managing director' had led her to expect.[31] Her anxieties about maintaining the sense of herself as an equal and respected participant in the interaction with Vic were eased by the fact that he seemed quite ordinary and approachable. In other words, she was relieved to feel that her sense of herself (i.e. the 'Me') would not be seriously undermined in the way that her 'generalized other' stereotypes of MDs had led her to fear.

The human organism, symbolic interactionists contend, does not simply respond according to previous patterns of reinforcement as behaviourists claim. Rather, the world is actively and creatively interpreted in ways that cannot be reduced to stimulus–response chains, or a past history of cause and effect:

> By virtue of engaging in self-interaction the human being stands in a markedly different relation to his environment than is presupposed by the widespread conventional view [e.g. behaviourism]. Instead of being merely an organism which responds to the play of factors on or through it, the human being is seen as an organism that has to deal with what it notes. . . . Its behaviour with regard to what it notes is not a response called forth by the presentation of what it notes but instead is an action that arises out of the interpretation made through the process of self-indication.[32]

From this perspective, actions arise out of processes of interpretation in which the individual 'I' creatively calls on the symbols to define and assess situations. From this it follows that: 'One has to get inside the defining process of the actor in order to understand his action'.[33,g]

Consider how Tomas defined and ascribed value to his professional and private life. He went to considerable lengths to construe sex as a purely physical act, devoid of any human significance or responsibility. However, the reverse of this attitude occurred in his professional role as a surgeon, where he was weighed down by responsibilities to the point of losing his sexual appetite:

---

f   Stereotypes of the 'Other' may also be used to perceive selectively only those aspects of a person or situation that comply with particular expectations and are extensively drawn on by those who are prejudiced (e.g. racism, sexism etc.). Such prejudice resulted in the dismissal of the Jewish maids in Ishiguro's novel *The Remains of the Day*, which is discussed in Chapter 4.

g   A vast range of methodological approaches and techniques (e.g. ethnographic, case study, personal construct theory, participant observation, depth interview etc.) have been developed to discover the nature of meaning as perceived by subjects. These 'qualitative' approaches contrast sharply with research methods (e.g. questionnaires or publicly available statistics) in which, directed by the demand for quantification and generalization, meanings are imposed on subjects by the investigator's categories.

Whenever anything went wrong on the operating table, he would be despondent and unable to sleep. He would even lose his taste for women. The 'Es muss sein!' (it must be) of his profession had been a vampire sucking his blood.[34]

'Professional work' tends to carry with it a generalized meaning that can weigh heavily on people as they strive to meet superhuman standards of conduct. To the extent that the 'I' invests the 'Me' with expectations drawn from the 'generalized other' (e.g. the competent surgeon), the professional self is acutely vulnerable. This is because the real or imagined demands of others invariably exceed the capacity of ordinary human beings to meet them. Tomas had successfully developed a means of evading conventional expectations attaching to central features of his private life – notably, a transgression of normal behaviour in his serial conquests of women. But he had found it impossible to stop his professional obligations as a surgeon from acting as a 'vampire sucking his blood'.

Later, Tomas fell from political favour, lost his position as a surgeon and took a job as a window cleaner. Only then did he experience work with the same abandon as he had pursued 'erotic friendship', as he then lost the compulsion of an internal 'Es muss sein!' (see above). By embracing a job with a low self-image, Tomas freed himself of professional responsibilities:

> Here he was, doing things he didn't care about and enjoying it. Now he understood what made people (people he always pitied) happy when they took a job without feeling the compulsion of 'Es muss sein' and forgot it the moment they left for home every evening. This was the first time he felt that blissful indifference.[35]

Precisely because a lower symbolic value is ascribed to such work as window cleaning, Tomas was less inclined to identify his 'Me' in it. There was correspondingly less risk of becoming 'weighed down'. For Tomas, window cleaning provided him with an identity of very limited commitment and responsibility that he enjoyed as 'simply a long holiday'.[36,h]

For symbolic interactionists, it is the claimed absence of autonomy declared by behaviourists that is a myth. It is a myth that becomes dangerously totalitarian, they argue, when behaviourists set out to engineer social systems. For these systems are based on schedules of reinforcement that are designed to deny the freedom of individuals to interpret or challenge them. Such a denial carries the political danger of the erosion of 'civil society' or 'community', as we know it. It is therefore resassuring that, from a symbolic interactionist perspective, every attempt to pro- gramme 'the good society' may be subverted and miscarry, as people ascribe alternative meanings to given stimuli – for example, by attributing

---

h   Although Van Morrison does not explore the erotic opportunities of the job, its carefree qualities are brilliantly expressed lyrically and musically in his song *Cleaning Windows*.

a diminishing (or even negative) value to those 'rewards' that behaviourists take to be positive reinforcers. One possibility is that the trappings of 'success' that are intended to reinforce certain, desired kinds of behaviour among working people, for example, may be redefined as 'greed'. When this happens, economic or status incentives may be diminished to the point at which the cost of securing compliance from employees is highly inflationary. Or these incentives may be inverted altogether, as individuals give greater priority to leisure than the extra effort required to secure economic or status rewards. In Tomas's case, the values associated with being a surgeon and being a window cleaner became reversed as he began to feel relief from the burdens of professional responsibility. These responsibilities had weighed heavily on him for so long and had contributed to a hedonistic promiscuity that served as a means of relief and escape.

Critical reflections on symbolic interactionism

The basic premises of symbolic interactionism can be summarized as follows:

1 People act on the basis of the meanings they ascribe to the objects in their world, not in terms of the stimuli given off by these objects.
2 Communications between people evolve through processes of interaction in which they make and interpret symbolic indications to one another, in the form of speech and gestures.
3 Social action is accomplished as individuals mobilize meanings to interpret and enact the situations in which they are involved.

As with behaviourism, a number of criticisms can be levelled against symbolic interactionism. First, when examining the process of self-formation and the process of interaction, symbolic interactionism treats individuals as curiously disembodied. Little consideration is given to how human experience comprises sensations, feelings, emotions, desires and so forth. The symbolic interactionist model of self-consciousness appears overly abstracted and detached from the 'lived experience' of human beings with bodily desires. In this regard, our illustration of symbolic interaction, through the character of Tomas in *ULB*, might seem to be misleading. Tomas is clearly keen to experience certain desires and feelings, yet he also contrives a degree of distance from them and, in at least this respect, the example is apposite. His behaviour can perhaps be said to reflect and reinforce a masculine conception of human existence in which the rational control of externalities, including the way that one perceives oneself, is dominant. In effect, the 'I' is charged with the task of creating and controlling the 'Me'. This masculinity takes insufficient account of the many occasions when bodily or emotional desires override any cognitive concern to secure a socially derived self-image or identity.

Second, symbolic interactionists fail to explore how the 'Me' emerges from the active 'I'. There is no explanation of what prompts this process or how it is accomplished, except to say that it involves reciprocal processes in which people respond to what they perceive to be others' attitudes towards them. The initial and recurrent process of (re)producing self out of it-self is taken for granted rather than critically examined and explored. We shall return to this criticism when we attempt to develop a conception of identity that is directly attentive to the existential problems of freedom and control.

Third, it is assumed that the process of interpreting the environment is necessarily structured (and constrained) by a concern to affirm a stable and continuous 'Me'. There is minimal discussion of how inconsistencies between others' definitions of self are accommodated. Is the 'Generalized Other' as uniform as symbolic interactionists seem to assume? It takes no account of how, for example, external and internal dialogues occur in which individuals construct boundaries or divisions within the 'Me' in order, paradoxically, to retain a sense of unity. Because the 'Me' is assumed to be comparatively integrated, symbolic interactionism does not explore the processes of self-interaction between different, and difficult to reconcile, views of self. For example, Tomas contrives to compartmentalize his political proclivities from his professional life as a surgeon. In contrast, those subscribing to a poststructuralist understanding of identity formation challenge the concept of a unitary self and argue that there are multiple, conflicting selves. Potentially, the problematizing of the unified self can expose the arbitrary and, in a sense, illusory, boundaries of reality that are created and maintained as individuals strive towards a consistent sense of self or identity. Compartmentalization serves to prevent conflicting and incompatible identities from confronting each other. A prominent example is the case of President Clinton's sexual misdemeanours with Monica Lewinsky. Seemingly, he contrived to separate the expectations ascribed to his office and marital status from his desire for oral sex, partly by defining a 'blow job' as not being a form of sexual intercourse.

Fourth, symbolic interactionism has almost nothing to say about the historical conditions that are at once a medium and an outcome of the process of symbolic interaction. Lichtman,[37] for example, has argued that 'the channelling of interpreted meanings is class-structured and is formed through lived engagement in the dominant institutions of society which are class-dominated and bear a specific class structure'. Even if one is sceptical of the deterministic claims of such analysis, it is difficult to dismiss the view that power and inequality are a condition as well as a consequence of the self and identity formation process. Having said that, the value of symbolic interactionism is that it usefully prompts reflection on how our sense of reality is mediated through symbols and, more particularly, how our selves are socially constructed through interactions with others. Our taken-for-granted sense of reality and selfhood is seen to be held together by a precarious set of symbols with which we just happen to have identified.

Beyond behaviourism and symbolic interactionism

What can be learned from behaviourism, symbolic interactionism and the criticisms that have been levelled against them? To begin with, it is worth noting that their respective perspectives are by no means novel. Consider the example of employees going on strike. When strike action is characterized in terms of a predictable response to a given set of stimuli, assumptions shared by behaviourism are implicitly invoked. Alternatively, assumptions shared by symbolic interactionism are mobilized when strike action is seen as reflecting the 'mood' of the workforce, who interpret their situation as unfair or unreasonable. To this extent, behaviourism and symbolic interaction do not so much challenge common sense as clarify, and make more available to critical reflection, the premises that guide its reasoning.

For behaviourists, the heart of the difference between behaviourism and symbolic interactionism, we have argued, is a disagreement about human autonomy. For behaviourists, this autonomy is a myth that obstructs the development of a more rational society. In such a rational society, environments would be redesigned to produce the stimuli that elicit socially desired responses. For symbolic interactionists, in contrast, autonomy is at the very centre of what it is to be human. Autonomy enables human beings to interpret stimuli in novel, imaginative ways that elude or defy behaviourist control.

It is unlikely, and perhaps undesirable, that the debate will ever be settled between those who believe in human autonomy or 'free will' and those who deny its existence. This is because both accounts are based on metaphysical assumptions that cannot be conclusively falsified. Such undecidability can invite despair, but only if there is a (naive and scientistic) expectation that social science will deliver absolute answers rather than provide fuel for continuing debate. The value of social science can be understood to reside in its capacity to clarify, and press to their limits, common-sense understandings of everyday life. Its tolerance of any inconclusive investigations helps keep alive debate on the moral and political legitimacy of the various competing frameworks that have been developed to guide our actions in the world.

The way this chapter has been structured in a linear developmental fashion may suggest a 'progressive' history of ideas approach. While that is not intended, we do see the theory of identity that we are now about to develop as an amalgamation of social-psychological and sociological ideas about, or theories of, human behaviour. While it captures elements of both behaviourism and symbolic interaction theory, it should not be regarded as superior but simply different and equally open to critique. For example, it is possible to be critical of the implicit masculinity of identity theory.[38]

Our own inclination is to emphasize how both behaviourists and symbolic interactionists assume human nature to be plastic. How people behave depends on the design of the reinforcement schedules or (re)construction of interpretive frameworks. Building on their shared assumptions about the plasticity of human nature, we now outline a theory of identity that builds on our critical reflections on behaviourism and symbolic interactionism. In particular, we draw on behaviourism to expose the limits of humanistic formulations that assume the centrality of human autonomy in a way that exaggerates its power. But equally, we are sympathetic to the symbolic interactionist emphasis on the mediation of human action and self-formation through processes of interpretation.

The precariousness of identity in the context of work and society

The limits of rational control

It is in the world of management and formal work where we expect to find the most refined form of rational, planned action. Yet empirical research repeatedly reveals a more chaotic scenario.[39] Even the best-laid plans cannot anticipate all conceivable contingencies or take full account of the interactive and contingent quality of relationships. For example, in *The Unbearable Lightness of Being*, Teresa did not expect to feel nauseous when emulating her husband's adultery.

As a consequence of unanticipated events, personal and corporate plans are often discredited. They fall into disuse or assume a purely formal ceremonial quality. Having been commended as the key to successful business in the 1970s and 1980s, elaborate, detailed planning has fallen into disrepute in an age where increased importance is attached to general strategic intent and direction, corporate agility and incremental progress.[40,i] Arising out of the development of 'flexible specialization',[41] the 'flexible firm'[42] and other systems of corporate responsiveness to changing markets and more demanding customers, management has been at pains to demonstrate intra- and entrepreneurial skills in the pursuit of customer service. In Kundera's terms, the pendulum has swung away from the 'heaviness' of grand strategic planning to the comparative 'lightness' of husbanding competencies and, in Tom Peters's words, 'thriving on chaos'.[43] Such injunctions invite managers to construct their sense of identity and to direct their actions in a specific manner, albeit one that is less wedded to the formulation and implementation of bureaucratic procedures.

Compared to the corporate arena, the private world of sex is widely assumed to be less amenable to planning on account of the volatility of

---

i   An extended study of rational planning occurs in Ishiguro's novel *The Remains of the Day*, which is discussed in Chapter 4. Stevens, the butler, devises an elaborate, comprehensive staff plan for running a large country house. In practice, the operation of this plan was seriously wanting on account of Stevens's failure to recognize his own limits.

human emotions. Nonetheless, Tomas's fear of women fuelled his desire to possess them in a way that was purely physical, devoid of any human significance or responsibility. He therefore developed a working plan or method:

> He considered [t]his method flawless: The important thing is to abide by the rule of the threes. Either you see a woman three times in quick succession and then never again, or you maintain relations over the years but make sure that the rendezvous are at least three weeks apart. The rule of threes enabled Tomas to keep intact his liaisons with some women while continuing to engage in short-term affairs with many others.[44]

Tomas planned his sex life to conform to a self-consciously designed strategy.

Identity formation in conditions of uncertainty

We have illustrated how behaviour is facilitated and constrained by routines or methodical ways of organizing human affairs. Self-consciousness allows, yet also demands, that human behaviour be purposive. For this reason, self-consciousness is a condition of anxiety and insecurity. Under conditions of material scarcity (e.g. lack of food), the desire to survive directs our purposiveness towards the production or the appropriation of the means of remedying this scarcity. Precisely how this desire is fulfilled depends on the cultural (e.g. religious) practices that develop to interpret and regulate processes of production or appropriation (see Figure 3.3). Except in the most extreme circumstances, meanings – such as customs and moral and religious beliefs – mediate desire and its satisfaction. It is impossible to separate out material or biological survival from the concerns that human beings have with symbolic meaning and identity as mediated through language.[j]

Feelings of insecurity about physical survival can be aroused when material scarcity is identified. Of equal if not greater importance, especially in materially affluent societies, are the anxieties aroused by threats to symbolic survival in the form of social encounters that unsettle a stable or secure sense of self. Our sense of self is endangered by situations where we perceive ourselves to be vulnerable to social or interpersonal rejection or denial. Whereas (other) animals tend to react instinctively to stimuli in the environment, human beings interpret every situation through a self-conscious perception of what it means for symbolic, as well as material, security. The formation of a sense of identity within social institutions

---

j   The focus on language is somewhat neglected or perhaps taken for granted by both behaviourists and symbolic interactionists, and yet it is through rational reflections or rationalizations of behaviour that behavioural reinforcement and identity construction take place.

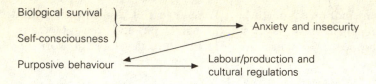

FIGURE 3.3 *Human nature*

means that the 'appropriateness' of behaviour can be challenged or may shift unpredictably from one moment or situation and context to another. This is what makes for the 'lightness of being' – a lightness that can be experienced as 'unbearable'. Perversely, it is precisely this experience, or its anticipation, that strengthens our commitment, or attachment, to established routines and obligations ('Es muss sein').

In *The Unbearable Lightness of Being*, Teresa is always uncertain about how to behave in response to Tomas's promiscuity. At first, she simply complained about it in a passive way. Later, becoming more assertive, she left him temporarily and also experimented with adultery. Finally, though perhaps only because Tomas himself came to regard womanizing as a form of enslavement, there was an agreement to move to the countryside. There, she anticipated that a 'harmonious world' would exist in which 'everyone came together in one big happy family with common interests and routines',[45] such as dancing in the local tavern on Saturdays and attending church on Sundays.

What she found, in contrast, was a suspension of the traditional way of life by a communist state that had turned the tavern into offices, shut down the local church and forbidden religious holidays. There was nowhere for the villagers to 'come together'. Their evenings were now spent watching television and (ironically) dreaming of moving into town to escape the boredom. Yet, unlike those living in the urban areas of Czechoslovakia, the villagers were not overseen or directly controlled by state officials, precisely because their passivity posed little threat to the state. The authorities were willing to allow the workers a degree of 'self-determination', so that they were able, for example, to elect the chairman of the collective farm[46] – a move that has its parallels in the empowerment programmes imposed on employees by the managers of capitalist enterprises.

Clearly, the lives of the country people were intensely affected by their interpretation of the changes associated with the reimposition of Soviet-style communism in Czechoslovakia. They serve to illustrate how different systems of ownership and control exert a pervasive influence on diverse aspects of everyday life – from entertainment to religious practice.

The response of the villagers to the loss of 'the age-old pattern' of the countryside was not one of rebellion or an active quest to re-establish their traditions. Instead, they retreated into their private worlds and fantasies of leaving the place that 'offered them nothing in the way of even a minimally interesting life'.[47] They adapted by willingly surrendering their identity as members of a rural community. Instead of resisting the authorities, they emulated the lives of city people, even in the way in which they furnished their homes.

The context of capitalism

Slavery, feudal obligations, market transactions and state control are examples of different structures of social relations through which the productive potential of human labour is translated into goods and services. Since most readers of this book are likely to live in regimes of market capitalism, more or less supported and regulated by institutions of the modern state, we now focus attention on how capitalist social relations condition the lives of individuals and communities. Central to capitalist production is a division between those who own capital (e.g. plant and equipment) and those who are obliged to sell their labour to achieve an adequate level of subsistence for themselves and their dependants.

Initially, the transfer of productive activity from artisans to capitalist manufacturers did not involve any major shifts in the division of labour. Nonetheless, new relationships of employment were established. In turn, these enabled capitalists to exert increasing control over the labour process:

> Through the co-operation of numerous wage-labourers, the command of capital develops into a requirement for carrying on the labour process itself, into a real condition of production. That a capitalist should command in the field of production is now as indispensable as that a general should command on the field of battle.[48]

Just as it became increasingly difficult for the villagers described in *ULB* to secure control over their lives through the maintenance of their traditions, it becomes almost impossible for individual producers, or even for small groups of artisans, to compete with the concentrations of capital to be found in factories. Ownership of capital becomes 'a real condition of production'.

Investors expect managers, as their agents, to organize work in a way that achieves an acceptable rate of return on their capital. This is contingent on success in the marketplace but also on restraining costs, especially those of labour. The relationship between capital and labour is thus founded on a fundamental conflict over the control of work and the economic rewards that it yields (see Figure 3.4). In these circumstances, managers struggle to organize work according to the preferences and priorities of capital. And since managers are also sellers of labour, capital struggles to ensure that their career interests do not override the quest for profitable growth.

A parallel can be drawn here between the appropriation and control of the means of production by capitalists and the collectivization of land by a state socialist regime. Under state socialism, popular support relies on

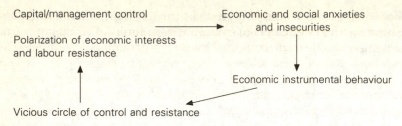

FIGURE 3.4   *Capitalist society*

appeals to the 'god' of the state, buttressed by social security for those who conform. Under capitalism, training and education, combined with market competition, transform sellers of labour into more or less compliant employees that are willing to embrace corporate values and objectives – such as improved customer service, productivity or quality (see Chapter 5). Sophisticated propaganda is adopted by capitalist corporations to promote employee productivity – notably, the cult of the individual and the pursuit of enterprise.

Resistance and control   To the extent that employees organize themselves and struggle to exert or expand their control over the labour process, they engage in forms of resistance. Alternatively, they may cooperate in return for benefits such as increased wages and/or shorter working hours. To the extent that such bargains are restricted to the terms and conditions of employment, they assume and reinforce the exclusion of labour from decisions about the organization of work. This approach to securing the cooperation of labour limits the opportunity for employees to be creative and self-managing. It also deflects their creative energies into recalcitrance and resistance. In turn, this resistance provokes a reassertion of managerial control and surveillance. The polarization between management and labour is reaffirmed as each side becomes increasingly instrumental in relation to the other and their respective economic interests (see Figure 3.4).

Employees resort to economically instrumental behaviour when, to paraphrase Oscar Wilde, capitalism puts a price on everything (i.e. labour as a commodity) while valuing nothing. Employees rarely feel satisfied as opposed to just 'knackered'.[49] They also become resentful when the exercise of management control is thought to undermine their sense of themselves as autonomous agents – an expectation nurtured by a long tradition of enlightenment philosophy in western civilization. One way they cope with this is by distancing themselves mentally[50] from the experience of subordination – just as the villagers in *ULB* had done in response to the privations of the communist regime (see earlier). Employee indifference is a form of resistance that lacks visibility since it is routinely, yet imperfectly, concealed in acts of compliance. Indifference and apathy are most common in situations where other channels for expressing dissatisfaction or dissent have been 'closed off' or restricted by the coercive threat of unemployment or social ostracism. Within the capitalist employment relationship, there have been a series of attempts to overcome these forms of resistance – from human relations, through corporate culture programmes to total quality management. All of these seek to 'bring employees back in' by securing their commitment to redesigned processes, quality products, customer service and the strategic goals of the organization (see Chapter 5).

Such innovations are intended to secure the commitment of both employees and managers. While more sophisticated than carrot-and-stick methods of control, they continue to rely on a coercive organization of work. As a consequence, they encounter resistance, not least when introduced against a background of restructuring, cost cutting and redundancy programmes. Such developments present a threat to the symbolic as well as material survival of employees, including the middle managers who may be required to preside over their own demise. Historically, management identity has been less threatened by the treatment of managerial labour as a commodity. But today, managers have become vulnerable to the degrading impact of programmes of corporate rationalization previously suffered largely by non-managerial labour. Some managers are able to avoid or limit such degradation by virtue of their specialist expertise, social connections or networking skills. But the uncertainty arising from recurrent reorganization renders managerial identity increasingly unstable and insecure.

Identity and exploitation   The dynamics of control and resistance endemic in capitalist relations of production are symptomatic of problems of trust and attendant anxieties relating to, for example, hours worked or access to tools and materials. However, the treatment of employees as an expendable commodity within the capitalist labour process generates anxieties about continuing employment, skill acquisition and renewal, and career development. These can be demoralizing and demotivating. But they can also be productive, in so far as they induce compliance and output. Unlike the slave who works 'under the spur of external fear' as manifest in the lash of the slave driver, the 'free' labourer of capitalism 'is impelled by his wants', including a desire to consume the products that she or he can freely purchase in the marketplace.[51] Marx continues:

> The consciousness (or better: the idea) of free self-determination, of liberty, makes a much better worker of the one than the other, as does the related feeling (sense) of responsibility; since he, like any seller of wares, is responsible for the goods which he delivers and the quality that he must provide to ensure that he is not driven from the field by other sellers of the same type as himself.

A number of points are incisively made in this passage. First, it is noted how the ascription of autonomy – 'free self' – to employees makes them work more productively. It instils, or conjures up, within them a sense of personal responsibility for their fate (and that of their dependants). Second, rugged individualism is assumed and promoted. Each person is represented

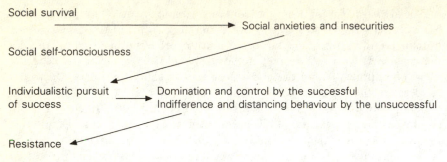

Social survival

Social anxieties and insecurities

Social self-consciousness

Individualistic pursuit   Domination and control by the successful
of success   Indifference and distancing behaviour by the unsuccessful

Resistance

FIGURE 3.5   *Advanced capitalist society*

as an independent, autonomous agent – a sense of identity that each employee is impelled to develop as they compete to provide the quality of skill and reliability demanded by the market. The emphasis on the 'free self-determination' of each seller of labour is strongly promoted by markets where, in principle, each individual is obliged to develop ways of outwitting or undercutting competitors. What is interesting in terms of our earlier discussion of human nature is that Marx's analysis makes clear how individual self-interest is not an essential element in human existence. It is conditioned and sustained by the very workings of capitalism, the market and enlightenment conceptions of the autonomous individual.

Identity and consumption   Marx was critical of the divisive, exploitive and destructive consequences of capitalism. But he also stressed its superior productive efficiency relative to previous economic regimes. This understanding leads Marx to identify a contradiction in the capacity of capitalism to produce a quantity of goods far exceeding the (unstimulated) demand for their use and/or the disposable income available for their purchase. The growth of credit and the advent of mass advertising have addressed this contradiction. People are encouraged to identify consumption as a meaningful, pleasurable activity through which they can establish themselves as rational autonomous agents. This they do by making choices between a proliferating range of products, services and diverse lifestyles. Demand is stimulated so as to absorb supply.

   Building a unique, style-sensitive brand image is also regarded as a more effective means of securing profitable growth than engaging in price wars. Unless price cuts succeed in increasing market share by pushing smaller players out of the market, price-based competition risks reductions in margins that, once lost, can be difficult to regain. Price wars are also a possible self-defeating outcome of price competition. But the degree of price competition is exaggerated by 'free market' rhetoric; by inducing imperfect knowledge where it does not already exist, price competition can be avoided. Because of the contradictory nature of price competition, companies much prefer to seek customer loyalty through service quality. Again, this helps to account for the proliferation and seductive nature of

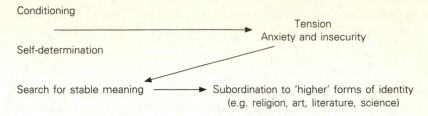

FIGURE 3.6 *Freedom and control*

initiatives intended to secure or enhance 'quality'. Advertising is deployed to boost demand, often by associating a product with 'lifestyles' (i.e. identities) to which potential consumers are believed to aspire and with which they are encouraged to identify.

Advertising appeals to and contrives to stimulate a multiplicity of human 'needs' that would otherwise not exist or be disregarded. These 'needs' are constructed or elaborated through symbols and images that arouse concerns about status and self-esteem. This observation echoes the central claim of symbolic interactionism that self-consciousness is at the centre of human life. As aspirations are raised and anxieties amplified by advertising, individuals are seduced and their energies directed narcissistically toward the acquisition of the symbols or attributes that signify a successful (self) image. In the context of an advanced capitalist society, the most compelling and legitimate means of relieving anxieties about social position and self-identity is through an individualistic pursuit of the material and symbolic indicators of success. This narcissistic project takes the form of domination and control in the spheres of both production and consumption (see Figure 3.5).

Coveted positions in organizations and society – from playing football for Manchester United to being appointed as chief executive of a major corporation – are socially acclaimed and respected, at least in formal (i.e. hierarchical) terms. These positions promise to provide material and symbolic privileges that enable their occupants to cope with anxiety and insecurity. Such privileges serve as generic institutional substitutes for those interpersonal confirmations of self that traditionally have bestowed on identities a degree of stability and security. Yet the presence of these privileges rarely eradicates existing anxieties and insecurities. Indeed, they invariably engender new and even more intense preoccupations with the search for stable meaning in identities that transcend conventional material and symbolic success (see Figure 3.6). For example, in *Nice Work*, Vic Wilcox lies awake in the small hours as 'worries streak towards him like enemy spaceships'. In *The Bonfire of the Vanities*, Sherman McCoy, self-appointed Master of the Universe, is anxious lest his wife discover his adulterous deception.

Like Vic and Sherman, we find ourselves searching for, or striving to protect, a valued set of meanings (e.g. a job or a marriage) that makes us feel wanted, superior or seems somehow to transcend the ephemeral character of such ambitions. This requires us routinely and recurrently to contrive ways of neutralizing or eliminating eventualities that pose a threat to these meanings and thus of the sense of self-identity derived from them.

Summary

In this chapter, we have explored 'identity at work' in a multiplicity of ways, how identity 'works' and, more importantly, how identity has to be 'worked at' in contemporary organizations and everyday life. We have drawn principally on Kundera's metaphor of 'lightness' and 'weight' to frame our reflections on the 'openness' of human existence, the conditional quality of autonomy, the centrality of self-consciousness, the virtue and necessity of interpretation, and the operation of power/knowledge within institutional and economic life.

Weight is added to our being by responsibilities and obligations that attend the development of a sense of purpose or mission, however grandiose or prosaic. In moments of reflection we may be relieved of some or all of this weight. Certain philosophies or religions (e.g. Buddhism) inspire us to shed the weight of our attachments to material and symbolic existence, so as to enter a world where the grasping of ego and the anxious preoccupation with making reality comply with its demands are dissolved.

However, the lightness of being can become unbearable when the jettisoning of attachments renders life meaningless and individuals find themselves floundering in a directionless void. When this happens, there can be a breakdown of established routines as people lose a sense of control and even escape into a world devoid of everyday meaning and normalized expectations. This is conventionally understood as mental illness. Alternatively, and more commonly, an encounter with the void manifests itself in a compulsive and self-defeating desire to escape.

For Teresa, the void took the form of intense and completely debilitating jealousy caused by Tomas's repeated infidelities. Over many years she was overwhelmed by a preoccupation with this problem, as it destroyed her identity as a married woman. At the end of her tether, the intensity of her suffering drove Teresa to engage in a casual extramarital sexual encounter. She fully expected that sex without intimacy would be suffused with a lightness that would ease the burden of her compulsive preoccupation with Tomas's promiscuity. Instead, it produced a weight of such proportions that she had the immediate urge to void her bowels.

In the context of advanced capitalist societies, a consumerist orientation generates a comparable experience of temporary gratification followed by a sense of continuing, oppressive emptiness. This is addressed through a variety of stratagems, such as workaholism, indifference and renewed consumption. Both in the novel and in our theoretical deliberations, we have emphasized the awesome but also inspiring ambivalence of human existence where we are caught between, and struggle to reconcile, the lightness of irresponsible autonomy on the one hand, and the burdensome desire for a secure identity with its attendant weight of responsibility on the other.

Notes

1 Kundera, M. (1989) *The Unbearable Lightness of Being*. London: Faber and Faber. p. 12.

2 *The Unbearable Lightness of Being*, p. 200.

3 *The Unbearable Lightness of Being*, p. 200, emphasis added.

4 *The Unbearable Lightness of Being*, p. 5.

5 *The Unbearable Lightness of Being*, p. 33.

6 See Schwartz, B. (1986) *The Battle for Human Nature*. New York: W.W. Norton.

7 See Dawkins, R. (1989) *The Selfish Gene*. Oxford: Oxford University Press.

8 See Turnbull, C. (1984) *The Ik*. Harmondsworth: Penguin.

9 Lepper, M.R. and Greene, D. (eds) (1978) *The Hidden Costs of Reward*. Hillsdale, NJ: Erlbaum.

10 *The Battle for Human Nature*, p. 240.

11 Watson, J.B. (1913) 'Psychology as the behaviourist views it', *The Psychological Review*, 20: 158–77, p. 10.

12 See, for example, Skinner, B.F. (1953) *Science and Human Behaviour*. New York: Macmillan; Skinner, B.F. (1971) *Beyond Freedom and Dignity*. Harmondsworth: Penguin; Skinner, B.F. (1976) *Walden Two*. New York: Macmillan.

13 *Beyond Freedom and Dignity*, p. 200.

14 *Beyond Freedom and Dignity*, p. 206.

15 *Beyond Freedom and Dignity*, p. 209.

16 *Beyond Freedom and Dignity*, p. 206.

17 *Beyond Freedom and Dignity*, p. 46.

18 Popper, K. (1963) *Conjectures and Refutations*. London: Routledge and Kegan Paul.

19 Chomsky, N. (1970) 'Recent contributions to a theory of innate ideas', in L. Hudson (ed.), *The Ecology of Human Intelligence*. Harmondsworth: Penguin.

20 Goldthorpe, J., Lockwood, D., Bechhofer, F. and Platt, J. (1968) *The Affluent Worker: Industrial Attitudes and Behaviour*. Cambridge: Cambridge University Press.

21 Sandberg, A. (ed.) (1995) *Enriching Production*. Aldershot: Avebury.

22 See Giddens, A. (1984) *The Constitution of Society*. Cambridge: Polity Press.

23 'Recent contributions to a theory of innate ideas'.

24 Foucault, M. (1982) 'The subject and power', in H. Dreyfus and P. Rabinow, *Michel Foucault: Beyond Structuralism and Hermeneutics*. Brighton: Harvester Press.

25 Mead, G.H. (1934) *Mind, Self and Society*. Chicago: University of Chicago Press.

26 Blumer, H. (1969) *Symbolic Interactionism*. Englewood Cliffs, NJ: Prentice-Hall. p. 5.

27 *Symbolic Interactionism*, pp. 2–3.

28 *The Unbearable Lightness of Being*, p. 12.

29 *Mind, Self and Society*.

30 Lodge, D. (1989) *Nice Work*. Harmondsworth: Penguin. p. 109.

31 *Nice Work*, p. 109.

32 *Symbolic Interactionism*, p. 14.

33 *Symbolic Interactionism*, p. 16.

34 *The Unbearable Lightness of Being*, p. 197.

35 *The Unbearable Lightness of Being*, p. 197.

36 *The Unbearable Lightness of Being*, p. 197.

37 Lichtman, R.T. (1973) 'Symbolic interactionism and social reality', *Berkeley Journal of Sociology*, 15: 75–94, p. 83.

38 See Kerfoot, D. and Knights, D. (forthcoming) *The Hidden Agenda: Masculinity in Management and Organization*. London: Sage.

39 See Knights, D. and Murray, F. (1994) *Managers Divided*. London: Wiley.

40 See Mintzberg, H. (1994) *The Rise and Fall of Strategic Planning*. Englewood Cliffs, NJ: Prentice-Hall.

41 See Piore, M. and Sabel, C. (1984) *The Second Industrial Divide*. New York: Basic Books.

42 See Atkinson, J. (1986) 'Manpower strategies for flexible organizations', *Personnel Management*, 16 (8): 28–31.

43 See Peters, T. (1989) *Thriving on Chaos*. London: Pan.

44 *The Unbearable Lightness of Being*, p. 12.

45 *The Unbearable Lightness of Being*, p. 128.

46 *The Unbearable Lightness of Being*, p. 283.

47 *The Unbearable Lightness of Being*, p. 283.

48 Marx, K. (1867/1976a) *Capital: a Critical Analysis of Capitalist Production*, trans. S. Moore and E. Aveling, ed. F. Engels. London: George Allen & Unwin. p. 448.

49 See Nichols, T. and Beynon, H. (1997) *Living with Capitalism*. London: Routledge.

50 Goffman, E. (1961) *Role Distance*. New York: Bobbs Merrill.

51 Marx, K. (1867/1976b) *Capital, Volume 1*. Harmondsworth: Penguin. p. 1031.

Recommended further reading

Identity

Casey, C. (1995) *Work, Self and Society*. London: Routledge.

Cohen, S. and Taylor, L. (1992) *Escape Attempts*, 2nd edn. London: Routledge.

Collinson, D. (1992) *Managing the Shopfloor*. Berlin: de Gruyter.

Henriques, J., Holloway, W., Urwin, C., Venn, C. and Walkerdine, V. (1984) *Changing the Subject*. London: Methuen.

Human nature

Becker, E. (1969) *Birth and Death of Meaning*. New York: Free Press.

Becker, E. (1973) *The Denial of Death*. New York: Free Press.

Giddens, A. (1991) *Modernity and Self-Identity*. Cambridge: Polity Press.

Shibutani, J. (1962) 'Human nature and collective behaviour', in A.M. Rose (ed.), *Human Behaviour and Social Processes*. London: Routledge & Kegan Paul.

Watts, A. (1973) *Psychotherapy East and West*. Harmondsworth: Penguin.

Behaviourism

MacKenzie, B.D. (1977) *Behaviourism and the Limits of Scientific Method*. London: Routledge and Kegan Paul.

Skinner, B. (1971) *Beyond Freedom and Dignity*. Harmondsworth: Penguin.

Smith, L.D. and Woodward, W.R. (eds) (1996) *B.F. Skinner and Behaviourism in American Culture*. Bethlehem, PA: Lehigh University Press.

Symbolic interactionism

Blumer, H. (1969) *Symbolic Interactionism*. Englewood Cliffs, NJ: Prentice-Hall.

Charon, J.M. (1995) *Symbolic Interactionism: an Introduction, an Interpretation, an Integration*. Englewood Cliffs, NJ: Prentice-Hall.

Manis, J.G. and Meltzer, B.N. (1967) *Symbolic Interactionism*. Boston: Allyn & Bacon.

References

Atkinson, J. (1986) 'Manpower strategies for the flexible firm', *Personnel Management*, 16 (8): 28–31.

Blumer, H. (1969) *Symbolic Interactionism*. Englewood Cliffs, NJ: Prentice-Hall.

Chomsky, N. (1970) 'Recent contributions to a theory of innate ideas', in L. Hudson (ed.), *The Ecology of Human Intelligence*. Harmondsworth: Penguin.

Clark, H., Chandler, J. and Barry, J. (1994) *Organizations and Identities*. London: Chapman and Hall.

Dawkins, R. (1989) *The Selfish Gene*. Oxford: Oxford University Press.

Foucault, M. (1982) 'The subject and power', in H. Dreyfus and P. Rabinow, *Michel Foucault: Beyond Structuralism and Hermeneutics*. Brighton: Harvester Press.

Giddens, A. (1984) *The Constitution of Society*. Cambridge: Polity Press.

Goffman, E. (1961) *Role Distance*. New York: Bobbs Merrill.

Goldthorpe, J., Lockwood, D., Bechhofer, F. and Platt, J. (1968) *The Affluent Worker: Industrial Attitudes and Behaviour*. Cambridge: Cambridge University Press.

Kerfoot, D. and Knights, D. (forthcoming) *The Hidden Agenda: Masculinity in Management and Organization*. London: Sage.

Knights, D. and Murray, F. (1984) *Managers Divided*. London: Wiley.

Lepper, M.R. and Greene, D. (eds) (1978) *The Hidden Costs of Reward*. Hillsdale, NJ: Erlbaum.

Lewis, M. (1989) *Liar's Poker*. London: Hodder and Stoughton.

Lichtman, R.T. (1970) 'Symbolic interactionism and social reality', *Berkeley Journal of Sociology*, 15: 75–94.

Marx, K. (1867/1976a) *Capital: a Critical Analysis of Capitalist Production*, trans. S. Moore and E. Aveling, ed. F. Engels. London: George Allen & Unwin.

Marx, K. (1867/1976b) *Capital, Volume 1*. Harmondsworth: Penguin.

Mead, G.H. (1934) *Mind, Self and Society*. Chicago: University of Chicago Press.

Mintzberg, H. (1994) *The Rise and Fall of Strategic Planning*. Englewood Cliffs, NJ: Prentice-Hall.

Nichols, T. and Beynon, H. (1977) *Living with Capitalism*. London: Routledge and Kegan Paul.

Peters, T. (1989) *Thriving on Chaos*. London: Pan.

Piore, M. and Sabel, C. (1984) *The Second Industrial Divide*. New York: Basic Books.

Popper, K. (1963) *Conjectures and Refutations*. London: Routledge and Kegan Paul.

Sandberg, A. (ed.) (1995) *Enriching Production*. Aldershot: Avebury.

Schwartz, B. (1986) *The Battle for Human Nature*. New York: W.W. Norton & Co.

Skinner, B.F. (1953) *Science and Human Behaviour*. New York: Macmillan.

Skinner, B.F. (1971) *Beyond Freedom and Dignity*. Harmondsworth: Penguin.

Skinner, B.F. (1976) *Walden Two*. New York: Macmillan.

Thompson, P. and McHugh, D. (1995) *Work Orgnaizations: a Critical Introduction*, 2nd edn. London: Macmillan.

Turnbull, C. (1984) *The Ik*. Harmondsworth: Penguin.

Watson, J.B. (1913) 'Psychology as the behaviourist views it', *The Psychological Review*, 20: 158–77.

4   Power and Inequality at Work

In previous chapters we touched on questions of power and inequality when discussing Vic Wilcox's treatment of his workforce in *Nice Work* and Tomas's relationship with his wife Teresa in *The Unbearable Lightness of Being*. In this chapter, we draw primarily on Ishiguro's, *The Remains of the Day*. This novel provides an exceptionally sensitive account of power and inequality at work, as it explores the 'professionalism' of domestic service against a background of the English aristocracy in decline.

Ishiguro offers a moving story of Stevens, a butler, who has devoted his life to the service of those whom he deems to be his 'betters'. He portrays how a sense of status and dignity is achieved and sustained by those in the lower reaches of an aristocratic household. Despite the servile character of his work, Stevens ascribes to it a great depth of personal meaning and social significance, hierarchical importance and prestige. He takes personal pride in, and enjoys the power associated with, his role as a professional butler. Ishiguro also shows how a sense of dignity that is too closely allied to a preoccupation with status and duty can be disastrous for human well-being, especially when the aristocratic object of Steven's loyalty no longer seems to be as deserving as had initially been thought. In the twilight of his life, Stevens recognizes that the trust he had placed in his master had perhaps been unwarranted, since there was, after the fact, clear evidence that Lord Darlington had flirted with German Nazism.

Another novel considered in some detail in this chapter – Tom Wolfe's *The Bonfire of the Vanities* – has as its focus big city life in modern America. In contrast to Ishiguro's sensitive recording of the more subtle and less visible aspects of power and inequality in domestic service, the canvas of *The Bonfire of the Vanities* is the 'open society' of New York, where stable traditions are as rare as snowstorms in a desert. In the 'Big Apple', power and wealth are portrayed as the product of struggle, deceit, corruption and luck. The author paints a devastating picture of crude, lewd, immoral and violent egos battling it out for a slice of the 'apple' – one that Wolfe presents as rotten to its core. Only the street-wise survive as the 'characterless' rich, especially the 'nouveau riche', and the not-so-rich are all seemingly swallowed up, or burnt alive, in *The Bonfire of the Vanities*: a bonfire of contemporary American and indeed western civilization.

The chapter is organized as follows. First, we provide brief excerpts from these two novels to reflect respectively the distinct worlds of deference in the form of devotion to a master and difference in the form of devotion to success.[a] The second section is concerned with a conceptual analysis of power and the third with an analysis of inequality. Throughout, we seek to integrate the insights drawn from the novels with views on management and identity that have been introduced in the previous chapters.

Devotion to a master

The Remains of the Day describes a form of subordination that involves living one's life through the expectations of others. Stevens dedicates his life to being, or becoming, the perfect butler. This, for him, means devoting himself unreservedly to 'the great gentlemen of our times in whose hands civilization had been entrusted'.[1] Despite its focus on the life of a butler, the novel has contemporary relevance and potency well beyond its historical specificity. For example, there are important parallels between Stevens's devotion to the aristocracy and forms of adherence to 'authority' within corporations. In each case a notion of 'professional competence' is mobilized to secure the employee's conformity to household or corporate objectives.

Stevens justifies the dedication of his life to providing a professional service to Lord Darlington by stressing, somewhat perversely, that respect for the personal qualities of his master is a precondition of his unreserved devotion and deference:

> I would be among the last to advocate bestowing one's loyalty carelessly on any lady or gentleman who happens to employ one for a time. However, if a butler is to be of any worth to anything or anybody in life, there must surely come a time when . . . he must say to himself: 'This employer embodies all that I find noble and admirable. I will hereafter devote myself to serving him'.[2]

Much of the novel explores Stevens's understanding of what makes a perfect and most professional butler. In an effort to specify the qualities of supreme professionalism, Stevens reflects on his knowledge of this or that butler of 'great' repute,[3] their standards of proficiency and 'demeanour'.[4] Perhaps the most critical feature of 'professional demeanour', in Stevens's assessment, is the capacity to retain one's 'dignity' by never displaying private or personal emotions, even when put under the most severe kind of pressure. Stevens becomes so attached to this 'virtue' that he ends up sacrificing (personal) life for the sake of his professional obligations.

---

a It will not be missed by those who have a smattering of knowledge of poststructuralism that difference and deference are intimately tied to one another in the term différance, where what is different is simply a deferral of the absent 'other' to that which is present and thus privileged. Stevens's definition of a professional butler privileges the ability to *defer* emotions in order to perform his duties in a competent manner. An example of this is when he distances himself from the emotional trauma and turmoil surrounding his father's death in order to maintain an uninterrupted service to his lordship. See Derrida, J. (1967/ 1968), *Writing and Difference* (trans. Alan Bass). London: Routledge and Kegan Paul.

For Stevens, the only source of self-worth is to serve a virtuous master with loyalty and devotion. 'What is there undignified in this so long as this service is intelligently bestowed?' he asks. Accepting as 'an inescapable truth'[5] that people like himself will never be able to comprehend the great affairs of today's world, he concludes:

> Our best course will always be to put our trust in an employer we judge to be wise and honourable, and to devote our energies to the task of serving him to the best of our ability.[6]

For Stevens, a major crisis of confidence in the old, aristocratic order occurs when it becomes clear to him that his master had been a Nazi sympathizer and, thereby, perhaps contributed indirectly to the rise of fascism. Much effort is then required to rationalize or justify the devotion of his life to serving Lord Darlington. During the twilight of his years, Stevens finds himself contemplating a lifetime of service devoted to his master. In the end, he is forced to admit to himself that his service and devotion had been to no good purpose:

> Lord Darlington wasn't a bad man. He wasn't a bad man at all. And at least he had the privilege of being able to say at the end of his life that he made his own mistakes. His lordship chose a certain path in life, it proved to be a misguided one, but there, he chose it, he can say that at least. As for myself, I cannot even claim that. You see, I trusted. I trusted in his lordship's wisdom. All those years I served him, I trusted I was doing something worthwhile. I can't even say I made my own mistakes. Really – one has to ask oneself – what dignity is there in that?[7]

Stevens had consumed a lifetime believing his subordination to be necessary and dignified. His admission of a 'wasted life' was therefore extremely hard to bear. Yet this admission is a moment of the greatest dignity and grace as, perhaps for the first time in his life, he draws his own conclusions instead of relying on a formula provided by others. The pain of this admission must have been compounded by a realization that his professional devotion to duty had extended to a refusal to become emotionally involved with his master's housekeeper, Miss Kenton. She had made several subtle efforts to encourage such a liaison and later admits to 'thinking about a life I might have had with you'.[8] Instead of his professional service being a 'cause for pride and contentment'[9] as he reflects on his life, it became a source of some regret. A tragic figure, Stevens discovers that he has sacrificed his life, including any deeply personal or romantic relationship, for a career in service that, in the end, he could not defend. On reflection, his life turns out to be a huge disappointment as a consequence of his misplaced allegiance to an indefensible cause.

Devotion to success

The Bonfire of the Vanities also draws attention to the precarious character of status, wealth, inequality and power. The storyline involves Sherman McCoy's downfall from the pinnacle of affluence and success as a Wall Street bond broker. This follows a car accident in which a black youth is seriously injured. McCoy takes a wrong turning when driving his mistress, Maria, from the airport after dark. They find themselves lost in the nightmare territory of the Bronx. After several failed attempts to retrace their steps to the freeway for Manhattan, they eventually find themselves on a dark road under an expressway that they believe will lead them back to 'civilization'. Suddenly, what appears to be a large wheel is blocking their path. Getting out to remove the obstacle, Sherman sees two black youths walking towards him. Fearing that they might attack and rob him, Sherman throws the tyre at one of the youths before rushing back into the car. 'Human existence had but one purpose: to get out of the Bronx.'[10] In the frenzy to drive off, Maria, who had by now taken over the wheel, runs over and seriously injures the smaller boy:

> The skinny one standing right there. . . . The rear end fishtailed . . . thok! . . . the skinny boy was no longer standing.[11]

In discussing what to do, and whether to report the incident, Sherman was willing, though reluctant, to notify the police. He was anxious that this would result in his wife finding out about his illicit relationship. Maria refused even to contemplate telling the police. Street-wise, she had no 'hang-ups' about doing 'the right thing'. So far as she was concerned, whatever may have happened was not her responsibility:

> Sherman, I'm gonna tell you what happened. I'm from South Carolina, and I'm gonna tell you in plain English. Two niggers tried to kill us, and we got away. Two niggers tried to kill us in the jungle, and we got outta the jungle, and we're still breathing, and that's that.[12]

With a reputation and a marriage to protect, Sherman did not need much convincing. But once the police had knowledge that the car was a Black Mercedes and that the first letter of the registration plate was an *R*, he was in deep trouble.

Sherman's job as a bond dealer, the source of his success and wealth, exemplifies a type of 'yuppie' work where there is an exceptionally arbitrary relationship between reward and effort. His fall is equally contingent and accidental. Had he not been picking his mistress up from the airport, he would have had no reason to drive close by the Bronx. Had Sherman not been scared of an attack, he would not have aggravated one. Had Sherman and Maria not been so anxious to leave the Bronx, the car would have been driven less recklessly. Had they not been in an illicit relationship, they could have reported the incident without fearing the consequences for their respective marriages. Had the boy not been black, there would not have been the same degree of community sensitivity and public outrage that subsequently politicized the case. Had the case not become such a political *cause célèbre*, personal security costs would not have been added to an already escalating set of legal defence fees. This and many more contingencies were the conditions that eventually condemned Sherman to an impoverished, and incarcerated, existence. Unable to raise the bail money and abandoned by Maria, the novel ends tragically with Sherman destined to lose his case because he lacked the necessary funds to hire a good attorney.

This story is told against a background of greed, sex, envy, racial tension, political intrigue and corruption. Consider, for example, Sherman's thoughts and feelings, early in the novel, as he begins a day's work:

> Sherman sat down before his own telephone and computer terminals. The shouts, the imprecations, the gesticulations, the fucking fear and greed, enveloped him, and he loved it. He was the number one bond salesman.[13]

And when walking down Fifth Avenue:

> It was in the air! It was a wave! Everywhere! Inescapable! . . . Sex! . . . There for the taking! . . . It walked down the street, as bold as you please! . . . It was splashed all over the shops! If you were a young man and halfway alive, what chance did you have? . . .
> Technically, he had been unfaithful to his wife, Well sure . . . but who could remain monogamous with this, this, this *tidal wave* of concupiscence rolling across the world?[14]

For many people, including Sherman, the pursuit of power is appealing because it seems to offer a way of avoiding others imposing *their* meanings and desires on us. Yet it is also precarious. Although Maria ran over the skinny black kid, it was Sherman who fell victim to political and physical harassment. This fate befell him as a result of becoming caught up in racial tension and conflict, which were themselves a condition and a consequence of the wealth and status that he pursued. Such harassment combined with the scale of his legal fees ultimately destroyed Sherman. Despite wealth and status, he could not withstand such an onslaught. In the end, his sense of identity – as Sherman McCoy – could no longer be sustained in the face of the press and television portrayal of him as a hit-and-run criminal:

> I'm not Sherman McCoy anymore. I'm somebody else without a proper name. I've been that other person ever since the day I was arrested.[15]

A parallel, though not as complete, loss of power, wealth and status befell Vic Wilcox in *Nice Work*. As a result of Pringle's being sold off by its parent company, Vic joined the swelling ranks of redundant executives in the recession of the late 1980s. His demise was also partially caused by an illicit relationship. In the gossip around Pringle's, Vic's growing familiarity with Robyn, a female academic whom he had taken on a business trip to Frankfurt, had not passed unnoticed. Prior to presenting Vic with his redundancy notice, Baxter, the chairman of the foundry division of the parent company, couldn't resist making the innuendoes:

> I gather she's quite a dish, this shadow of yours. . . . You seem to be inseparable. I hear you took her with you to Frankfurt.[16]

In different ways, then, the novels considered in this chapter demonstrate the precariousness of power, wealth and status in contemporary western society. The novels, however, do not provide us with an analytical framework. As we attempt to remedy this, we draw selectively on theories of power and inequality, which we illustrate by reference to the novels.

Conceptualizing power

We have already observed how, in *The Remains of the Day*, the relationship between Stevens and his master epitomized traditional forms of power and subordination. As long as Stevens never questions the validity of what he serves, his life is comparatively stable and secure. This is not so for Sherman McCoy in *The Bonfire of the Vanities*. Instability and uncertainty are manifest *in extremis* in the bond markets where Sherman works. They also pervade his entire life: his marriage, his extramarital affair, on the street where he risks physical assault and, eventually, in the courts where he is reduced to a common, though high-profile, 'professional defendant'[17] who felt like a criminal. His self-image as Master of the Universe (who looks on Wall Street lawyers as mere functionaries) allows Sherman to ignore or deny the precariousness of his position until he is arrested. The inflated and parasitic nature of his employment is hinted at by Judy, Sherman's wife, when she is asked by their daughter what her father does for a living. As Judy hands someone a slice of cake, she explains to her daughter that selling bonds is like collecting 'golden crumbs' that fall off pieces of cake that the bond salesman hasn't made but is happy to profit from.[18] Judy is critical of the abstract and intangible nature of bond selling, an activity that Wolfe contrasts with her own interest in interior design, an interest that Sherman dismisses as 'decorating'. In her own defence, Judy retorts:

> Even if interior design is for people who are shallow and vain, it's something *real*, something describable, something contributing to simple human satisfaction, no matter how meretricious and temporary, something at least you can explain to your children.[19]

Despite the differences between bond selling and interior design claimed by both Sherman and Judy, each is engaged in a way of life where the acquisition of the material prizes and privileges of the rich is routinely assumed to be *the* way of achieving a degree of security and status. In the cosmopolitan world of New York, there is a comparative permeability of class boundaries and increased opportunities for social mobility. Yet the relationship between talent, effort and reward (e.g. lifestyle) is not that much more transparent than in the aristocratic world displayed in *The Remains of the Day*. The shift from aristocracy to meritocracy does not bring about an easy truce between the 'haves' and the 'have nots'. The poor are often resentful, occasionally militantly aggressive, sometimes criminal, but almost always indifferent to the system that sustains the structures of inequality of which they are the most disadvantaged victims.

Nonetheless, the routine pursuit of power, wealth and status stems from the belief that it facilitates a sense of control, or at least limits the degree to which one has to subordinate oneself to others. This preoccupation with the control of meaning, although not always conscious, is prevalent within all areas of inequality (e.g. relations of gender, ethnicity and class). It occurs in the domestic household, in relations of sexuality and in work. It is, in effect, the medium and outcome of power relations. It is at the root of Sherman's annoyance – 'he wanted to strangle her'[20] – when his role of Master of the Universe is redefined by his wife as collector of golden crumbs. Whether as a means to some other end (e.g. cooperation in production) or merely as an end in itself (e.g. adulation), defining reality for others is an exercise of power. Yet even where those exercising power control resources, definitions of reality may be less effective than they appear.

In the aristocratic household of Lord Darlington, there was never any questioning of the definition of reality and its hierarchical order. Only in retrospect did Stevens begin to regret such subservience and servility. Such a traditional control of reality is, of course, a rarity today. Employees, for example, frequently comply with management definitions of reality for fear of losing their jobs. But compliance does not mean subservience or servility, let alone commitment. For this reason, corporations repeatedly search for, and introduce, organizational innovations (e.g. quality management, employee involvement, business process reengineering, customer care) that, by attempting to control the meaning of reality, promise to bring about a more efficient system of work (see Chapter 5).

So far, we have explored the two systems of power described in *The Remains of the Day* and *The Bonfire of the Vanities*. The first, represented by the aristocratic household of domestic service, is dependent on established traditions of inequality where everyone knows their place from birth. No one aspires to change either their own position or the structure of social relations in which they are embedded. The second, by contrast, is one where accidents of birth present no necessary or insuperable obstacle to social mobility. Mobility is heavily dependent on individual achievement, where anything is permitted so long as its dubious legality is not detected or likely to be challenged. In the one case, members of society are wholly respectful of established and traditional power relations. In the other, they are comparatively disdainful, yet covetous, of those who enjoy the prestige and privilege of power. This typology provides only a limited insight into power relations and their dynamics, so we now turn to a more sophisticated academic analysis.

Lukes's three-dimensional model

Following Lukes,[21] power is conceptualized as having three dimensions. These extend from comparatively self-evident and overt forms of its exercise to forms of power that are more subtle and institutionalized. These are as follows:

- *Dimension 1.* Power that is exercised to secure a decision in situations where there is some observable conflict or disagreement.
- *Dimension 2.* Power that is exercised to keep issues on or off the decision-making agenda, so that potential conflicts or disagreements are precluded and therefore unobservable.
- *Dimension 3.* Institutionalized power that is exercised to define social reality. To the extent that norms and meanings are internalized, people accept and thereby reproduce the power-invented definition of reality, even when this is against their 'real' interests.

The *first dimension* comprises the observable behaviour of individuals or groups that are seen to determine, or at least to influence, the form and content of decision making. An example of this is the decision of Abe Weiss, the district attorney, to treat McCoy like anyone else who is arrested, regardless of what his social status leads him to expect:

> How *do* we treat some hotshot from Park Avenue? Like anyone else, that's how! He gets arrested, he gets the cuffs, he gets booked, he gets fingerprinted, he waits in the pens, just like anybody down there on those streets.[22]

The *second dimension* of power concerns the non-observable behaviour implicit in keeping issues on or off the agenda. For example, in *The Bonfire of the Vanities*, there were behind-the-scenes negotiations between various parties (lawyers, politicians and community leaders) that resulted in Sherman's case being investigated and becoming high profile. Where observable behaviour and conflicts are examined, some important aspects of power are unacknowledged, since the exercise of power can prevent a controversial issue from being discussed so that it never reaches the public domain of decision making.

Consider the way in which Sherman McCoy's case was placed so prominently on the agenda via the mass media. For Weiss, the equitable treatment of McCoy was not simply a matter of demonstrating the impartiality of the law but of gaining the support of the community to keep him in office. Weiss had an election coming up in five months. McCoy's trial was a means of demonstrating to the 70 per cent of the Bronx who were black or Latin that they were being represented: 'I think that sends a helluva good signal. It lets those people know we *represent* them and they're a part of New York City.'[23]

The McCoy case became part of Weiss's agenda to retain his position. He milked it for all it was worth while defending this action in terms of fairness and justice. No matter that the trial did nothing to change the materially disadvantaged and symbolically devalued position of the black and Latin population of the Bronx. Weiss calculated that transforming Sherman McCoy into Public Enemy Number One would be a vote winner, as it kept more difficult issues – of poverty and discrimination – off the agenda.[b]

This brings us directly to a consideration of Lukes's *third dimension* of power. This dimension is attentive to how those in positions of power may define reality so as to secure the general support of others, including those who are most disadvantaged. Weiss appreciated how the media could be deployed and manipulated to define reality in ways that shape perceptions, expectations and demands:

> Abe Weiss was one of a long line of New York district attorneys whose careers had been based on appearing on television and announcing the latest paralysing wallop to the solar plexus of crime in the seething metropolis. Weiss, the good Captain Ahab, might be the object of jokes. But he was wired to the Power, and the Power flowed through him.[24]

Lukes contends that the 'real' interests and potential grievances of those subjected to power are obscured or distorted, as they are preoccupied with immediately understandable events. One example of this is Weiss's use of the sensation of the McCoy case to deflect the disadvantaged away from thinking about, and acting on, their 'real' interests. Lukes's third dimension of power is Stevens's dogged devotion to duty. His unquestioning loyalty and trust are grounded in the idea that only members of the aristocratic elite, like Lord Darlington, are capable of making informed decisions. Musing on the qualities of a 'great butler', Stevens reflects:

> The more one considers it, the more obvious it seems: association with a *truly* distinguished household *is* a prerequisite of greatness. A great butler can only be, surely, one who can point to his years of service and say that he has applied his talents to serving a great gentleman – and, through the latter, to serving humanity.[25]

---

b   It has been claimed that leaders in both the UK and US have been 'trigger happy' when domestic difficulties threatened their popularity or authority (e.g. Thatcher's Falklands and Clinton's Gulf War).

Whereas Stevens's loyalty to his master arises from an internalization of aristocratic norms and values, Sherman McCoy's predicament is a product of his preoccupation with an ethic of success. By focusing on how power may be exercised outside of specific points of conflict or decision making, Lukes's third dimension of power usefully draws attention to its institutionalization. When institutionalized, power operates in ways that cannot be convincingly ascribed to the choices made by individuals who directly influence decisions (the first dimension) or who manoeuvre, behind the scenes, to exclude consideration of controversial issues (the second dimension).

There is a questionable assumption, however, underlying Lukes's discussion of the three dimensions of power. Throughout, he conceptualizes power as the property of people polarized around those who have power and those who do not. For Lukes, the powerful are those who define reality in such a way as to *control meaning* so that others – such as the black and Latin populations of the Bronx or Stevens the butler – are rendered powerless. The 'powerless' are no longer capable of recognizing, let alone expressing, their own 'real' interests.

The question of 'real interests' A question remains, therefore, as to how far Lukes's formulation of the third dimension of power advances our understanding of its exercise. Lukes's analysis focuses on the manipulations of the powerful as if they are not themselves subject to its exercise. For him, the powerful are not themselves victims as well as perpetrators of the social practices that form the backdrop to their own and others' preoccupations with success. He assumes that the powerful are unequivocally the beneficiaries of their position of privilege and influence. His analysis also excludes consideration of how the trappings of power and status offer a *precarious* basis for happiness and fulfilment. Weiss, for example, is paranoid about how he is being portrayed by the media: 'If Abe Weiss or anything concerning Abe Weiss or anything concerning crime and punishment in the Bronx was on television, Abe Weiss wanted it on tape.'[26] Lord Darlington was sufficiently threatened by critical newspaper coverage of his appeasement-seeking efforts with the Germans that he issued a libel action. This he lost, resulting in the destruction of his 'good name' and social ostracism. The loss of a sense of identity was so profound that he effectively gave up the will to live, becoming a reclusive invalid.[27]

Conceptually, the fundamental problem with Lukes's perspective is that it assumes *a priori* knowledge of the 'real', objective interests of particular individuals, groups or classes in society; and further assumes that these exist prior to, or independently of, power relations. We would question this. Following Foucault,[28] we contend that 'interests' are a product of the exercise of power. It is not that 'interests' pre-exist power relations, and that power relations articulate, express or obscure these interests. Rather, 'interests' are identified and pursued through relations of power, in which case, we find unpersuasive the attribution of 'real' interests that somehow lurk behind 'false' interests (or consciousness).

This perspective leads us to appreciate how reference to 'real' interests assumes, and thus privileges, a certain kind of thinking and associated intellectual identity. In radical humanist thinking, assumptions about human nature ascribe an essential autonomy to the self (see Chapter 3). 'Power' is located in actions or institutions that are understood to impede or restrict the freedom of individuals. When interpreted in this light, each dimension of power can be seen as an increasingly potent and insidious threat to human autonomy. So, for example, the internalization of aristocratic values can be understood as placing severe constraints on Stevens's freedom to express his feelings or to act counter to his professional obligations. Were the assumption of *essential* autonomy to be rejected, attention could shift to a consideration of the role of power in constituting a sense of autonomy for individuals as well as the limits to its scope.

Stevens derives a sense of autonomy from his investment in the values of a professional ethic. One consequence of embracing this ethic is a diversion into what is seen as a disordered world and what is perceived as a remedy for it. To the extent that his emotions are effectively controlled so that the project of maintaining an orderly household can be fulfilled, Stevens's sense of autonomy is routinely affirmed. For him, preventing emotions from disrupting the attainment of the professional ideal enables him to sustain a perception of himself as autonomous. However, this commitment to a professional ethic does not just define his autonomy. In so far as Stevens is obsessed by living up to these ideals, his autonomy is abnegated or renounced.

As intimated earlier, we have a series of related reservations about Lukes's assumption of 'real' interests. He believes that these are distorted or denied by the exercise of power. In contrast, we understand that it is easy to attribute 'real interests' to people but difficult to justify such attributions. *The Remains of the Day* highlights this difficulty. The novel alludes to some of the contradictions of Stevens's unquestioning devotion to a master who turns out not only to have sympathies with the fascist movement, but supports an influential line of political appeasement to Hitler. In justification of these sympathies, Lord Darlington says to Stevens: 'Democracy is something for a bygone era. . . . Look at Germany and Italy, Stevens. See what strong leadership can do if it is allowed to act'.[29]

In the end, Stevens accepts that, with the benefit of hindsight, his master's efforts may have been 'misguided, even foolish',[30] but refuses to concede that it was contrary to his own interests to serve Lord Darlington to the best of his abilities: 'It is hardly my fault if his lordship's life and work turned out today to look, at best, a sad waste – and it is quite illogical that I should feel any regret or shame on my own account.'[31] Here, Stevens rejects any suggestion that his 'real' interests could have been better served or realized by pursuing a different vocation or by serving a different master. We are not suggesting that Stevens is better able to judge his own interests than we are or than Lukes is. Rather, we are arguing that 'interests' are contestable and not something essential or given.

Whatever interests are elevated or claimed as more 'real' than others, their formation as well as their identification are conditioned by relations of power. In Sherman McCoy's case, power was exercised by a variety of individuals and groups – his mistress, his wife, the mayor, the kid's mother, the press, community groups and so on. Power cannot then be identified on the basis of whether someone acts against their 'real' interests, as is assumed by those who subscribe to Lukes's third dimension of power. This is not to deny that power is most potent in its institutionalized form. In this respect, we share Lukes's view that power is not adequately conceptualized in terms of the first two dimensions alone. We have simply questioned the assumption that 'real' interests are self-evident or pre-exist their identification. Underpinning this challenge to Lukes's radical humanist belief in 'real' interests has been our rejection of autonomy as an *essential* feature of human nature. Our view is that human interests are neither formed nor identified independently of relations of power. These relations are both a condition and a consequence of social inequalities, to which we now turn our attention.

Conceptualizing inequality

Two of the most prevalent understandings of the inequalities that pervade contemporary society can be traced to the thinking of Marx and Weber (see Table 4.1). In the class analysis of Marx, a fundamentally polarized struggle between capital and labour is assumed. In the stratification analysis developed by Weber, there are multiple dimensions of inequality (e.g. wealth, status) around which competition and conflict are centred. Weber's pluralistic model stresses the multiple points of competition and the diverse ways in which groups might mobilize around particular inequalities.

In liberal democracies, the pluralistic model is widely embraced and promoted. From a Marxian standpoint, support for this model can be explained in terms of the legitimacy that it bestows on the structure of the inequalities prevailing between the privileged and the underprivileged. Expressions of unrest continue to exist despite, or because of, liberal reforms based on meritocratic principles, including equal opportunity legislation. When a belief in equal opportunity is widely and uncritically accepted and embraced, those individuals who do not succeed are invited to blame themselves alone for what is viewed as their personal failure to compete. Equal opportunity legislation, then, has the paradoxical effect of amplifying feelings of personal inadequacy, as it leaves those at the bottom of the heap even less equipped to compete on equal terms with those who are more successful.[32] In short, the application of meritocratic principles can easily result in inequalities that are even more insidious and destructive than those found in societies based on 'good breeding' or property ownership.

From time to time, however, the blocked mobility experienced by the underprivileged surfaces in the form of widespread industrial or civil

TABLE 4.1 *Conceptions of inequality*

Polarity (conflict) Model	Plurality (competition) Model
Class system	Stratification system
Two-dimensional	Multidimensional
Polarization	Pluralization
Blocked mobility	Equal opportunity
Conflict or traditional acceptance	Competition
Change occurs through:	
Rebellion/revolution	Reform
Problem:	
How to allocate scarce resources	Meritocracy

unrest. Such resistance suggests the presence of underlying polarities in the distribution of wealth, status and power that invariably provoke a coercive and punitive response from those who either enjoy privilege or are employed (e.g. managers) to protect it on behalf of others. Order may be restored, but at the expense of damaging the inclusive claims of liberal democracy and the pluralist model. Violent reactions to protest tend to lend credibility to the polarized view of social inequality (e.g. the miners' strike in the early 1980s in the UK, race riots in Los Angeles in the late 1980s). They also give succour to the view that revolution is the only solution, since reform does little more than protect the system of inequality from fundamental change.

The polarized model of inequality assumes the existence of deep-seated divisions in society that can erupt into major social conflicts. Reforms, such as welfare provision for the unemployed, or regulations governing health and safety at the workplace, may serve to moderate, constrain or institutionalize conflict. But when push comes to shove – notably during economic recessions – those who suffer most as welfare provision is cut or jobs are lost are those who lack the capital, in the form of property or savings, to tide them over during hard times.

The Remains of the Day illustrates how a polarized model of inequality can be sustained, at least for a period. In the aristocratic household the 'lower orders' endorse the inequality by virtue of tradition or an institutionalized set of deferential values. However, as the thoughts and actions of Miss Kenton indicate in her opposition to Lord Darlington's racist sacking of the Jewish maids, this deference is by no means complete or secure. Only the worry of having nowhere to go made her draw back from abandoning her professional duty to carry out the instructions of her employer or to fulfil her threat of resignation. As times change and modern values and practices develop, the aristocratic virtues are reinterpreted by modernizers as amateurism: 'Today's world is too foul a place for fine and noble instincts' when these instincts result in becoming 'the single most useful pawn Herr Hitler has had in this country for his propaganda tricks'.[33]

By contrast, *Bonfire of the Vanities* displays strong elements of the pluralistic model of competition for society's material and symbolic resources. It illustrates the array of dimensions through which inequalities are expressed, contested and reproduced. At the same time, the novel provides the reader with a sense of the illegitimacy and corrupt ways in which power is often exercised, and the injustices involved in how material and symbolic rewards are allocated. Those favouring a polarized model would argue that beneath the surface of the diversity and dynamism of New York life, where rags-to-riches stories are glamorized (e.g. Maria, Sherman's mistress, is a high-class hooker who married an elderly millionaire) and riches-to-rags stories are sensationalized (e.g. Sherman's downfall), there remain an institutionalized racism and blocked mobility. It is notable that in the bond department where Sherman worked, 80 people were employed but not one of them was black or female.[34]

The two distinctive conceptions or models of inequality not only are the basis of much academic theorizing but also inform lay understandings of society, as we will illustrate in the following section through more extended reference to the novels. In the polarized model, inequality is understood in terms of two dimensions – wealth and power. Society is seen to comprise advantaged and disadvantaged groups whose interests are diametrically opposed (e.g. capital versus labour, men versus women, white versus black). In this model, the former category in each antinomy is understood to exercise power so that its material and symbolic advantage is sustained over the latter. Social mobility is not impossible, but it is exceptional. For this reason, those who adopt the polarized model as a basis for political action do not have greater equality of opportunity or social mobility as their primary objective. Rather, their aim is to transform the established social order with a view to eradicating social inequalities altogether.

Polarized notions of conflict are rejected by the pluralistic model. Social differences are understood to occur with respect to status, fame, prestige, lifestyle, family background, education, sport, leisure etc. All these factors distinguish and grade people. It is assumed that numerous, often competing, values and beliefs coexist in creative tension. Given this continuous gradation of often overlapping economic and status inequalities, it is believed that any remaining obstacles to mobility between strata are either inescapable or will eventually be removed through the introduction of appropriate reforms.

Rereading the novels through an understanding of inequality

In this section, we selectively examine incidents in the four novels that illustrate the polarized and pluralistic models of inequality.

Nice Work   In *Nice Work*, Robyn asserts her belief in the conflict model when she perceives workers on the shopfloor at Pringle's to be suffering from the violent exploitation of their labour and the repression of capitalist production. However, this polarized view of inequality is somewhat at odds with her postmodernist views. From the latter perspective, no fundamental or absolute meaning can be attached to workers' experience or their position in the workplace. To the extent that the postmodernist view undermines the polarized model, it indirectly lends credence to a conception of society as pluralistic.

Perhaps reflecting his 'working-class-lad-made-good' origins, Vic Wilcox, in contrast, subscribes to the pluralistic model. Even so, he has occasional feelings of uneasiness about how 'the system' works, particularly in its allocation of rewards. He is highly critical of those who do not work hard for a living. He is incensed when, for example, he discovers that his marketing director and the chairman of the parent company have together been building up a business in hiring sunbeds, often using company time to pursue this venture. The irony, of course, is that Vic, the self-styled 'hard-headed' businessman, conqueror of the Real World, had not seen or recognized how the world of manufacturing industry (e.g. Pringle's) is being dismantled and displaced in favour of service industries, such as the hiring of sunbeds.

The Remains of the Day   Stevens has a polarized conception of society. In this model, there are those who understand the 'great affairs of today's world' and servants, like himself, who can only deploy their 'energies to the task of serving' their 'masters'.[35] But Stevens's version of this model of polarization does not carry with it the Marxist undertow of conflict and revolution. Instead of understanding human dignity to be conditional on the eradication of inequality, it is seen to derive from providing an impeccable service for those who possess the breeding and ability to assume responsibility for mastering the decisions of state. Stevens is unsympathetic to demands for reforms intended to ameliorate inequalities. It is sufficient to serve someone who is contributing to 'humanity'[36] and the development of a 'better world'.[37]

Stevens believes that the great political decisions are made in the informal and private surroundings of 'great houses', and not necessarily in the formal, official and public hierarchies of power. This view provides him with a rationale for taking pride in his occupational position. It also supports a belief that, in his words, loyalty to his master is 'intelligently bestowed'.[38] Further, his belief in the informal influence of aristocrats on decisions of state offers a defence against a growing threat to those traditions to which Stevens owed his allegiance. Stevens's conception of society is that of a wheel in which the great houses are at the hub. Yet, as the narrative of the novel proceeds, it becomes clear that the patrician basis of government is in decline. It is being overhauled by career politicians. These modernizers seek to supplant amateurish (and self-serving, if not degenerate) aristocratic virtues and practices with a more professional, managerial approach. At an informal but high-level conference attended by 50 international delegates organized by Lord Darlington in 1923 – a conference designed to discuss the effects of First World War reparations against Germany (demanded by the treaty of Versailles) – an American participant (a senator) commented:

> The days when you could act out of your noble instincts are over. . . . Gentlemen like our good host still believe it's their business to meddle in matters they don't understand. So much hog-wash has been spoken here these past two days. Well-meaning, naive hog-wash. You here in Europe need professionals to run your affairs.[39]

Such 'professional' developments would, of course, displace or marginalize aristocratic status polarities in favour of greater equality of opportunity and other forms of meritocratic inequality.

The Bonfire of the Vanities In *The Bonfire of the Vanities*, Sherman McCoy prided himself on his professional élan: 'He considered himself a part of the new era and the new breed, a Wall Street egalitarian, a Master of the Universe who was a respecter only of performance'.[40] In believing himself to be successful as a result of his abilities, Sherman McCoy subscribes to a pluralistic model of inequality. Following his downfall, he becomes painfully aware of widespread corruption. He comes to understand that the corruption in New York is a direct and unbridled expression of ambition, desire, envy, greed and immorality. It has become a way of life. The espoused intent of the 'hidden hand' of free market capitalism is to produce beneficial effects for all who participate in it. But success at any cost results in a displacement of the moral and social order (i.e. rules and norms) on which the social benefits of competition depend. Competition and the 'success ethic' become dominant, all-consuming values. At the same time, the 'beneficiaries' of the success ethic seek an ethereal and exclusive life that affords them a degree of distance and protection from its underside. They live in secure apartments guarded by doormen and travel everywhere by car. Though comparatively plastic and flimsy, the lifestyle emulated by Sherman McCoy and his wife is, ironically, imitative of the privileged existence found in the great houses served by Stevens.

In contrast to Lord Darlington, however, Sherman McCoy struggles to realize his aspirations to become a member of an elite New York social set. Despite his million dollar a year income, he experiences considerable discomfort in attending 'society' dinner parties. He assumes, often incorrectly, that a majority of the guests at these parties are truly upper class; and that they would look down on a mere bond salesman.[41] In this respect, his discomfort suggests a polarized model of inequality where success and money cannot ultimately secure entry to the ranks of the truly upper class. Sherman believes that a status above that of a bond salesman – the collector of 'golden crumbs' – is required to gain entry to the elite social set. For this reason, Sherman hired a black Buick limousine and driver at enormous expense to drive him and his wife Judy to a party being held only four blocks away from their apartment. Judy's fashionable but non-functional dress prevented them walking. There was an even more compelling reason for the hired car and chauffeur:

> It would be perfectly *okay* for the two of them to *arrive* for dinner at a Good Building (the going term) on Fifth Avenue by taxi, and it would cost less than 3 dollars. But what would they do *after* the party? How could they walk out of the Bavardage's building and have all the world, *tout le monde*, see them standing out in the street, the McCoys, that game couple, their hands up in the air, bravely, desperately, pathetically trying to hail a taxi? The doormen would be no help, because they would be tied up ushering *tout le monde* to their limousines.[42]

Sherman clearly feels a strong social obligation to 'pass' as a member of a privileged class for whom money is not a consideration when pursuing, or rather exhibiting, an elite lifestyle.

In part, Sherman's discomfort arises from not having quite enough income to participate without anxiety in the lavish, and ostentatious, rituals of the social set to which he, and especially his wife, aspires. Yet Sherman's own somewhat cultured, upper-middle-class upbringing leads him to have twinges of doubt and guilt about this lifestyle. He also projects the values of his solid upbringing on to the members of the social set to which he and his wife aspire, even though their lifestyles were vacuous and brash. He wants the trappings of wealth that serve to reassure him that he is indeed a Master of the Universe. But at the same time, as a mere employee, albeit a highly paid one, Sherman's income is not so secure and sufficient to be untroubled by the expense of hiring a limousine. There is then the additional complication that his background made Sherman feel uncomfortable among people for whom all the world, including themselves, is reducible to a commodity. His job as a bond salesman is not recognized or respected by the members of the class into which he was born, including, most importantly, his father. So how else is Sherman to acquire respect for himself except by consuming his wealth conspicuously? The obvious route is to seek membership of the *nouveau riche*.

Here, issues of insecurity and identity explored in the previous chapter are apparent in Sherman's struggles to meet the socially competitive demands of the success ethic. At work, his achievement as the leading bond salesman allows him to think of himself as a Master of the Universe. But elsewhere, this self-image is undermined by his own belief that his job and achievements at work secure no respect from others. When, for example, the woman sitting next to him at the dinner party asks Sherman what he does for a living, he struggles to find a 'winning' answer:

> *I want to impress her!* The possible answers came thundering through his mind . . . *I'm a senior member of the bond division at Pierce and Pierce* . . . No . . . makes it sound as if he's a replaceable part in a bureaucracy and proud to be one . . . *I'm the number one producer* . . . No . . . sounds like something a vacuum-cleaner salesman would say. . . . There's a group of us who make the major decisions . . .

No . . . not accurate and an utterly gauche observation . . . I made $980,000 selling bonds last year. . . . That was the true heart of the matter, but there was no way to impart such information without appearing foolish . . . I'm – a Master of the Universe! . . . Dream on! – and besides there's no way to utter it![43]

Sherman peers into the abyss as he senses the gulf between his self-image as Master of the Universe and what he anticipates others will understand by different possible accounts of what he does for a living. In essence, he is a salesman who works in a bureaucracy selling things that few people can understand, and that he himself cannot explain (see above), but for which he receives an enormous salary. It transpires that Gene Lopwitz (Sherman's boss) is a client of his fellow dinner guest. On discovering that Sherman is unaware of her firm's existence, she immediately turns 90 degrees to her left and resolutely ignores him for the remainder of the meal. Sherman is left stranded, believing that his neighbour had 'devoted all the time she cared to devote . . . to a mere bond salesman!'[44]

The Unbearable Lightness of Being   In *The Unbearable Lightness of Being*, issues of inequality are related to questions of individual autonomy, moral responsibility and power. Tomas's friends, including Sabina and Franz, are members of an intellectual and cultural elite. This elite has a distaste for the totalitarian regime of communism, which it regards as philistine and oppressive. Tomas and his friends subscribe to a conflict model of inequality. In place of the polarization of capital versus proletariat, their view counterposes the party and its bureaucratic machine with the 'ordinary' people or the public at large.

Tomas's vocation as a doctor and his sexual exploits leave him little time or inclination for any active involvement in politics. The extent of his involvement was limited to writing a satirical commentary on the regime. This intervention was stimulated by a growing frustration with public debates over the question of who was responsible for the judicial killings associated with the establishment of the communist regime in the early 1950s. Debate circled around the question of whether party activists knew about the crimes against humanity. The dominant view was that those who could be shown to have known about these crimes were guilty and should be punished, while those who were genuinely ignorant bore no responsibility. Tomas believed that the distinction between knowledge and ignorance of the murders was largely irrelevant. Why? Because to remain ignorant by turning a 'blind eye' was a function of passively endorsing the regime rather than challenging its propaganda. Naiveté, in Tomas's assessment, was an accomplice to the guilt, not an alibi for it. That is to say, those involved could not be excused on the basis of their ignorance of the consequences of their support, since the regime traded on, or made a virtue of, such ignorance:

When Tomas heard Communists shouting in defence of their inner purity, he said to himself: As a result of your 'not knowing', this country has lost its freedom, lost it for centuries, perhaps, and you shout that you feel no guilt? How can you stand the sight of what you have done? How is it you aren't horrified? Have you no eyes to see? If you had eyes, you would have to put them out![45]

The reference to putting out their eyes is an allusion to the Oedipus tragedy. Oedipus plucked out his own eyes because he could not bear to see the suffering of his subjects once they had knowledge that he (albeit unknowingly) had killed his own father and slept with his mother. Tomas's satirical commentary was subsequently published as a newspaper article. This drew parallels between Oedipus and those who had established and maintained the Czechoslovakian communist regime. The article was edited so as to sensationalize its content. It then read as if communists should literally put out their eyes.

Instead of acting as a way of challenging institutionalized inequalities and associated forms of repression, the article was employed, by those who felt themselves to be on trial, as a means of discrediting the critics of the regime. Tomas's act of literary resistance had been transformed by the newspaper editor into an instrument of power. The events that followed are too complex to describe here but, in essence, Tomas became the subject of an investigation by the secret police. Eventually, this led to a demand that he retract the article. In addition, he was pressed to affirm his love for the Soviet Union, his fidelity to the Communist Party, his condemnation of the intelligentsia and his denunciation of the editor of the newspaper in which his article had appeared. Unwittingly, Tomas had incriminated this editor in an earlier interview with a ministry official.

Tomas did not reject these demands outright, for he feared that this would result in the police publishing their own prepared statement over his signature without his consent. When making this decision, Tomas drew on his polarized model of society. He reasoned that he was in no position to challenge the police should they attribute the statement to him. He decided that the only course of action was to cut his ties with any position that gave the secret police some hold over him. As a surgeon, it was his position in the social system that made him, and other dissenters occupying prestigious posts, a target of secret police activity. This was not just, or even primarily, because the police sought to silence him. It was also because statements supportive of the regime made by those occupying positions of authority, such as surgeons, had a demoralizing effect on the people as a whole. By resigning his post and taking up a job as a window cleaner, descending to 'the lowest rung of the social ladder',[46] Tomas escaped harassment by the police and the pressure to compromise himself and others:

Once he had reached the lowest rung on the ladder, they would no longer be able to publish a statement in his name, for the simple reason that no one would accept it as genuine. Humiliating public statements are associated exclusively with the signatories' rise, not fall.[47]

In offering this extended reflection on an episode in *The Unbearable Lightness of Being*, we have sought to demonstrate how power and inequality operate in ways that can rarely be anticipated. Secret police exercise their power in ways that are directed at extracting confessions from dissidents whose social status would count in terms of communication credibility. If Tomas had been in an occupation with little public status, his satirical comments on the regime would probably have been ignored.[c] This example illustrates how high status is not unequivocally advantageous. In western democracies too, public figures may be disgraced by media investigations that expose 'misdemeanours' that would be ignored if perpetrated by those with less notoriety.[d]

While locating the central characters of our novels in one or other of two models of inequality, we have also noted some tensions that would suggest that the models themselves are not unproblematic.

Discussion

We anticipate that many readers will find elements of the two models within their lay understandings of inequality in society. A majority may accept that there are numerous social strata and a multiplicity of dimensions of inequality. Even when this pluralist view is held, it may also be accepted that the upward mobility of manual or women employees is often impeded by class and gender barriers. Despite equal opportunity legislation, it may be believed that race as well as sex discrimination is prevalent in industry and elsewhere, but these inequalities can as readily be understood to arise from the (as yet) imperfect operation of the pluralist model. However, it is not altogether clear whether the models represent the actual structure of inequality or simply common beliefs about it.

We take the view that accounts of the world that aspire to have scientific and academic credibility are not independent of the political and moral beliefs and assumptions that guide their construction. For example, Marx held political beliefs about the inevitability of a class-based revolution. In his scientific analysis, this belief demanded a view of polarized class inequality and conflict as a condition of the dynamic necessary for fermenting radical change. Weber, in contrast, was less sanguine than the populist Marx about

---

c   In the West, people are not used to the level of interference in 'free speech' that is recorded in Kundera's novel. While there are no doubt similar devious tactics employed by CIA and MI5 agents, one would not expect the same level of effort to be targeted at someone who had done no more than write an allegorical newspaper article.

d   Despite negative media reaction, it is remarkable how, in the West, infamy makes public figures attractive to other institutions (e.g. the media) or how frequently they re-accommodate themselves. For example, in the UK, David Mellor, a Conservative minister who was obliged to resign following a sexual scandal, became a successful media celebrity and was coopted by the Labour government to chair a national football (soccer) taskforce. This is not to say that 'trouble makers' have a free hand. Usually, however, their voices are smothered in a plurality of diverse views that have a tendency to regress to the mean that coincides with the moral majority in most communities.

the ability of the masses to make moral choices (e.g. to struggle to create a communist society) that transcend their self or sectional interests. In his analysis, this assumption was translated into a focus on exposing and limiting manifestations of inequality without radically changing the status quo. The models of inequality, then, are perhaps best understood as useful but limited teaching aids that provide divergent frameworks for examining social relations. When deploying the models, we are equally as involved in constructing the reality of inequality as in observing its manifestations.

The insights provided by the models can guide a process of reflection on how to ameliorate inequalities. Suppose we find that our beliefs correspond more closely to the conflict model. We may then conclude that class, gender and racial inequalities can be eradicated through rebellion (e.g. radical rather than liberal feminism) or revolution (e.g. Marxism). Assuming that a revolution would remove the market system, so fundamental to capitalism, it is unclear how scarce resources would then be allocated without creating more problems (e.g. corruption and waste) than it aspires to solve. If these problems are addressed by reverting to the market, there is a danger that over time, small inequalities become compounded into huge disparities of wealth and status. On the other hand, if we are convinced by the pluralist model, we may conclude that the removal of constraints on competition will enable the market to operate efficiently. From this perspective, the market ensures that people are rewarded equitably on the basis of the demand for their skills and their contribution to wealth production, rather than on the basis of their class, gender and/or ethnic membership. However, those who subscribe to the pluralistic model anticipate that the removal of constraints on the operation of markets will also benefit those who are already privileged. Reformists therefore argue that legislation (e.g. equal opportunities) is needed to curb the divisive effects of the market mechanism so as to avoid reinforcing an extreme polarization of wealth.

Dynamics of inequality

Having examined two somewhat static models of inequality, we now turn our attention to a more dynamic approach to its study. This approach is summarized in Table 4.2, which enumerates the what, who and why of inequality. We shift our focus to an examination of everyday strategies and practices through which relations of inequality are sustained and/or changed. In doing so, our account of how inequality is managed is developed through a focus on five central concepts – stereotyping, domination, subordination, indifference and resistance.

Stereotyping

Identifying other individuals or groups as a 'type' is a habitual feature of everyday life. It is the way in which we organize perceptions when making

TABLE 4.2 *The what, who and why of strategies of inequality*

What?	Who?	Why?
Stereotyping	Everyone	Uncertainty
Domination	Mainly advantaged	Self-interest
Subordination	Mainly disadvantaged	Deference and self-blame
Indifference	Mainly disadvantaged	Impotence
Resistance	Mainly disadvantaged	Dignity and collective self-interest

sense of the world (see Chapter 3). When encountering a stranger, we ordinarily typify them as male/female, young/old, black/white. This practice of typifying places a *temporary* closure on how we perceive others and their behaviour. In contrast, *stereotyping* is distinguished by ascribing fixed and unchanging characteristics to the other. Here, the same typifications may be used but they contain a much stronger evaluative element. So, for example, in some contexts men may be assumed to be superior to women and blacks may be thought to be inferior to whites (or vice versa).

Stereotyping is a process that emphasizes one part of the make-up or behaviour of another individual or group so as to *reduce* their particularity to a cartoon-like quality. A well-known example is the stereotyping of Margaret Thatcher as the 'Iron Lady'. This amusing stereotype enabled men, in particular, to reconcile their perceptions of her as feminine while implicitly celebrating her exceptional displays of aggressive and determined masculinity. In *Nice Work*, Robyn's description of her academic interests prompts Vic to respond in a way that stereotypes women:

'My field is the nineteenth century novel,' said Robyn. 'And women's studies.'

'Women's studies?' Wilcox echoed with a frown. 'What are they?'

'Oh, women's writing. The representation of women in writing. Feminist critical theory.'

Wilcox sniffed. 'You give degrees for that?'

. . . 'It's an option.'

'A *soft one* if you ask me,' said Wilcox. '*Still I suppose it's alright for girls.*'[48]

When told that boys also take the women's studies options, Vic says that they must be homosexual or, as he puts it, in a more stereotypical fashion, 'nancy boys'. On being told that they are 'normal, decent and intelligent young men', Wilcox asks:

'Why aren't they studying something useful, then?'

'Like mechanical engineering?' and Robyn sighs . . .[49]

Stereotyping frequently involves a negative evaluation or pejorative labelling of the 'other'. It is a way of showing that one's own behaviour, lifestyle, reality or identity is better, more real or socially valued. Robyn's explanation of her field is grasped by Vic as evidence to confirm his prejudice that many university courses (e.g. studying novels or feminism) are not 'proper' subjects and are certainly not for men. Stereotyping 'rubbishes' other realities and identities as one's own is elevated over the alternatives.

Domination

An individual, group, corporation and indeed a nation state may accumulate scarce material resources as a way of dominating and controlling others. The accumulation and control of symbolic 'goods' can be equally important. In hierarchical relations, symbols are developed and mobilized so that subordinates defer to, or comply with, the wishes or demands of those in 'authority'. In *The Bonfire of the Vanities*, Sherman is intimidated by Pollard Browning, 'a true Knickerbocker' who enters the apartment lift wearing immaculately laundered clothes. These clothes gave Browning a presence which conveyed a message that Sherman, in his raincoat, was 'letting down our new mahogany panelled elevator'.[50]

Controlling meaning is a routine practice for those seeking to dominate other groups, as was noted earlier when discussing Lukes's third dimension of power. This control is further strengthened when the exercise of power is managed through the control of scarce and valued resources, such as education, housing, jobs and even sexual favours. In *The Unbearable Lightness of Being*, Tomas was told that unless he retracted the newspaper article, he would risk losing his job as a surgeon. The chief surgeon reasoned with Tomas that making a retraction was no more than 'mere verbal, formal sorcery'.[51] 'In a society run by terror,' he added, 'it is evident to everyone that such a retraction is meaningless.'[52] The retraction would not have to be public. A note for the files of the bureaucrats would be sufficient. There was no reason not to retract, especially as it would mean that Tomas could continue to care for his patients.

No one at the hospital doubted that Tomas would comply, not least because he was seen to be immediately in line for the job of the chief surgeon, who was about to retire. Tomas was shocked that his colleagues 'were ready to bet on his dishonesty rather than his virtue'.[53] Whether out of fear of losing his job or of not securing promotion, they expected Tomas to fall in line with the oppressive demands of the authorities, as so many had done in the past. But Tomas knew that irrespective of whether the retraction was treated as just a note for the files, its effect would be to inhibit dissent:

> Even after the statement is safely filed away, the author knows that it can be made public at any moment. So from then on he doesn't open his mouth, never criticizes a thing, never makes the slightest protest. The first peep out of him and into print it goes, sullying his name far and wide.[54]

Ironically, Tomas was convinced that even 'dissidents' who had been per-
secuted for refusing to, or believed themselves to be above, compromise
would prefer that he retracted the article. This was because his retraction
could confirm for them a sense of their own heroism. These 'heroes',
Tomas believed, secretly nurtured a love of cowards, without whom their
courage and stoicism would become reduced to 'a trivial, monotonous
grind admired by no one'.[55] He had no more time for these self-righteous
'heroes' than he had for the villains, the collaborators. He felt increasingly
isolated.

Thomas's relationship to women also provides a dramatic illustration of
(male) domination. It could be argued that, in his sexual encounters, he
was seeking to break patriarchal conventions that privilege exclusive,
permanent and possessive sexual relationships. However, this challenge to
conventionality is governed by sexual domination and conquest, in which
no obligations or responsibilities are acknowledged. Traditionally, men of
wealth and status have had mistresses with whom they have usually
enjoyed sex without the obligation of a long-term and/or financial commitment, as well as wives who have provided them with the appearance of
respectability through the family and a line of inheritance. Sherman is a
classic case. He believes that a mistress is nothing but a reasonable reward
for a Master of the Universe who feels that he 'deserve(s) more from time
to time'.[56] However, Maria's spell-binding qualities trap him into a spiral
of devastating lies that ultimately destroys him. The irony, of course, is
that the manslaughter of a black kid in Brooklyn, for which he eventually
goes to jail, was committed by Maria. She drove Sherman's car into the
boy when feeling threatened by the possibility of an imminent attack. The
seducer has such power over the bewitched and guilt-ridden Sherman that
she involves him in a series of attempted cover-ups, resulting in his being
prosecuted for a crime for which he was only indirectly responsible.

Subordination

Subordination is often the only way to respond to power and domination,
especially in societies where certain traditional values of hierarchical
superiority and inferiority prevail. Most people will experience some degree
of subordination – finding themselves in a position where frequently they
have to deal with the dominant reality, as defined by others. However,
people can respond in a variety of ways, as is evident in our novels. Stevens,
the butler, subordinated himself to the expectations of his master, basking in
his glory or what he (mis)understood to be his service to humanity. An
internalized deference made this subordination 'natural' and unquestioned.

The subordination willingly embraced by Stevens is something that many
of us have experienced: the adulation of the teenager for a pop idol, the
believer in romantic love who recurrently becomes infatuated by someone
who always seems to escape their grasp, the admiration for a charismatic
leader. These forms of subordination have in common an impulse to

resolve the tensions and uncertainties of contemporary life. Yet tensions invariably resurface as the seductive qualities of these forms of subordination fade. In an achievement-oriented society, deference may still occur where subordinates blame themselves for not having achieved positions of authority and status. They are thereby inclined to believe that those who have become successful deserve their deferential respect.[57]

On the other hand, Tomas in *The Unbearable Lightness of Being* refused to be deferential to the regime he despised, preferring in the end, on principle, to sacrifice his status as a surgeon and his likely career progress to chief surgeon. Ultimately, this led to his taking on a job with no status at all – as a window cleaner – although probably the reduction in income was negligible.[e]

Indifference

The response to power may not necessarily take the form of subordination; indifference is an alternative. Such a response may involve a self-conscious process of mental distancing[58] (see Chapter 3). Where this occurs, people deny or disregard the reality of their situation as they comply, but without any commitment to the demands of those who exercise power over them. Typically, they daydream or think about those parts of their life in which they do not feel subordinate to someone or something, or in which their feelings of impotence are not overwhelming. At work, the extremes of this kind of behaviour usually occur at the factory or the office or where the conditions of work leave individuals feeling dejected and depressed, so that 'cutting off' is a kind of relief.

This way of categorizing behaviour may, however, be interpreted as ascribing excessive intentionality to people who may simply slide into a 'world' of indifference, without being aware of what they are doing and its implications. Indifference provides a precarious and ultimately destructive means of self-protection, since individuals can never wholly evade the socially constructed processes through which a sense of identity is maintained. Self-inflicted isolation may indeed render individuals more vulnerable to the threatening consequences of change. It also reproduces (and often intensifies) the conditions of subordination, from which indifference is an escape.

Brian Everthorpe, the marketing director at Vic's factory in *Nice Work*, frequently turns up late for work, is running the sunbeds business on the side and often in company time, and has no qualms about making love to Shirley, Vic's secretary, on the reception lobby sofa. All this suggests a lack of interest in his job or the company. This indifference is also displayed in Brian's greater concern to spend time chatting rather than getting on with

---

e   Although Kundera makes no mention of it, the East European regimes had reduced or even reversed income differentials such that doctors often earned less than bus drivers.

his work – a trait that clearly aggravates the work-obsessed Vic. But then Vic has got used to coping with indifference towards his authority. Despite clear principles concerning the work ethic, his own son Raymond spends half the day in bed and has absolutely no interest in getting a job.

Almost all the characters in *The Bonfire of the Vanities* are indifferent to the fortunes of others. Their aim in life is simply to stay one step ahead of the game and protect their every flank against the numerous physical and symbolic attacks on their precarious social position in the success stakes. Indifference is also exhibited by Tomas in *The Unbearable Lightness of Being*, when he resigns from his job as a hospital consultant to take up window cleaning. This affords him extra space and opportunity to engage in his sexual exploits. It also relieves him of the massive burden of a job with responsibility. As a window cleaner, he experienced the

blissful indifference of doing a job that he didn't care a damn about, and enjoying it.[59]

This is indifference experienced not as an escape from, but as an escape into, the indignity of subordination. It is an escape from the responsibility of a demanding job that Tomas felt had dominated his life, and one with which Vic Wilcox could doubtless identify. In contrast to our example of the indifference of shopfloor workers, however, Tomas did appear to choose rather than drift into indifference. He chose to be indifferent to his work in the same way as he had always chosen to be indifferent to his sexual partners and largely for the same reason: the absence of responsibility made the experience more enjoyable.

Resistance

Resistance is another alternative response to the domination of others, whether this be individually or collectively organized. Here, the disadvantaged resist as a means of pursuing their collective and individual self-interest, but also for purposes of retaining a sense of dignity in conditions of its continuous erosion. In a sense, the indifference discussed above is itself a covert form of resistance but one that rarely changes, as opposed to reinforcing, the conditions that give rise to domination. But we should not necessarily see resistance as the opposite of power, as if it is a mechanical force operating in the opposite direction to the energy that it is pitted against.[60] Power relations are much more messy than many conventional texts suggest when they presume power to be the property of individuals or groups. Everyone exercises power and is also its target to some degree and at some time. For this reason, there is resistance to power occurring at various points and involving agents who might otherwise be seen as dominant in relations of power.

In social relations, resistance often operates in the same direction as the power that it opposes; and indeed, it is often more effective as a result.

Resistance can be seen as an alternative means of achieving a given goal that agents share, or as redefining a goal so as to make it more readily achievable. Resistance is not the sole prerogative of those at the bottom of organizational hierarchies nor of those without wealth. Instead, it is as dispersed throughout populations as power itself. In many ways, resistance is just another way of looking at power and its effects.

In *The Unbearable Lightness of Being*, Sabina exhibited a certain resistance when her lover wanted to move in with her. An artist who had also been one of Tomas's sexual partners, she had been a frequent lover of Franz, a university lecturer. Franz had taken her on several of his foreign visits, not least because, unlike Tomas, he was unable to make love to her in the same town where he lived with his wife. Unable to continue living a lie with his wife, to whom he had been married for 23 years, Franz sought a divorce, expecting Sabina to welcome his sharing a home with her. Although extremely upset, he was not entirely shocked by her disappearance when faced with the reality:

> Sabina felt as though Franz had pried open the door of their privacy. . . . Franz would ask for a divorce, and she would take Marie-Claude's place in his large conjugal bed. Everyone would follow the process from a greater or lesser distance, and she would be forced to playact before them all instead of being Sabina, she would have to act the role of Sabina, decide how best to act the role. Once her love had been publicized, it would gain weight, become a burden. Sabina cringed at the very thought of it.[61]

Paradoxically, after settling in Paris, Sabina reflected on a life of betrayal (or should we say resistance?) that had led to a strange emptiness, where there was nothing left to betray, because she had betrayed (resisted) her parents, husband, country, love:[62]

> She had left a man because she felt like leaving him. Had he persecuted her? Had he tried to take revenge on her? No. Her drama was a drama not of heaviness but of lightness. What fell to her lot was not the burden but the unbearable lightness of being.[63]

Having resisted everything, especially those weighty burdens such as living with your lover, Sabina was left with the emptiness of the lightness of being.

There was no such lightness of being for Stevens in *The Remains of the Day*. Miss Kenton challenged his privacy by trying to confirm that underneath the ritualized and depersonalized role and demeanour he adopted was a man of real flesh and blood. In response, Stevens insisted on restoring the highly formal working relationship that had been slightly transgressed, partly or ostensibly to improve communications between the two sides of the service household that was split on lines of gender. What then happened was that Miss Kenton 'invaded' Stevens's pantry and insisted on seeing the book that he was reading, suspecting it to be a ravenous and racy text of sexual adventure. As she discovers it to be nothing more than a romance, she exclaims:

> Good gracious, Mr. Stevens, it isn't anything so scandalous at all. Simply a sentimental love story.[64]

Stevens was indignant at this invasion of privacy, failing to recognize that it was only a faintly disguised 'pass' at him by Miss Kenton. But not only did he feel the need to rationalize his reading the book to improve his command of the English language, he also resisted any further attempts by Miss Kenton to break from the extreme formality of their relations:

> [A] butler who aspires at all times to a 'dignity in keeping with his position', as the Hayes Society once put it, should never allow himself to be 'off duty' in the preserve of others.[65]

Miss Kenton also (unsuccessfully) attempted to resist the demands of Lord Darlington to have two Jewish girls dismissed from the staff at Darlington Hall, despite threatening Stevens with her own departure. However, this episode was probably instrumental in her decision eventually to leave her employment for marriage; and perhaps this was also because her attention towards Stevens ultimately failed to be reciprocated.

In *Nice Work*, Robyn engages in resistance as she challenges the taken-for-granted reality of factory life. In particular, she questions the cavalier way in which Vic contrives to ensure the dismissal of an ethnic minority worker. However, in forewarning the individual, and thereby inadvertently prompting a strike, her resistance produced some unintended consequences. Vic forces her to withdraw the accusation, but only when she realizes that a prolonged strike could result in the closure of the plant, with the loss of all jobs. Nonetheless, this enabled her to extract a promise that Vic would never act in such a coercive and underhand manner and, in her terms, this was a solid and positive outcome resulting from the orchestrated resistance.

These examples have sought to show how inequalities and resistance to them take diverse strategic and tactical forms in the dynamics of everyday life. They also indicate how the conflict and competition models of inequality fail to capture the complexity and subtlety of the processes of its reproduction. While we all tend to engage in stereotyping as part of an ordering of reality, and negatively as a way of elevating ourselves over others, strategies of domination are restricted to those who, because of extreme inequalities, control universally valued resources. In the sphere of sexuality, for example, women have frequently been dominated by men, especially when, through the gaze or sexual conquest, they are treated as little more than objects of sex. The response to power and domination takes the form either of subordination, indifference or resistance. We have

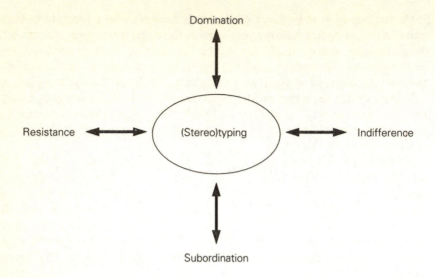

FIGURE 4.1   *Forms of stereotyping*

provided illustrations of each of these strategies from the novels. In place of the rather static diagram presented earlier (Table 4.2), the dynamics may be better summarized as follows (see Figure 4.1).

Summary

Both resistance and power are exercised most effectively when framed within a definition of reality that is widely shared. The exercise of power then secures a measure of collective solidarity and support. Political parties, trade unions, employers' associations, trading blocks and multinationals all work on this simple principle where their members feel bound to one another.

   Of course, the mere existence of an institution cannot guarantee collective solidarity that is the source of its power. Internal divisions frequently result in competing power/resistance strategies and tactics that limit or restructure the broader objectives. The working class, feminist and ethnic minorities have all suffered setbacks as a result of these rifts in their ranks. If, however, we focus more on the localized circumstances where resistance actually arises, we may find that change can occur despite the absence of unified and coherent perspectives. For example, through various strategies and tactics of a collective as well as an individual nature, some limited changes were secured in Pringle's. Robyn shamed Vic into taking down the girlie pin-ups; and she took actions that led the workforce to act together to threaten the withdrawal of their labour if Vic pursued his intent to dismiss an employee on the trumped-up grounds of incompetence.

On the face of it, the actions of Tomas and others who attempted to resist oppression in Eastern Europe would seem to be quite marginal. In the end, those regimes simply imploded under the weight of their own internal contradictions. We cannot attribute the collapse of communism directly to specific instances of dissent and resistance, such as Tomas's refusal to collaborate with the secret police. Nonetheless, pockets of resistance clearly energized the spirit of opposition and the public expression of demands for change that eventually contributed to the political disintegration and demise of these oppressive regimes.

Elements of resistance can also be seen in *The Remains of the Day*; notably, there was Miss Kenton's opposition to Lord Darlington demanding the dismissal of her Jewish maids. However, her self-interest prevented the protest extending beyond the confines of the service area and the butler, Stevens. Both Miss Kenton and Stevens acted to sustain the structure of inequality represented by the Darlington household. This they did partly by constructing their own hierarchy and sense of identity and dignity within it.

In contemporary society, the market and 'professional' practice have gradually displaced much of the aristocratic system of inequality in favour of a more meritocratic system. This new bourgeois meritocratic order – in which control, competition and conquest predominate – is vividly portrayed in *The Bonfire of the Vanities*. The precariousness of social status in this dog-eat-dog world is reflected in the downfall of Sherman McCoy. He was a victim of several discrete and incoherent powers and associated fields of resistance that converged when, in the words of Sheldon, the Mayor's assistant, McCoy 'hit the wrong kind of kid in the wrong part of town with the wrong woman, not his wife'.[66] There were lawyers trying to make a name for themselves, a mayor looking for the black vote, community protest groups looking for a cause around which to organize, journalists with an eye on what sells newspapers, a mother seeking to revenge her dead son etc. Of course, 'bringing down' an individual such as Sherman hardly constitutes a change in the structure of inequality in New York, but that is hardly the point. Not only does Sherman's downfall highlight the limits to wealth and power even in a society that deifies them, it also illustrates how a focus on individual misdemeanour serves, through the sensationalizing mass media, simultaneously to galvanize and distract oppositional forces from engaging in more radical forms of dissent.

Clearly, relations of power and inequality may be quite robust but they are also dynamic, ever changing as a result of unpredictable and uncontrollable events. Few would have predicted the collapse of the Soviet Union, including those who were most acutely aware of its internal cleavages and contradictions. Without claiming that the world is rendered more controllable through the study of power and inequality, we have suggested that a focus on them is no less central to the study of management and organization than it is to other aspects of society. Yet most textbooks in the field treat the study of power and inequality, as well as identity and insecurity, as irrelevant or, at best, peripheral to the under-standing of management. This is so except in a managerialist sense, when techniques are prescribed for ensuring that the power of managers is effective in controlling employees and securing profits – for example, by exploiting economic and psychological insecurities. The application of these techniques sustains existing systems of inequality in which power, insecurity and identity are taken as givens rather than studied as a con-dition and consequence of management and organization.

Notes

1 Ishiguro, I. (1990) *The Remains of the Day*. London: Faber and Faber. p. 116.
2 *The Remains of the Day*, p. 200.
3 *The Remains of the Day*, pp. 29–31; 116.
4 *The Remains of the Day*, p. 43.
5 *The Remains of the Day*, p. 201.
6 *The Remains of the Day*, p. 201.
7 *The Remains of the Day*, p. 201.
8 *The Remains of the Day*, p. 239.
9 *The Remains of the Day*, p. 244.
10 Wolfe, T. (1988) *The Bonfire of the Vanities*. London: Picador. p. 99.
11 *The Bonfire of the Vanities*, p. 102.
12 *The Bonfire of the Vanities*, p. 108.
13 *The Bonfire of the Vanities*, p. 69.
14 *The Bonfire of the Vanities*, p. 65.
15 *The Bonfire of the Vanities*, p. 692. See also Chapter 5.
16 Lodge, D. (1989) *Nice Work*. Harmondsworth: Penguin. p. 364.
17 *The Bonfire of the Vanities*, p. 727.
18 *The Bonfire of the Vanities*, p. 260.
19 *The Bonfire of the Vanities*, p. 261.
20 *The Bonfire of the Vanities*, p. 262.
21 Lukes, S. (1973) *Power: A Radical View*. London: Macmillan.
22 *The Bonfire of the Vanities*, p. 544.
23 *The Bonfire of the Vanities*, p. 544.
24 *The Bonfire of the Vanities*, p. 419.
25 *The Remains of the Day*, p. 117.
26 *The Bonfire of the Vanities*, p. 420.
27 *The Remains of the Day*, p. 235.
28 Foucault, M. (1980) *Power/Knowledge: Selected Interviews and Other Writings*, ed. C. Gordon. Brighton: Harvester Press.
29 *The Remains of the Day*, p. 198.
30 *The Remains of the Day*, p. 201.
31 *The Remains of the Day*, p. 201.
32 Sennett, R. and Cobb, J. (1977) *The Hidden Injuries of Class*. Cambridge: Cambridge University Press.
33 *The Remains of the Day*, p. 224.
34 *The Bonfire of the Vanities*, p. 74.
35 *The Remains of the Day*, p. 201.
36 *The Remains of the Day*, p. 117.
37 *The Remains of the Day*, p. 115.
38 *The Remains of the Day*, p. 201.

39 *The Remains of the Day*, p. 102.
40 *The Bonfire of the Vanities*, p. 74.
41 *The Bonfire of the Vanities*, pp. 369–400; 614–23.
42 *The Bonfire of the Vanities*, pp. 369–70.
43 *The Bonfire of the Vanities*, p. 389.
44 *The Bonfire of the Vanities*, p. 390.
45 Kundera, M. (1989) *The Unbearable Lightness of Being*. London: Faber and Faber. p. 177.
46 *The Unbearable Lightness of Being*, p. 192.
47 *The Unbearable Lightness of Being*, p. 192.
48 *Nice Work*, p. 114, our emphasis.
49 *Nice Work*, p. 114.
50 *The Bonfire of the Vanities*, p. 21.
51 *The Unbearable Lightness of Being*, p. 180.
52 *The Unbearable Lightness of Being*, p. 180.
53 *The Unbearable Lightness of Being*, p. 181.
54 *The Unbearable Lightness of Being*, p. 182.
55 *The Unbearable Lightness of Being*, p. 183.
56 *The Bonfire of the Vanities*, p. 20.
57 See *The Hidden Injuries of Class*.
58 Goffman, E. (1961) *Role Distance*. New York: Bobbs Merrill.
59 *The Unbearable Lightness of Being*, p. 197.
60 See Knights, D. and Vurdubakis, T. (1994) 'Resistance, power, Foucault and all that . . .', in J. Jermier, D. Knights and W. Nord (eds), *Resistance and Power in Organisations*. London: Routledge.
61 *The Unbearable Lightness of Being*, p. 115.
62 *The Unbearable Lightness of Being*, p. 122.
63 *The Unbearable Lightness of Being*, p. 122.
64 *The Remains of the Day*, p. 197.
65 *The Remains of the Day*, p. 169.
66 *The Bonfire of the Vanities*, p. 626.

Recommended further reading

Inequality

Berger, P. and Luckmann, T. (1964) 'Social mobility and personal identity', *Archives of the European Journal of Sociology*, 3–31.
Heller, C.S. (1969) *Structured Social Inequality*. London: Collier-Macmillan.
Savage, M. (1992) *Property, Bureaucracy and Culture: Middle Class Formation in Contemporary Britain*. London: Routledge.
Sennett, R. and Cobb, J. (1977) *The Hidden Injuries of Class*. Cambridge: Cambridge University Press.
Westergaard, J. (1975) *Class in Capitalist Society*. London: Heinemann.

Power

Clegg, S. (1989) *Frameworks of Power*. London: Sage.
Foucault, M. (1980) *Power/Knowledge: Selected Interviews and Other Writings 1972–1977*, ed. C. Gordon. Brighton: Harvester.
Jermier, J., Knights, D. and Nord, W. (eds) (1994) *Resistance and Power in Organizations*. London: Routledge.

Knights, D. and Roberts, J. (1982) 'The power of organisation or the organisation of power?: management–staff relations in sales', *Organisation Studies*, 3 (1): 47–63.
Knights, D. and Willmott, H.C. (1985) 'Power and identity in theory and practice', *Sociological Review*, 33 (1): 22–46.
Lukes, S. (1974) *Power: A Radical View*. London: Macmillan.

References

Derrida, J. (1967/68) *Writing and Différance* (trans. Alan Bass). London: Routledge and Kegan Paul.
Foucault, M. (1980) *Power/Knowledge: Selected Interviews and Other Writings 1972–1977*, ed. C. Gordon. Brighton: Harvester.
Goffman, E. (1961) *Role Distance*. New York: Bobbs Merrill.
Knights, D. and Vurdubakis, T. (1994) 'Resistance, power, Foucault and all that . . .', in J. Jermier, D. Knights and W. Nord (eds), *Resistance and Power in Organisations*. London: Routledge.
Lukes, S. (1974) *Power: a Radical View*. London: Macmillan.
Sennett, R. and Cobb, J. (1977) *The Hidden Injuries of Class*. Cambridge: Cambridge University Press.

5   Managing to Manage

In this chapter, our attention turns more directly to the subject of management. The terms 'manage' and 'management' are used in two broad senses – an everyday and a specialist sense. This chapter is concerned to acknowledge rather than deny the links between these common-sense and specialist uses of the term management.

Commonsensically, managing describes what people do as they go about 'managing' their everyday lives. For example, as we interact with relations, friends and others, we are more or less deliberately involved in acquiring and managing a morally and emotionally charged sense of who we are and what we are doing – a sense of identity, meaning and purpose. We are not programmed beings governed entirely by instinctual impulses (see Chapter 3). Instead, we continuously interpret and 'manage' numerous competing desires, demands and obligations. For example, we may ask an acquaintance: 'Did you *manage* to see my father?' Or we might inquire of a friend: 'And how did you *manage* to get out of that situation?' This everyday sense of managing is examined in the first section of the chapter. Here we consider how Sherman McCoy, self-styled Master of the Universe in *The Bonfire of the Vanities*, spectacularly mismanages the task of phoning his mistress from a public telephone booth under the pretext of taking his dog for a walk.

Of course, we are rarely conscious of the fragility and complexity of social identity or its active management. We only become aware of this on occasions when routines and relationships break down or become full of tension and conflict. Then we may be prompted to reflect more deeply on the political character of even our own relationships. Most poignantly, this happened to Sherman McCoy when, following his arrest and trial for manslaughter, he says: 'I'm not Sherman McCoy anymore. I'm somebody else without a proper name'.[1]

The everyday meaning of managing exists as a *resource* and as an *obstacle* in work organizations. The practicalities of coordinating and controlling work – conventionally defined as central to the tasks of specialist or professional management – are always made possible and yet constrained by conventions and expectations drawn from everyday life. In workplaces, managing and management have specialized and historically specific meanings, where the management of people or activities is associated with processes of coordinating and controlling the organization of work. Certain employees are assigned management titles such as 'production manager' or are identified as members of 'the management team'. In this context, the meaning of management is defined in relation to specific activities and responsibilities, such as the design and implementation of procedures and systems deemed necessary (by managers at least) to provide an efficient and/ or effective means of realizing organizational goals. These include, *inter alia*, procedures and processes that enable staff to be recruited and trained, technologies to be introduced and maintained, products to be developed and distributed etc.

We examine the development of modern work organizations and their consequent refinements in the two central sections of the chapter. In doing so, we continue to use examples drawn from the novels, especially, *The Bonfire of the Vanities* and *The Remains of the Day*. The first of these sections addresses the growth of formal rationality and its associated effects in eroding personal obligation and 'moral community' in work organizations. We then focus on the recent managerial disaffection with the impersonal, amoral and soulless character of formal, bureaucratic rationality and its capacity to maintain profitability in a fast-changing world. Finally, we draw on an exchange between Vic Wilcox and his boss, Stuart Baxter, in Lodge's *Nice Work* to recap on the central concepts and themes of earlier chapters and show how these have general relevance for understanding both senses of the words managing and management.

Everyday managing

When, in *The Bonfire of the Vanities*, we are introduced to its (anti) hero Sherman McCoy, he is down on both knees, in the front hall of his very expensive New York apartment, struggling to get his reluctant dachshund on to its leash. Eventually, he '*managed* to hold on to the leash and struggle into his raincoat'.[2] But it quickly becomes evident that Sherman is also managing appearances, as his interest in walking the dog is a subterfuge for phoning his mistress, Maria. And, as a consequence of the anxiety and guilt he feels and seeks to hide, he is also engaged in managing himself.

Observing this scene, Sherman's wife, Judy, remarks that he is being surprisingly nice to the dog 'all of a sudden', volunteering to exercise the hound on a wet and windy evening. As their daughter would like her father to read a bedtime story, Judy suggests that either she or Eddie the doorman could exercise the dog. Sherman wonders anxiously if his wife suspects something. Then, reassured by a (non-verbal) smile that suggests the sincerity of her suggestion, he feels trapped by the logic of her counsel. He is consumed with guilt about depriving his daughter of a story. But he also feels angry because he – a virile, handsome male from an established family, possessing a Yale education and able to make $50 000 as commission for trading just one lot of bonds – is being deflected from his goal by a woman, his wife, a mere housewife.

Privately, Sherman thinks of himself as one of the Masters of the Universe – a person for whom there is no limit whatsoever. Yet he finds himself wrestling on the floor with a dog, 'hog-tied by sweetness, guilt and logic'.[3] Surely, Sherman thinks to himself, he should be able to manage his adultery by calmly explaining to his wife that he loves her, their daughter and their home and doesn't want to lose them. It is just that, as a Master of the Universe, he simply 'deserves *more* from time to time, when the spirit moves me'.[4]

Feeling trapped and put upon, Sherman '*managed* to manufacture just enough resentment to ignite the famous McCoy temper'.[5] Instead of attempting to explain his actions or to respond directly to Judy's suggestions, he substituted violence for communication. He roared that he was ready to walk the dog and that was what he proposed to do. In response, his wife simply says, 'Please do what you want' – a reaction that makes his mastery of the situation a hollow victory and produces yet another spasm of guilt. At which, 'the Master of the Universe stood up and *managed* to hold on to the leash and struggle into his raincoat'.[6] And at the same time, he realized that his worries about managing the situation were groundless. In the event, there was 'nothing to it': he had 'run right over her' – an image that was soon to haunt him.

Sherman McCoy's everyday managing skills were tested and again found wanting before he reached the street. First, there is an unexpected encounter with Pollard Browning, another resident in the sumptuous apartment building. Browning had attended the same school as Sherman. Since their schooldays, he had looked (down) on Sherman as a 'Mountain Boy'. As Browning gets into the lift, he says 'Hello, Sherman' in a way that communicates the message: 'You and your animal are unfit to be in this mahogany panelled elevator'.[7] Sherman is furious at this put-down, yet he finds himself obeying the unspoken instruction delivered by the patrician Browning, to pick the dog off the floor. Then, silence. When they reach the ground floor, Browning looks at the dachshund, shakes his head and says: 'Sherman McCoy. Friend to man's best friend'[8] – the implication being that McCoy is a desperately sad case, reduced to lavishing his affection on a dumb animal. In retaliation, Sherman makes an unsuccessful attempt to 'trump' the put-down with the sarcastic observation that Browning has taken eight floors to 'think up something bright'.[9] However, in delivering the insult, Sherman is undone by his temper which 'had slipped out around the edges'.[10] Browning demonstrates his indifference to the likes of Sherman by saying: 'I don't know what you are talking about'.[11] Once again, the Master of the Universe is brought down to earth with a bruising bump.

Out in the rain, Sherman encounters another problem: the dog does not relish the wet or the wind and will not budge. It is a tug of war between Sherman and the dachshund, with the doorman and anyone else on Park Avenue as unwelcome spectators. Sherman expects the dog to start walking if he jerks hard enough on the leash. The hound's toenails scrape along the pavement. Sweating and soaked by the rain, Sherman at last reaches the call box. He dials the number. A woman's voice answers, but the voice isn't

Maria's. Sherman assumes that it's Germaine who sublets the apartment to Maria. He asks to speak to Maria. The voice then says: 'Sherman? Is that you?' In his eagerness and confusion, Sherman has dialled his own apartment. It's not Maria or even Germaine. It's Judy, his wife! Paralysed, he hangs up. How is he going to manage *that* situation?

Analysing mundane managing

We now explore in more detail Sherman's efforts to manage his relationships with Judy, Browning and Eddie the doorman. Sherman, we suggest, is not particularly unusual or socially 'maladjusted'. On the contrary, he exemplifies a form of mundane narcissism that is widespread in modern, competitive, individualized societies. It is not difficult to recognize our own versions of Sherman's self-centred mindgames and anxieties about his status. Being open about these anxieties and subterfuges is no less problematic for many of us than it is for Sherman. As the British comedian Ben Elton would say, 'We are all "farties"', masquerading as Masters of the Universe who are cool and in control. To the extent that we lack the insight and/or courage to acknowledge this to ourselves, let alone to others, it can appear that we are indeed secure. This only fuels others' feelings of inadequacy and insecurity, giving rise to a redoubling of efforts to appear confident and 'in control' which, if successfully managed, are at once intimidating and seductive. Needless to say, it is precisely this effect that is engendered by allegedly charismatic leaders and management gurus who simultaneously amplify insecurities as they offer to provide a remedy for them.

Sherman McCoy, Master of the Universe, deems himself to be deserving of a degree of freedom from the moral obligations of marital fidelity and fatherhood. Despite being 40, he looks on himself as 'a young man still in the season of the rising sap'.[12] This self-image allows him to justify the acquisition of a beautiful, young mistress, in the ravishing form of Maria. Through his sexual exploits, Sherman finds a means of dissolving his anxieties about his 'mastery' through the momentary ecstasies engineered by Maria's professional lovemaking. But, at the same time, Sherman fears the insecurity and loss of status associated with the threat posed to his marriage by his adulterous relationship. He has perhaps even greater concern for his daughter, on whom he dotes (but with whom he has only fleeting contact) and whom he displays to his acquaintances (Sherman seems to have few friends) as an attractive accessory to his magisterial, masculine self-image.

Sherman's fears and insecurities are precisely what undermine his ability to act consistently and decisively. They are also qualities that make him a warmer and more attractive character than his calculating mistress. Lacking the necessary degree of calm and clarity to execute the simple task of making a phone call, Sherman discovers that his freedom to act is seriously impeded by emotions that he is unable to control. The formal rationality of his plan to outwit his wife is undermined by a series of unanticipated events, such as meeting Browning in the elevator and struggling with the dog. The resulting emotional turmoil leads him to make the elementary mistake of dialling the wrong number.

Social interactions of all kinds, however mundane or trivial, are potentially fraught with difficulty – not least when, egotistically, we aspire to convey an impression that we struggle to sustain. Since social relations are never programmed, even when they are formal and closely scripted (as in the case of Stevens's interactions in *The Remains of the Day*), they are necessarily 'managed' . Consider Sherman's initial exchange with his wife in which she observes that he is being unusually nice to the dog. It is unclear to him how this is to be taken or 'managed'. It could be a casual comment, or an intended compliment, or an irony. Its meaning is *ambiguous* – an ambiguity to which Sherman is hypersensitive precisely because, of course, he fears that his deception will be unmasked. The threat posed to his magisterial self-image makes him angry: this should not happen to him! Only the non-verbal signal – his wife's smile – leads him to believe (but perhaps not fully) that no irony is intended. But then, her very sincerity is itself painful to Sherman.

Sherman knows that he has no rational means of contesting her logic that Eddie should walk the dog. Sherman is rendered speechless because 'there weren't enough white lies to get around such logic!'[13] Bereft of logical argument, he resorts to verbal aggression. The reality of his definition of the situation is violently asserted. Sherman insists that because he is ready to walk the dog, he is going to do precisely that. At the same time, he senses that his insistence is an overreaction fuelled by anxiety, guilt, anger and resentment. But (how perverse!) this Master of the Universe is powerless to moderate his aggression. Faced with this contradiction, Sherman justifies his violence by silently intoning his treasured, intensely private belief that intemperance is 'the secret of the McCoy temper . . . on Wall Street . . . wherever . . . the imperious excess'.[14] In other words, because verbal bullying has proved to be a winning formula at the workplace, its very success provides a way of rationalizing (and legitimizing) the use of verbal violence in other spheres, including his marriage.

Events – such as his failure to control his dog, his inability to match his wife's logic, his encounter with Browning and finally his failure to dial the required phone number – cast doubt on Sherman's self-identity as a Master of the Universe. These experiences do not, however, lead him to reflect on how he has become enslaved to his own self-deception. Instead, they simply make him feel angry and resentful because the world – that is, other people, his dog and Sherman himself – is not behaving or responding in a way that confirms his magisterial self-image. While contemptuous of Browning as a snob, Sherman nonetheless finds himself responding to his unspoken commands. Though indifferent to the likes of Eddie, the doorman, Sherman is still anxious about what Eddie thinks of his efforts to manage his dog. Blinded by self-deception, Sherman is unable to see how his paranoid feelings about what he believes Judy, Browning and Eddie the doorman to be thinking about him are fuelled by his vanity and associated insecurity. Sherman identifies himself as a Master of the Universe who can have (and has a right to get) whatever he wants – from a top-of-the-range Mercedes to a ravishing mistress. Perversely, however, this beguiling and seemingly powerful self-image is, in practice, a source of continuous discomfort. Paradoxically, the sense of identity that gives him the greatest satisfaction and feeling of omniscient security is also what renders him repeatedly impotent and insecure. What, potentially, are humorous events (e.g. the encounter with Browning and his attempts to walk the dog) are experienced by Sherman as direct assaults on his self-image.

In everyday life, interactions are often conditioned by a sense of moral commitment and personal obligation to others or a wider community. Judy, for example, clearly expects Sherman to respond positively to the suggestion that he could read their daughter a story or, at least, that he will offer some plausible explanation for preferring to take the dog for a walk on a wet and windy night. Sherman's sense of guilt at overriding this expectation indicates knowledge of, and a degree of subscription to, his membership of a moral community of family members. Likewise, when Sherman picks up Marshall in response to Browning's unspoken instruction, he reluctantly acknowledges the unwritten moral duty to keep his dog from fouling the elevator. Finally, when Sherman reaches the street and struggles to make the dachshund walk to the call box, he feels the disapproving or contemptuous eyes of Eddie and other passers-by on him as he throttles the dog into obedience.

Even though inequalities of class, status and power are rarely far beneath the surface of social niceties that may quickly lose their veneer, everyday interactions can also be friendly, informal, spontaneous, warm and personal. Seemingly, Judy's suggestion that she or Eddie might exercise the dog was spontaneous and sincere. Within the employment relationship, by contrast, interactions are comparatively formal, planned and impersonal. Employees are often strangers; they are not generally relatives or friends. They surrender personal control over how they spend their time when their labour is exchanged for a wage or salary. Friendships and informal relations may develop. They may even be selectively nurtured by corporate policies such as 'awaydays', teamworking, conferences and other such initiatives. The remoteness and anonymity of workplace relations may be diluted, especially in situations (e.g. in work groups) where an open expression of feelings is less likely to jeopardize employment or promotion prospects. Yet work relationships invariably remain conditioned by other, less personal (e.g. commercial or statutory) values and priorities that militate against the development of interpersonal and moral or collective solidarity.

In everyday business practice, employees routinely discover that they are expendable when there is a demand for cost cutting as a means of boosting short-term profits. Alternatively, the competition for status and career fuelled by emotional and economic insecurity results in the denial or exploitation of collegial or trusting relationships in the interests of self-advancement. 'Rational' and emotional spheres become decoupled as a consequence of the organizing of productive activity into a hierarchically based division of labour. Emotional expression and the development of friendships within workplaces are contained within a dominant ethos of formal hierarchical authority that is established, policed and selectively relaxed by those who occupy managerial positions within organizations. Although there are important parallels between hierarchical relations within the family (e.g. patriarchy) and within work organizations, they are differentiated by the contractual nature of the employment relationship. Nonetheless, as *lived experience*, there remain continuities between the process of managing (in) organizations and the process of managing mundane everyday activities. Indeed, as service work expands and employers strive to mobilize the enthusiasm and commitment of employees, there are attempts to bring about a managed reunification of the 'rational' and emotional spheres of life. Human emotions become a target of colonization by the 'rationality' of businesses as empathetic and socially skilled labour, which is often gendered, is hired to provide a superior level of 'customer service', for example.

Insights into managing mundane activities are therefore increasingly pertinent for interpreting the dynamics and contradictions of managing in work organizations. Yet, the interlinking of management, as a specialist activity in bureau-corporate spheres and managing everyday life (as part of what it is to be human), could be dangerous if it encourages a further extension of the former to the latter. For the specialist meaning of management then becomes a lens, and even an ideal, for interpreting and assessing everyday ways of managing. This is certainly not what we intend when we draw attention to the continuities between the practice of management and managing in everyday life. The parallels drawn between management at work and in everyday life do not assume or imply an absence of differences; nor, more importantly, are we suggesting that the activity of managing is exhaustive of what it is to be human.

We hope that our treatment of management practice as little more than an elaboration, and to some extent obfuscation, of the universal human attributes of managing everyday life will stimulate reflection on the authority and privilege ascribed to managerial expertise. In the contemporary context, there is a sense in which, as a consequence of 'delayering' and 'empowerment', management as a distinctive, specialist expertise is being demystified as its boundaries are blurred. That said, it is hardly the case that senior executives are undermining their power and privileges when they champion new management practices. For it is mainly the middle-ranking managers who suffer a loss, downgrading or intensification of their jobs through this kind of rationalization. Any ensuing increase in profitability that corporate rationalizations are intended to produce is of benefit largely to shareholders, including senior managers who receive profit-linked bonuses or share options.

On the other hand, we have noted how the comparatively impersonal and calculating practices developed within the context of work organizations exert an influence on how we 'manage' our everyday lives. Ideas and techniques absorbed at work can influence the development of a cognitive style (e.g. orderliness, emotional control, life planning, political correctness etc.) that is extended to the private sphere.[a] A strong articulation of this argument would suggest that the terms 'managing' and 'management' are increasingly saturated with managerial meanings, so that the everyday sense of managing is colonized by them. Without going quite this far, we have stressed how the management of work organizations and the management of everyday life are inextricably interlinked. They exist in a relationship of some tension to each other. For example, in *Nice Work* Vic is unsettled by the playful familiarity of his secretary, Shirley; and in *The Remains of the Day*, in catching Stevens secretly reading a romantic novel, Miss Kenton exposes the private self beneath the public mask. Without denying the differences – for example, the relative impersonality and formality of work compared to everyday life – we believe that it is unhelpful to deny or ignore their connections.

Having drawn attention to the centrality of processes of managing in both everyday life and work organizations, we now focus directly on the historical and contemporary development of the modern organization.

Making the modern organization

We noted in Chapter 2 how, during the period of the Industrial Revolution, the location and organization of work shifted from domestic/craft to factory production, and control changed from the family or guilds to the owners or managerial agents of capital.[15] As factory production progressively

---

a   Instrumental reasoning and the perfection of systems are incorporated into everyday life as individuals now routinely assume responsibility for 'family planning', 'career planning' 'diet planning' etc. Complex calculations are made about where we should live, whom our children should associate with, what sort of car 'fits' our self-image and so on. The disciplines, languages and paraphernalia of modern management are applied within the home – with budgets, lists, noticeboards, scheduling, the use of computer software and other bureaucratic devices to 'manage' the household. For some commentators, such as Habermas (1984, 1987), in this colonization of everyday life instrumental reason is met with unequivocal censure and regret. While sharing some of his reservations, we believe that this hostile assessment must be balanced by an appreciation of the positive aspects of signs of convergence between the workplace and everyday life. On the one hand, the appeal to cultural values within the workplace (albeit selective and exploitive) presents an opportunity for challenging the rationality of established workplace disciplines. On the other hand, the adoption of management disciplines in the home can potentially facilitate an enrichment of everyday life rather than its impoverishment. Unless these reservations are entered, then the critique of convergence comes very close to a reactionary call for a return to traditional values. Management disciplines are then too easily and simplistically viewed as essentially sinister or immoral. We take the view that, if wisely (rather than slavishly) applied, they can be of positive value in the husbandry of scarce resources.

displaced cottage industry, work and family life were separated into more distinct spheres. They did not simply occupy different time periods but became increasingly spatially segregated. As the residues of feudal society were progressively dissolved, people were obliged to treat their own labour as a commodity to be exchanged with employers who competed over its purchase. Work in the factories was no longer subject to the everyday rhythms of nature, tradition and domestic existence. A condition of employment (as a wage labourer) in the new factories and offices was the contractual obligation to set aside the customary right to work at one's own pace and place. Labour worked at a speed and was directed, formally at least, by owners or their managerial agents (e.g. the gang bosses of sub-contracted work groups). Traditional rhythms were progressively supplanted by the demands of an impersonal and bureaucratic workplace discipline, determined largely by the constraints of productive efficiency within competitive markets.

Traditional values were not abandoned wholesale as a medieval order governed by monarch, church and guilds gradually unfolded into a society regulated by markets and bureaucratic organizations.[16] Certain values – such as those associated with the Protestant ethic, which suggested that hard work could be interpreted as a sign of grace – were selectively promoted. Not least this was because of the 'elective affinity' between the value of industriousness and the productivity improvements demanded by the market imperatives of an emergent capitalist economy.[17] Conversely, within the home and community, a concern to protect private, personal and emotional life was reflected in a degree of antipathy to factory discipline and bureaucratic regulation. Its control was widely experienced as intrusive, coercive, degrading and divisive.

When contracting to sell their time to an employer, employees *formally* relinquish their rights over how their labour is applied. However, this contract does not eliminate, and may even stimulate or inflame, hostility to employer discipline and demands. Such hostility, expressed in diverse forms of resistance (e.g. absenteeism, sabotage, militancy), not only arises from perceptions of being materially undervalued (e.g. in terms of the relative wage level for the work performed). It is also aroused when an employee's sense of identity is threatened or devalued (e.g. when menial tasks are performed and/or impersonal and instrumental relationships are encountered). Today, the comparative intimacy and privacy of the domestic sphere are still upheld (in rhetoric if not always in reality) as a refuge where people can escape from the depersonalized demands of the competitive and 'dehumanizing' world of organized work.[18]

In response to an experienced lack or loss of control, employees may seek to 'escape' by distancing themselves mentally from their work, for example by daydreaming (see Chapter 4). Such 'escape' is a means of protecting individual identity against the erosion of a sense of dignity that is associated with employees' limited control over their treatment as commodified labour. As Vic Wilcox pointed out to Robyn in *Nice Work*, monotonous work allows employees to 'switch off' and 'daydream'. They can live out their fantasies of a private identity that feels less constrained or subordinated – precisely the opposite of what is experienced in the work environment. A sense of self can be protected at work through 'daydreaming', at least when the tasks are sufficiently routine and repetitive.

Employers may view daydreaming positively as something of a 'safety valve' that reduces the risk of more organized and challenging forms of resistance. However, distancing of all kinds can be a major obstacle to managerial initiatives that seek to mobilize the tacit and informal knowledge of employees for purposes of involving them more closely and actively in processes of organizing and managing work (e.g. in programmes of 'continuous improvement'). Such initiatives require employees to renounce the 'escapist' pleasures of daydreaming in favour of a disciplined engagement in their work. The effort and risk associated with the management of self-identity are, of course, by no means confined to the sphere of work (see the earlier account of Sherman McCoy's encounter with Pollard Browning). However, in the work sphere, the penalties – symbolic as well as material – associated with failures to manage one's self in a way that is acceptable to an employer (e.g. inappropriate expression of emotion such as anger or sullenness) are generally greater. The possible excuses or explanations for expressing such feelings are also more restricted.

Weber and bureaucracy

Max Weber (1864–1920) is widely regarded as an influential analyst of the modernizing tendency to regulate human actions by formal procedures that draw their authority from due legal process, that is, bureaucracy. The employment contract is an example of a key bureaucratic mechanism that regulates productive activity. The very condition of being modern, Weber contends, involves a movement towards an increased dependence on rational-legal principles of social and economic organization. While other bases for the regulation of human action – notably, tradition and charisma – continue to exert an influence on people, bureaucracy becomes increasingly pervasive and dominant.

Weber[19] did not assume or expect that, in practice, work organizations would faithfully follow or perfectly exemplify the bureaucratic ethos that requires employees to act in 'a spirit of formalistic authority . . . without hatred or passion, and hence without affection or enthusiasm'. On the contrary, he believed that there would be considerable resistance to bureaucratic organization because it suppresses human emotions and communal sentiment. For example, at the investment bank where Sherman worked, there were many opportunities in the trading room for light-hearted banter, though any display of idleness was not tolerated.[20] In any event, many unintended consequences flow from the application of bureaucratic principles. A preoccupation with refining organizational means (e.g. the elaboration of procedures) can take precedence over the pursuit of objectives to which the procedures are supposedly dedicated. In short, an obsessive and meticulous focus on formally rational means displaces the attainment of intended goals. When this occurs, compensatory measures of bureaucratic management, such as a resort to 'strong leadership' or a return to 'traditional values', may be invoked.

Weber stressed how, in the context of bureaucratic organization, any desire to do meaningful work, which involves passion and enthusiasm, is subordinated to a requirement to comply with rules and regulations. In *The Remains of the Day*, Stevens's refusal to acknowledge, let alone express, emotion or to allow personal life to intrude on 'professional' activity is an extreme example of impersonal devotion to duty. Stevens is determined to perfect the execution of his duties with all due speed, unambiguity, continuity etc. When considering the appointment of staff, for example, he observes that care should be taken to minimize the risk of staff falling in love, since this can have 'an extremely disruptive effect on work'.[21] While conceding that it would be churlish to apportion blame for such events, Stevens records that he considers particularly irksome those staff – particularly housekeepers – 'who are essentially going from post to post looking for romance. This sort of person is a blight on good professionalism'.[22] For Stevens, the consummate professional is the person who does not allow even a trace of personal feelings to intrude on the task in hand.

Stevens's devotion to the bureaucratic demands of his office, that in later life he much regrets, leads him to deny or refuse to acknowledge his attraction to Miss Kenton and to spurn her advances. Weber anticipated that the promise of bureaucracy to create a rational system of administration, unfettered, undistracted and uncompromised by irrational feelings or enthusiasms, would continue to seduce and captivate those responsible for designing and managing work organizations. Even when managers aspire to reform or redesign work organizations – by introducing programmes (e.g. human resource management, total quality management, business process reengineering) that avowedly eliminate the inflexibilities and perverse effects of bureaucracy – they are inclined to favour bureaucratic methods for implementing and monitoring their application.

Weber was highly ambivalent about the organizing power of bureaucracy. On the one hand, he acknowledged and celebrated its formal rationality and its related capacity to eliminate excess effort and waste from traditional work practices. On the other hand, he was deeply concerned about its disempowering consequences for employees who, he anticipated, would be 'dehumanized' by the rigidity of rules and procedures. The extension of a purely instrumental, calculating orientation dedicated to the refinement of means renders the very idea of reflecting critically on alternative possible ends 'irrational'. The more developed (or perfected) a bureaucracy becomes, he warned, 'the more completely it succeeds in eliminating from official business love, hatred, and all purely personal . . . and emotional elements which escape calculation'.[23] When working in bureaucracies, people would become reduced to 'small cogs' in large corporate wheels. The bureaucratic ethos offers no moral or intellectual basis for making informed judgements between competing value standpoints (e.g. consumerism or conservation; fascism or democracy).

Conversely, from Weber's perspective, the more an individual is committed to, and guided by, a particular value position 'the less he is influenced by considerations of the consequences of his action'[24] for advancing material or other self-interests. There is then less concern with satisfying immediate wants or pursuing what are calculated to be the most efficient or effective *means* of achieving a given end (e.g. 'profitability' or 'customer satisfaction').

The spirit of formalistic authority infused and directed Stevens's work in *The Remains of the Day*. Most dramatically, when hearing of his father's death, he steadfastly allowed no hint of his distress to interrupt the continuity of his dutiful, bureaucratic provision of a meticulous service. In *The Bonfire of the Vanities*, the spirit of formalistic authority is exemplified by Sherman's boss. When told that Sherman would be arrested the following morning, he reacts instantly by 'offering' Sherman leave of absence. For Sherman, it came as a shock to find that Lopitz wasn't disturbed by the prospect of losing a highly successful bond salesman. Lopitz was indifferent because he had made the instant calculation that Sherman was just another bond salesman, a mere factor of production that had become a liability and must therefore be discarded:

> Lopitz wasn't angry with him. He wasn't perturbed. He wasn't even particularly put out. No, *the fate of Sherman McCoy didn't make all that much difference*. . . . Everybody would enjoy the juicy story for a while, and bonds would go on being sold in vast quantities.[25]

It is worth stressing that, for Weber, the absence of hatred or passion, affection or enthusiasm, is the mark of the '*fully developed* bureaucratic apparatus'.[26] In most cases, this ideal is imperfectly realized. His focus on bureaucracy does not imply that all organizations are necessarily or relentlessly complying more closely with its principles. As Weber[27] notes, 'it would be very unusual to find concrete cases of action . . . which were oriented *only* in one or another of these ways' – that is, by traditional, charismatic or legal-rational forms of authority. Rather, it is Weber's contention that an attentiveness to bureaucracy can provide us with considerable insight into the key features and problems of modern organizations.

Anticipating a relentless process of rationalization, Weber questioned the plausibility of proletarian revolution. He anticipated that only a minority of people would receive the necessary (elite) education and possess the strength of character to sublimate the desire to satisfy their immediate material self-interests and thereby pursue volume-rational forms of action. Accordingly, Weber commended leadership by an educated elite capable of limiting the worst excesses of legal-rational authority. Guided by the insights of social science that would reveal the limits and paradoxes of bureaucracy, he urged the training of experts (e.g. managers) who would construct a more just and humane order *within* a modern, capitalist society.[c]

Weber's prognosis for modern society is nonetheless bleak. The masses, he believed, are destined to be controlled by large bureaucratic organizations – from the registry of births, through educational institutions and workplaces to the registry of deaths. Distracted and entertained by populist forms of sensuality involving instant gratification, Weber anticipated that few people would be capable of seeing beyond, and rising above, the tide of rationalization.

Taylor and scientific management

The application of legal-rational authority, in the form of bureaucratic organization, was exemplified in Taylor's *Principles of Scientific Management*.[28] As Weber himself put it:

> With the help of appropriate methods of measurement, the optimum profitability of the individual worker is calculated like that of any material means of production. On the basis of this calculation, the American system of 'scientific management' enjoys the greatest triumphs in the rational conditioning and training of work performances.[29]

In contrast to Weber, Taylor was uninterested in the historical and existential significance of the use of bureaucratic principles to organize work. He was concerned only with specifying and prescribing the principles, rules and procedures (e.g. very detailed time and motion studies) that would constitute the perfect, 'scientific' approach to managing shopfloor production. His primary objective was to facilitate a maximization of productivity and wealth. Taylor's 'principles' are directed at separating the conception of work (i.e. planning, designing and developing) from its day-to-day execution. The responsibility of shopfloor workers is limited to performing tasks predetermined by management. Taylor's own experience on the shopfloor led him to believe that when workers are allowed to plan and organize the work, they invariably preserve established practices based on traditional ways of working or what is known as custom and practice. This restricted output and productivity, as employees sought to regulate the pace of work to a level that they thought would not threaten their continuing employment.

---

c Weber did not anticipate the resilient capacity of market relations to override or stem the flow of bureaucratic regulation, including procedures (e.g. health and home safety, equal opportunity) that protected employees from the progressive 'commodification' of their labour.

Taylor assumed that people are motivated principally by money, and that the opportunity to earn more would induce greater output. He regarded workers as incapable of interpreting their lives except through an instrumental interest in money and the goods it can buy. He assumed that workers would accept 'scientific' methods of work organization and management as long as these demonstrably increased their earnings. It did not occur to him that employees might resist his system in defence of other values and priorities, or that there would be any difficulty in eradicating recalcitrance as long as managers were trained to apply his principles to the letter. Nor did it occur to him that managers acting on the demands of owners would adopt some aspects of his system without distributing to employees their 'fair' share of the economic rewards that followed from the increases in their productivity. Shortcomings with the practical operation of his principles were attributed by Taylor either to the reluctance of managers to acquire the discipline and techniques of his system, or to workers' pre-modern attachment to custom and practice. In short, any failure to subscribe to the bureaucratic regime of scientific management on the part of managers or employees was simply attributed to their ignorance or 'irrationality'.

Yet some employees may indeed welcome and respond positively to the sense of order and predictability produced by Taylor's principles or what Weber termed 'the rational conditioning and training of work perform-ances'. In *The Remains of the Day*, Stevens seemed to thrive on the equi-valent of a scientific approach to planning the household as if it were a well-oiled machine. According to Stevens:

> It is, of course, the responsibility of every butler to devote his utmost care in the devising of a staff plan. . . . Indeed, I can say I am in agreement with those who say that the ability to draw up a good staff plan is the cornerstone of any decent butler's skills.[30]

It is ironic that Stevens justified his painstaking care in devising his staff plans on the grounds that this would avoid emotional damage – in the form of 'quarrels, false accusations, unnecessary dismissals' etc. To the extent that it eliminates needless waste or the unnecessary toil arising from duplicated effort, a good plan may indeed lessen the burden of human misery. But the consumption of so much energy in perfecting the plan may equally be interpreted as an attempt to minimize the risk of being drawn into incidents that would carry an emotional charge or that would require 'unplanned', spontaneous involvement. In this respect, planning can be seen as a flight from, or defence against, emotional engagement, rather than simply a means of avoiding unnecessary conflicts.

In *Nice Work*, the treatment and attempted dismissal of a foundry worker who was not operating a machine correctly (discussed briefly in Chapter 1) exemplified Taylorism, but without incorporating even the rudiments of training. There was a clear separation of the design of machine operations from their execution by the operator. It was assumed that a system of piece-rate rewards would be sufficient to induce the worker to acquire the skills necessary to raise output and earnings, including those that would minimize machine breakdowns. As far as the manager, Vic, was concerned, repeated machine breakdowns were intolerable and the operative was at fault. The worker had demonstrated an incapacity to acquire and apply the relevant skills, despite the existence of material inducements. The obvious solution, to Vic, was to 'get rid of him'[31] immediately.

The denial of morality?

Following his attempt to dismiss the machine operator on the spot, Vic is confronted by Robyn (a woman academic who is 'shadowing' Vic one day a week), who questions the morality of such practices. Vic tells her that it is none of her business. In response, she asserts that such treatment of people is the business of anyone who 'cares for truth and justice'. Refusing to accept Vic's division of personal morality and workplace decision making, she asks: 'Don't you see how wrong it is, to trick this man out of his job?'[32] Vic responds by repeating his view that 'it is a management matter', a matter 'in which you have no competence', to which Robyn reasserts her opinion that it is 'not a management matter, it is a moral issue'.[33]

As 'private' individuals, Vic and other managers may or may not have agreed with Robyn that sacking the employee was morally wrong. As managers responsible for safeguarding shareholder interests, however, they are more likely to regard it as their 'professional duty' and responsibility to remove inefficient elements from production processes. The rational-legal authority of company law formally positions managers as guardians of shareholders' assets. In this position, they are justified in treating employees as means to the ends of capital accumulation. Other elements of legislation (e.g. the minimum wage) may constrain them in performing this (bureaucratic) function but, in principle, personal morality must not be allowed to colour or distort 'rational' decision making in the workplace.[34]

In practice, however, the denial of personal morality in organizational decision making is difficult, if not impossible, to sustain. Only the most brutalized or fanatical of managers is capable of consistently denying personal involvement in, and a degree of responsibility for, the decisions that he or she takes. In effect, they are positioned or 'imprisoned' in a discourse that ascribes intentionality and responsibility to their actions. In *Nice Work*, Vic's decision to remove all pin-ups from the factory was based on his personal (puritanical) morality, even though this was aroused by Robyn's feminist (and 'politically correct') objections to such blatant sexism. Significantly, it was Vic's puritanical action that was later used against him as evidence that his business judgement had become clouded and that his services were no longer required.

In a way that parallels Robyn's questioning of Vic's morality, Stevens is challenged by Miss Kenton in *The Remains of the Day* about his abdication of moral responsibility for carrying out their employer's instruction to dismiss a couple of Jewish maids. Stevens had been directed by Lord Darlington to dismiss the maids, whose Jewishness posed a potential embarrassment on account of his lordship's fascist connections.[35] Personally, Stevens experienced some misgivings about this order – 'my every instinct opposed the idea of their dismissal'.[36] Nonetheless, he carried out his master's instructions. Stevens did not convey his misgivings to Miss Kenton, the housekeeper, whom he was obliged to consult over the process of the dismissal. Perhaps sensing that Miss Kenton would be ill disposed to participate in the sacking of the maids, and that an exchange over this issue would risk unplanned emotional involvement, Stevens resolved to address the issue in 'as concise and businesslike way as possible'.[37] His proposal to Miss Kenton was that the maids should be sent along to the pantry the following morning where they would be told of their dismissal. Miss Kenton reacted strongly against this plan, arguing that the maids had been members of the staff for six years and that 'I trust them absolutely and they trust me'.[38]

Refusing to be drawn into a discussion of the merits of their case, Stevens reminded Miss Kenton that sentiment must not be allowed to cloud the issue. For her part, Miss Kenton was not willing to confine their discussion to the procedural matter of how the maids were to be dismissed. Instead, she demanded that they consider the ethics of their dismissal. Miss Kenton openly expressed her outrage that Stevens could deliberate over the fate of the maids as though discussing 'orders for the larder'.[39] To this Stevens replied, in the measured tones of the bureaucrat, that he had explained the situation fully to her, that the dismissal of the maids is the wish of 'his lordship'; and therefore that 'there is nothing for you and I to debate over'.[40] As Stevens reflects:

> A butler's duty is to provide a good service . . . those of us who wish to make a mark must realize that we best do so by best concentrating on what *is* within our realm; that is to say, by devoting our attention to providing the best possible service to those great gentlemen in whose hands the destiny of civilization truly lies.[41]

Stevens disclaims all personal responsibility for his actions by appealing to the idea that he is positioned in a hierarchical relationship to his employer. In this relationship, butlers and housekeepers execute the orders of their superiors and therefore bear no responsibility for such decisions. Their responsibility is confined exclusively to determining the most efficient and effective way of implementing instructions:

> This is a very straightforward matter. If his lordship wishes these particular contracts to be discontinued, then there is little more to be said.[42]

The legal contract permits the dismissal of the maids, so there is nothing to discuss. Miss Kenton then asks whether it occurs to Stevens 'that to dismiss Ruth and Sarah on these grounds would be simply – *wrong?*'. She tells Stevens that she will not stand for such practices and, indeed, that she will not work in a house where such things occur. To which Stevens replies:

> I am surprised to find you reacting in this manner. Surely, I don't have to remind you that *our professional duty* is not to our own foibles and sentiments, but to *the wishes of our employer*.[43]

Much like Vic in *Nice Work* who prefers to exclude moral issues from management matters, Stevens's dedication to the idea of professional duty is paramount. It allows him not only to deny responsibility for his actions – he is simply the servant of his master – but also to dismiss the notion that there is any moral or ethical issue at stake.

Slavish dedication to professional duty provided Stevens with a sense of order and security, as his responsibilities and associated anxieties were clearly circumscribed. By drawing boundaries around his life, a series of potentially troublesome issues and challenges were circumvented if not avoided. Stevens derived considerable satisfaction from the completeness of his subordination. He was able to take great pride in maintaining his composure in the face of all kinds of provocation and adversity. Great butlers, Stevens told himself, inhabit their professional role without being outwardly shaken 'by external events, however surprising, alarming or vexing'.[44] Still, while perfecting the suppression of his personal feelings, Stevens was unable to eradicate them.

When, for example, Miss Kenton's threatened resignation failed to materialize, Stevens takes sadistic delight in teasing her about this, but without acknowledging to himself that this teasing was a repressed or distorted form of flirtation. His avoidance of emotionally troublesome issues turned out to be an evasion of them. Not communicating his feelings had consequences for the mental health of Stevens and Miss Kenton. It also had ramifications for the management of the house. To have known that Stevens privately felt deeply uncomfortable about his lordship's decision to dismiss the Jewish maids would doubtless have brought Miss Kenton closer to him. This was something which Miss Kenton had sought to develop and which Stevens subsequently attempted to revive – in the remains of the day, when it was too late. Communication between them became restricted to purely business matters which, perversely, impeded the smooth running of the house. It minimized the opportunities for 'informal' discussions that had developed over a nightly cup of cocoa in Miss Kenton's parlour.

The break with this *tête à tête* occurred when Miss Kenton asked Stevens whether he was 'well-contented' as a bachelor dedicated to a life of service. Stevens responded by arguing that his mission in life would be fulfilled only when he has 'see(n) his lordship through the great tasks he has set himself'.[45] Only then will he be able to call himself 'well-contented'. At this point, Miss Kenton despairs of developing any personal or intimate relationship with Stevens and her communications become distracted. When Stevens remarks on this change, he is unable to deal with the disappointment and frustration expressed in her testy response that she was tired. Stevens's (unconscious) feelings of rejection are evident in his desire to avoid further discomfort by declining her offer to continue their informal meetings and instead substituting written messages:

> There are many alternative options for achieving the level of professional communication necessary without our meeting on this basis. . . . Should we not be able to find each other readily [during the course of the working day], I suggest that we leave written messages at one another's doors.[46]

Despite his obvious but unacknowledged attraction to Miss Kenton, Stevens reverts to impersonal forms of intercourse that neutralize any personal or moral obligation.

Refining the modern organization

For the past 50 years, and with increasing intensity during the last 10 years or so, the belief that the moral spheres of work and everyday life are, and should be, separate has come under sustained attack. This criticism stems from those who have been concerned about the effects of demoralization and inflexibility on the capacity of bureaucratic organizations to maximize productivity and respond sufficiently quickly to changing market conditions. Such 'dysfunctions'[47] had long since been identified in academic studies of bureaucracy.[d] During the 1980s and 1990s, these findings were rediscovered by management gurus.[48] The impersonality consequent on the adherence to bureaucratic rules and the attachment to positions deriving from the functional division of labour, they argued, are associated with needless inefficiency. By commending the reform of modern organizations, the gurus sought to raise morale and the standards of work performance in ways that would eliminate unnecessary delays in decision-making processes, inflexibility and indefensibly high managerial overheads.

Remembering Barnard

The concern to develop forms of leadership and culture that would induce employee cooperation can be traced to the seminal work of Chester Barnard (1886–1961). In *The Functions of the Executive*,[49] he provides an exceptionally penetrating diagnosis of the limits of a purely bureaucratic ethic of organizing. He notes how a willingness on the part of employees to

---

d More recently, they have been analysed as 'resistance' to management control in the labour
   process literature.

realize the objectives of the employer generally demands the (temporary) suspension of immediate, personal desires and impulses. Securing the willing cooperation of employees is recognized to be problematic because it 'means self-abnegation, the surrender of control of personal conduct'.[50] Achieving total, unconditional identification with an organizational purpose, Barnard argues, is rarely achieved in the family or in the patriotic or religious organization, let alone in work organizations. Nonetheless, he urges managers to do what they can to engineer a closer identification of employees with what he terms the 'organization purpose' (as contrasted with their immediate desires and impulses).

The main challenge for managers, Barnard contends, is not simply to provide a schedule of inducements that outweigh the burdens imposed by the scientific methods of job design, advocated by Taylor. It is to educate and train employees in ways that *lead them to transform their desires and preferences* in a direction that increases 'the disposition to make a personal act a contribution to an impersonal system of acts'.[51] While recognizing that tensions exist between the personal preferences of employees and the impersonal demands of bureaucratic organizations, Barnard clearly believed in the possibility of reducing these tensions. A key function for managers was to make participation in bureaucratic systems more personally meaningful for all employees.

Human relations theorists and some recent gurus have amplified and extended Barnard's ideas by emphasizing that social recognition and the confirmation of identity are important means of increasing employee commitment and raising organized performance. By paying attention to the emotional desires of employees, human relations thinking seeks to minimize the loss of self-esteem associated with employment in an impersonal system where personally meaningless tasks are performed. Instead it supports a humanization and even partial democratization of management style/leadership to provide an environment where individual employees can improve their self-esteem and self-worth.

What distinguishes 'human relations' from most of what went before is the simple recognition that men and women, except in the most extreme of circumstances (see Chapter 3), do not live by bread alone. Social recognition or identity is equally as important as economic reward if the commitment, rather than mere compliance, of employees is sought. Managers are urged to exercise, strengthen and extend their authority by providing the inducements – *symbolic* as well as material – that are effective in securing cooperation and commitment from employees. Human relations thinking does not, however, seek to transform employees into self-disciplined subjects of a managed corporate culture where the mantras of empowerment, commitment, involvement, teamworking and customer service are repeatedly recited. By contrast, contemporary gurus (e.g. Peters, Crosby, Hammer) have placed these ideas at the centre of organizational reforms in which *instrumentalism is extended* from the redesign of work to the reconstruction of employee subjectivity. The responsibility of managers is enlarged to include the shaping of employees' sense of identity in ways that are calculated to secure staffs' willing commitment to what managers require them to do.

These prescriptions are promoted as central elements of a more dynamic and energizing approach to managing modern organizations. Their requirement is for employees to become *emotionally* engaged with key tasks that are deemed essential for corporate success – such as passionately taking care of customers, deriving a real buzz from being successful, experiencing a strong identification with the product or service that is being sold. Contemporary gurus are particularly critical of established, bureaucratic forms of management where employees are dominated by rule-bound, analytical, numerical and calculative methods of organizing. Here, employee initiative, commitment and responsibility tend to be frustrated and deadened by a bureaucratic approach that fails to appreciate how 'strongly workers can identify with the work they do if we give them a little say-so'.[52]

'Post-bureaucratic' organization

Contemporary management gurus attempt to change organizations by reinventing Barnard's prescriptions. They seek to redesign and develop organizations so that, like idealized family units, everyone is emotionally involved, as well as committed to, a shared set of goals. Often buoyed up by superficial and apocryphal accounts of the success of Japanese corporations, these gurus promote a transformation of the culture of organizations so that employees come to work bringing the whole of their embodied selves to labour, and not just an abstracted rationality. This thinking begins to blur, if not reintegrate, the Taylorian separation of conception from execution through teamworking and other techniques of 'empowerment'. Associated with an extension of the salesperson's ethic[53] to all production activities, the gurus of 'quality management' (e.g. TQM) seek to convert every employee into the understanding that they are not a factor of production but a customer of somebody else within the organization. It is then not just a matter of complementing economic reward with social recognition, as advocated by the human relations theorists, but of striving to transform the identity and associated priorities of employees. Describing such organizations as *clan-like*, Ouchi[54] contrasts these with those espousing a human relations-type philosophy, suggesting:

> In a clan, each individual is effectively told to do just what that person wants. In this case, however, the socialization of all to a common good is so complete that the capacity of the system to measure the subtleties of contributions over a long time is so exact that individuals will naturally seek to do that which is in the common good.

Clan-like organizations are understood actively to value, foster and exploit emotional commitment, of the kind more generally found in clans or families, as a resource for enhancing corporate performance. In principle, there is a substitution of a strong corporate culture for the seeming robustness and security of hierarchic structure and bureaucratic procedures. In addition to their alleged value in addressing pressures for greater flexibility in rapidly changing environments, strong corporate cultures provide a set of core values on which all employees are expected to draw when faced with uncertainties in everyday work situations.[e] In this respect, a strong corporate culture is prescribed as a remedy for what employees experience as 'an uneasy, embarrassed or chronically anxious quest for knowledge about what [they] should be doing, or what is expected of [them], and similar apprehensiveness about what others are doing'.[55]

In effect, the proponents of strong corporate cultures argue that employee insecurity can be exploited as a largely untapped source of motivation and employee goodwill. An established focus on 'structure', 'systems' and 'strategy' should be supplemented by an attentiveness to 'staff', 'style' and 'shared values', they argue:

What our [7S] framework has really done is to remind the world of professional managers that 'soft is hard'. *It has enabled us to say, in effect, 'All that stuff you have been dismissing for so long as the intractable, irrational, intuitive, informal organization can be managed'.*[56]

Managers are urged to enlist the informal or 'soft' practices and processes of organizing to manage what much management theory had previously regarded as beyond the scope of managerial intervention. When following this advice, managers may appear to rehabilitate personal desires and preferences within the workplace that were excluded, officially at least, by theory that emphasized 'structure', 'systems' and 'strategy'.[f]

---

e   Insecurity is fuelled where turbulence and indeterminacy are increasingly the norm. Establishing a set of core values is viewed as a necessary condition of the effective functioning of organizations that rely on organic (e.g. clan-like) systems of regulation, as contrasted with the mechanical application of rules typical of bureaucracy. This is where organizations in western economies contrast sharply with the Japanese experience, from which the idea of clan-like organizations is derived. In Japan, job security in the primary sector is guaranteed for life, whereas in western economies it is either non-existent or rapidly declining as companies increasingly seek to adapt to their environments 'through flexible labour policies'. In the West, a culture of corporate identification and integration generally has to be engineered from a situation of weakness or non-existence.

f   In response to critics of his prescription on achieving excellence through the strengthening of corporate culture, Peters (1989) has shifted ground from the advocacy of a universal to a contingent framework in which any allegiance to a set of corporate values is subordinated to a continuous adjustment to changing circumstances. From this perspective, the strengthening of corporate culture is not necessarily an effective means of achieving shifting corporate goals. As he has expressed this view: 'Excellent firms don't believe in excellence – only in constant improvement and constant change' (ibid, p. 4).

Reflections on post-bureaucracy

An alternative interpretation of these developments focuses on the way that managerial power is being exercised. It is concerned to show how the 'private' or 'personal' aspects of subjectivity become a target of systematic managerial intervention, control and colonization. This extension of managerial control is for the instrumental purpose of bringing the individual employee firmly into the locus of calculability for the productive and profitable benefit of the corporation. From this perspective, the instrumental rationality at the core of bureaucracy is understood to be refined, revitalized and extended, rather than abandoned, in 'postbureaucratic', clan-like forms of organization. Instead of cogs within the machine, employees occupy cells within organic, 'learning organizations' where they are expected to adapt their lives to satisfy its demands. Zuboff[57] illustrates this scenario when discussing the role of information technology in facilitating the rise of new, organic forms of organization:

> The empowerment, commitment, and involvement of a wide range of organizational members in self-managing activities means that organizational structures are to be both emergent and flexible, changing as members continually learn more about how to organize themselves for learning about their business.[58]

Weber's[59] concerns about the corrosive effects of instrumentalism on value-rational choices (see above) are perhaps even more relevant and instructive today, when instrumentalism is being primed to penetrate deeply into the very 'souls' of employees.[60] This is not to argue that the prosecution of prescriptions for the postbureaucratic organization is necessarily successful. Rarely are outcomes identical to intentions. Resistance to such initiatives is a recurrent feature of organizational life. This is partly because of the tensions and inconsistencies in management practice where one policy often is contradicted by another; where career contests between managers frequently impede the coherence of policy; and where ignorance or arrogance can result in managers making demands that simply cannot be met. For example, where there is talk of 'empowerment' or 'customer service' in a context of cost cutting and increased work pressures, employees may be dismissive of such demands as empty managerial rhetoric. For employees, the rhetoric is vacuous because desired outcomes cannot be realized when cutbacks undermine employee morale and limit the time available to give personal services to the customer.[61] Past experience leads employees to form the view that their involvement and emotional well-being are rarely valued, nurtured or even tolerated *for their own sake*. Employees are not so trusting or naive as to be deceived by managerial claims to the contrary. Where labour market conditions render job security tenuous, managerial efforts to promote increased employee involvement and identification with corporate goals are more likely to stimulate scepticism and resignation, if not resistance, than they are to foster cooperation and commitment.

Moves to colonize or deny the personal and emotional dimensions of work simultaneously reaffirm and extend the orthodox view that organizational work is morally neutral. From this point of view, organizational work and managerial decision making are 'properly' judged according to their (instrumentally rational) effectiveness in achieving given ends, and not in terms of their (value-rational) consistency with ethical standards. No questions or doubts are therefore raised about the ethics of managing culture, so long as it is understood to make this contribution. As Roberts[62] articulates this understanding:

> Typically, it is the pursuit of the survival or growth of the 'organization as a whole' that for most managers is the *assumed* moral basis of their action and that provides them with a blanket justification for a whole variety of practices . . . their immediate practices are judged not by reference to moral standards or criteria but merely in terms of the effectiveness with which they secure these ends.[63]

Managers may strive to avoid courses of action that they believe to be inconsistent with, or abhorrent to, their personal values. However, when providing a formal justification of their actions to others – such as the funding of a programme that is intended to strengthen corporate culture or empower staff – this justification is invariably couched in terms of its intended contribution to survival, growth etc., and not in terms of the personal morality or inclinations of the individual manager. This is so even when personal values and moral imperatives have framed or influenced their decisions. Personal agendas continue to be pursued but must be expressed in the language of corporate performance and advancement. Rationales for action are illegitimate and counterproductive if they are not couched in terms that render them congruent with organizational goals.

From an instrumentally rational point of view, 'value-rationality is always irrational'.[64] The probable outcome of an extension of instrumental rationality into the realm of culture and subjectivity is increased cynicism or 'bad faith' and mere compliance or conditional commitment.[65] In the following section, we illustrate how, when finding themselves under pressure to 'get results', managers may engage in forms of reciprocal manipulation from which they derive some personal or career advantage. Through an extended analysis of an exchange in *Nice Work* between Vic Wilcox and his boss, Stuart Baxter, we show how Vic is persuaded to participate in a scheme about which he is personally antagonistic, partly because his agreement enables him to secure a compensatory benefit.

Managing to manage

Managerial manipulation

We begin by describing the interaction in *Nice Work* between two managers, Vic Wilcox and his boss. Vic Wilcox, MD of Pringle's, is working late in his

office. His phone rings. It's Stuart Baxter, the chairman of the corporate
division that owns Pringle's – Vic's boss. Stuart asks Vic if he's heard about
Industry Year. Vic has. Confident that his boss will also view such high-
minded government schemes as 'a waste of time and money', Vic's response
is quick, unambiguous and dismissive. Stuart agrees. But he then tells Vic
that, as a company, they *are* going to be involved since 'the Board feels that
we've got to go along with it', because 'it's good PR for the Group' and,
most decisively perhaps, because 'the Chairman is dead keen'. Vic immediately grasps that Stuart expects him, and will surely coerce him, to play a
part in enhancing the corporate image and fulfilling the chairman's desires.
Stuart then outlines the Shadow Scheme that forms part of the Industry
Year initiative. This involves an academic learning about industry by
following around a senior manager (e.g. Vic) for a day a week for a few
weeks:

> 'No way,' says Vic.
> 'Why not, Vic?'
> 'I don't want some academic berk following me about all day.'[66]

Stuart reminds Vic that its only for a day a week, and only for a few weeks.
Vic falls into a trap of his own making. Instead of stonewalling, Vic asks:

> 'Why me?'
> 'Because you're the most dynamic MD in the division. We want to show them
> the best.'[67]

Vic is not so stupid as to believe the sincerity of the compliment. But
equally, he is happy to take note of it as 'it could be useful to remind
Stuart Baxter of it some time in the future'. In response, Vic says he will
think about it. But Stuart insists that he must have an answer immediately
because (he says) he is seeing the chairman at a function later the same
evening. Vic can't resist the opportunity to comment on his boss's tardiness
in approaching him about the scheme: 'Left it a bit late, haven't you?'[68]
This can be interpreted as part of Vic's deeper resentment of the managers
of finance capital, like Stuart Baxter, who manage the buying and selling of
companies and therefore concern themselves with PR and share price
movements, but never become involved with, or feel any responsibility for,
the 'sharp end' of managing industrial capital.

Stuart concedes that it is late, but blames this on a subordinate: his
secretary 'fucked up' by losing the letter. 'Oh yes?' responds Vic, unconvinced by this explanation. Or, at least, even if he is convinced, Vic spots
an opportunity for putting Stuart on the defensive. Stuart then repeats his
request to Vic in a diplomatic and somewhat deferential way, although Vic
immediately translates the language of diplomacy into the language of
armed force:

'I'd be very grateful if you'd co-operate.'
'You mean it's an order?'
'Don't be silly, Vic. We're not in the Army.'[69]

Stuart may have been inclined to sympathize with Vic's view of the Shadow Scheme as 'a waste of time and money'. But he is not willing to debunk the understanding that he and Vic are players in the same team, and that his proposal is a request, not an order. Equally, Vic recognizes that Stuart is genuinely anxious to secure his cooperation. Identifying an opportunity to place Stuart under some obligation to him, Vic's response is to remind Stuart of his pressing need, as a manager of industrial capital, for an automatic core blower if he is to win orders against the competition. Stuart takes the hint. He immediately agrees to support Vic's demand for expenditure on this equipment and, in return, Vic acquiesces to Stuart's request that he participate in the Shadow Scheme.

Issues of hierarchy and accountability

This example from *Nice Work* serves to illustrate how much managerial work involves communicating with other managers and not just subordinates in the office or on the shopfloor. Communication takes place within hierarchical relations in which there is inequality as well as interdependence. In the above exchange, Stuart is dependent on Vic's willingness to participate in the Shadow Scheme. Ultimately, however, Stuart is able to 'pull rank' only because Vic is highly dependent on his boss for the reputation that he enjoys within Pringle's parent company.

Had Vic been approached by one of 'his' managers within Pringle's with an equally tiresome request, he would have had no difficulty in refusing or passing it on to someone else (as Stuart Baxter, his boss, was doing). Still, realizing that Stuart was himself in some difficulty because of the chairman's personal interest in the scheme, Vic spots the chance to 'trade' an agreement to participate for gaining Stuart's support for the core blower – something that he had been striving to get for some time.

Both the content and the form of their communication are mediated by each other's tacit understanding of their respective positioning in a corporate hierarchy. This becomes most explicit when, in response to Vic's attempts to shelve discussion of the Shadow Scheme by saying that he will 'think about it', Stuart insists that he's *got* to have an answer from Vic *now*. Vic had, until then, been unable to get from Stuart a positive answer to his demand for a piece of machinery that he regarded as critical for the survival of the company; yet Stuart can get an immediate answer from Vic over what, in purely economic terms, is a trifling matter.

It might be argued that the exchange between Vic Wilcox and Stuart Baxter does not merit further interpretation, since it is entirely predictable and mind-numbingly mundane. It is predictable because Baxter is bound to get his way and mundane because there is nothing at all remarkable in what either of them has to say. So why have we chosen to give it detailed attention? Precisely because it is so mundane and its outcome is so predictable. To do otherwise – for example, by considering something highly unusual, like the particulars of the negotiation with the German firm Altenhofer's over the purchase of a new automatic core blower in which Vic's shadow, Robyn, pretended to understand no German – would be to risk the charge that our analysis has relevance only for exceptional incidents. It has to be recognized that reality is constructed through the constant reiteration of mundanity – hence its mundanity! We now use the exchange between Vic and his boss as a springboard for exploring the relevance of ideas about identity and insecurity and further exploring the nature and dynamics of managerial and organizational work.

Identity and insecurity

As we suggested in Chapters 3 and 4, interactions between human beings are mediated by each person's self-image or self-identity. Through processes of interaction, identity is confirmed, challenged, defended or transformed. The shape and direction of interactions are influenced, in more or less intended ways, by each person's efforts to negotiate an outcome that is personally acceptable in terms of their own self-image or identity. Not infrequently, this involves efforts to defend or enhance self-identity in response to situations and communications, especially where these are 'open' or ambiguous.

In the exchange between Vic and his boss, their conversation begins with an affirmation of their shared sense of themselves as hard-headed businessmen who have little tolerance for initiatives (e.g. the Shadow Scheme) that waste their time and involve an unproductive expenditure of money. They live in the real world, and know much better how resources should be spent than those (civil servants and gong-seeking board members) who dream up such idiotic, time-wasting schemes. Sure of this common sense of reality, Vic is unhesitatingly dismissive of the Shadow Scheme, confident that his sense of its absurdity will be shared by his boss.

Yet self-identity is a social construction rather than biologically inherited or given. It is inescapably and continuously precarious, vulnerable to threats and challenges as well as supportive enhancement. Clearly, Vic did not know that Baxter was going to phone him; and the request to participate in the Shadow Scheme was unprecedented, as there had never been any directly comparable programme. As human behaviour is not programmed, responses to situations must be continuously negotiated in creative ways. All those who participate in routines actively work, more or less willingly or habitually, at maintaining their existence. Consequently, they become taken for granted as the 'natural order of things'. Requests and instructions from people in general, and his boss in particular, were certainly not unusual, so Vic was skilled at handling them.

Vic had learned and elaborated some routines for dealing with or declining such requests, an obvious one being to indicate a willingness in principle while insisting on its practical impossibility on grounds of work pressures. Baxter makes routine reference to 'coordinating initiatives' on behalf of the chairman, which Vic immediately recognizes as requiring him to do something: '"What do you want me to do?" Vic cuts in impatiently'.[70] However, even routines have to be 'worked at' if they are to be sustained and not disrupted by other possibilities. In the interaction between the two managers, each seeks to define the situation in a way that will confirm their competence in their own and others' eyes. Stuart Baxter deploys flattery and ultimately a veiled threat in order to avoid the embarrassment of failing to do the chairman's bidding. And Vic exploits Stuart's vulnerability by securing his support for the purchase of an expensive piece of equipment that will enable him to fulfil his key task of rationalizing the production process within the foundry.

The absence of any precedent or established set of routines for interacting with an 'outsider', such as a lecturer in English Literature, would pose a threat to self-identity for all but the most outgoing, open and socially skilled of managers. Vic's feelings of anxiety about how to deal with 'the shadow' are mixed with feelings of irritation about the inconvenience involved. As Vic tells Stuart, he has no desire to be followed around all day by 'some academic berk'. Baxter's parting shot to Vic, after he explains that the shadow is a lecturer in English Literature, is: 'Read any good books lately, Vic?', thereby pointing to a common-sense belief in a yawning gulf between managers as practical people who know how to get things done and academics whose knowledge is confined to what they read in books. Conceivably, Baxter could himself have elected to be the manager who is 'shadowed'. In fact, given the lateness of the request to Vic, and the prospect that Vic would wring some kind of *quid pro quo* out of him, Baxter may have been tempted to avoid this conversation by allowing himself to be 'shadowed'. But clearly, the inconvenience caused by a shadow and/or the insecurity aroused by the prospect of being shadowed were too great. In any event, the money for the core blower was not coming out of Baxter's pocket, whereas the inconvenience and anxiety associated with the shadow would hurt him personally. Baxter's hierarchical position in the company allows him to exercise power by virtually imposing this task on Vic.

The exchange follows a fairly expected pattern, as Vic deploys various well-established ploys that are aimed at blocking and then side-stepping his boss's moves without causing offence. In this process of negotiation, the two managers first affirm each other's managerial identity through the negation of others who lack their managerial insights – such as the champions of Industry Year and waste-of-space academics. Vic then invites and receives an explanation of the request in terms of his exceptional abilities (and, of course, Baxter's self-evident ability to identify 'the best'). For Vic, there is little that is problematic in the exchange until his boss insists that a decision has to be made immediately. It is only then that Vic recognizes that he cannot play for time in the hope of some other MD in the division offering less resistance to Baxter's requests than himself.

Social interaction always harbours the possibility of acting in ways that damage or augment the image that people have of themselves and, relatedly, the image that others have of them. Earlier, Vic had risked giving offence when Stuart Baxter told him: 'It's not worth investing in that foundry'.[71] Vic realized that his frustration with machine breakdowns, which meant that he failed to reach his production targets, led him to be curt with Baxter. He shrugged this off by *identifying* closely with the task of 'making J. Pringle and Sons profitable', and not with 'the business of ingratiating himself with Stuart Baxter'.[72] As it turned out, this identification had fateful consequences for Vic's continuing employment by Midland Amalgamated.

The possibility of enhancing or tarnishing self-image becomes more evident in (un)certain situations – such as approaching someone for a date, taking an examination or going for an employment or promotion interview. Then, the outcome is sensed to have major implications for the individual's self-image or identity and, relatedly, for how they are viewed by others (e.g. friends, potential employers). The two aspects are related, because it is through interactions with others that each human being selectively interprets and acquires the identity that others attribute to them (see Chapter 3). This includes the sense of being the occupant of a separate seat of consciousness to which identity is plausibly ascribed (by self as well as by others). For example, when Stuart Baxter says 'You know what a shadow is, don't you?',[73] he attributes to Vic a sense of his being competent and knowledgeable in respect of the Industry Year initiative. In these circumstances, for Vic to admit ignorance would damage his identity as a well-informed manager.

In contrast, when Vic is dismissive of those who contrive to 'do good' by forging links between industrialists and academics, he finds and confirms a common cause with his boss, as their contempt for such schemes serves to elevate their sense of shared identity as 'hard-headed' businessmen. Although Vic was not to know how the experience of the shadow scheme would change his life, it was clearly better not to avoid its disruptive impact. Yet, of course, it is precisely the disruption and the way in which Vic is forced to reappraise his sense of himself (i.e. identity) when confronted by the feminist, Robyn, that gives *Nice Work* so much of its dramatic tension. We now illustrate how this same exchange in *Nice Work* can help us to understand power and inequality.

Power and inequality

Managerial self-identity is founded on the understanding that only managers really know what business is about. Academics certainly do not, and neither do civil servants. Nor, in the view of Vic and his boss, do those who rise to a position where sight is lost of the self-evident basics of business. A case in point is the chairman of the company, who is seemingly happy to deploy corporate resources, in the form of Vic and Baxter's time, in pursuit of an ambition to transcend the identity of 'mere' manager by becoming a member of the 'great and the good'. To this end, the chairman backs a government-led programme on the grounds, or pretext, that it will be good for PR. His position in the hierarchy allows him to delegate the dirty work of 'coordinating initiatives' to Stuart Baxter and, ultimately, to Vic, who gets saddled with executing the Shadow Scheme.

As managing director of Pringle's, Vic clearly occupies a senior position. Yet he is subordinate in the hierarchy to those on the board of the parent company. Consequently, when responding to Baxter's request to take on the academic shadow by saying 'no way', Vic rationalizes his refusal in terms of the pressures of work, not simply in terms of personal preference. This is a tactic that individuals in work organizations regularly use to conceal or divert attention from activities, decisions or definitions of reality that are predominantly about staking a personal preference or career claim. As we noted earlier, if such claims can be couched in the universal language of corporate performance and profitability, they are more likely to secure legitimacy within the organization. Indeed, it could be argued that competence in doing this is the most important criterion for a successful organizational career. It also demonstrates that power (and, by implication, inequality) in organizations is precarious and is always subject to negotiation and renegotiation, dependent as it is on the legitimate consent of those over whom it is exercised.

However, Vic is not willing simply to accede to Baxter's request. For whatever reason – his sense of pride, his professionalism and/or his continuing irritation with Baxter's unwillingness to release the capital to purchase the machinery which, in Vic's judgement, is necessary to meet the production targets set by Baxter – he cannot resist commenting on Baxter's tardiness (and, by implication, ineptitude) in leaving it 'a bit late'. This tardiness is at odds with Vic's sense of managerial self-identity. It is not something that he is prepared to accept as normal or routine and therefore he feels compelled to comment on it, even though it is a direct criticism of his boss. Confronted with Vic's challenge to his competence, Baxter is either exceptionally quick at thinking on his feet or, more likely, had learned from previous occasions that his position could be defended by finding a scapegoat lower down the hierarchy – someone who would find it difficult to deny taking the blame even if innocent. So his secretary is blamed for losing the letter – an explanation that Vic might not find credible but one, equally, that he could not directly question or disprove. Vic suspected a cover-up (and with some good reason, since Baxter's deviousness becomes apparent as the novel develops), but could do no more than offer a sceptical 'Oh, yes?'.

For all his personal dynamism and hard-nosed talk about production and profits, Vic is shown to be as naive in his understanding of managerial politics as he is in his experience of sexual politics. He expects that his colleagues, notably Baxter and Brian Everthorpe, the marketing director, are as committed to the company, and possess as much personal integrity, as he does. It probably never occurs to Vic that Baxter may be inventing the story about going to a function later that evening with the chairman as a way of resolving the issue there and then. Certainly, Vic is astonished to discover later that his managerial colleagues appear to have no qualms about using company time and resources to develop a completely different business renting out sunbeds. Vic's sense of self-identity is immersed in his job as MD. In contrast, others are clearly prepared to use their position in the company as a basis for pursuing alternative ventures. Vic was so astonished by their behaviour because he had projected on to them his own sense of managerial self-identity as a loyal and dedicated executive, just as he had remained faithful to his wife.

In part, it is Vic's desire to have his self-image as a competent manager confirmed that enables Baxter to exercise power over him. It is this desire that Baxter exploits, as he approaches Vic to participate in the Shadow Scheme. Baxter anticipates that, despite the bravado of resistance, Vic's managerial pride will not allow him, when pressed, to say 'no'. Moreover, and of greater importance to Baxter, he has confidence that once Vic, the dedicated manager, has agreed to take on the job, he will see it through. This is important to Baxter's career if, as seems likely, it is the case that the chairman is 'dead keen' on the scheme. Here, then, Vic's managerial self-identity undermines his ability to resist his boss's request. It also provides Baxter with some assurance that Vic will not 'fuck up' in the way that his secretary is alleged to have done.

Responding to Stuart's request, Vic preserves a sense of self-esteem and dignity by declining to agree straight away. He is not going to make life especially easy for his boss, who appears to be anxious for a positive answer – anxious because his chairman is apparently expecting Baxter to have 'coordinated initiatives' with regard to the company's participation in Industry Year. Recognizing Baxter to be in a tight corner, and that he (Vic) can take some advantage from it, Vic savours the moment of a brief reversal of power as his boss waits for his answer. This gives him a moment to think about the way to press home his momentary advantage. Vic recalls the automatic core blower and successfully secures a verbal agreement (at least) to support its purchase. And, in doing so, he affirms for himself, and for Baxter, his identity as a hard-headed and effective manager who invariably negotiates a good deal. Similarly, and despite having to malign the competence of his secretary and agree to a major investment in return for what amounted to a personal favour, Baxter's sense of identity – one may surmise, as a successful operator or, at least, a survivor – is maintained by Vic's acquiescence. Once again, the senior manager gets what he wants and the means – insincerity, vilification and corruption – justify the ends of material self-interest. The hierarchy of power and inequality is preserved.

Summary and conclusion

In this chapter we have stressed the continuities between managing every-day life and managing work organizations, arguing that both can be more effectively understood when we explore their dynamics through a consideration of power, inequality, identity and insecurity. After discussing Sherman McCoy's attempt to manage a series of troublesome encounters that threatened his sense of control, we turned our attention to management in the context of work organizations. In the second section, we examined the development of the modern organization, focusing on how a bureaucratic ethos displaces traditional values and personal morality. Following this, the contemporary shift towards more flexible, adaptive and organic forms of organization was explored. There we argued that, through an appeal to the identity of the employee, organizations contrive to integrate personal values and organizational goals. Potentially, this reverses the tendency for bureaucracy to divide 'life' or personal morality from the impersonal, instrumental world of work. In practice, however, we argued that the extension of instrumental rationality into the realm of managing values and employee subjectivity may produce cynicism and resigned compliance, if not outright resistance. In the final section, we drew on an example from *Nice Work* to illustrate our conceptual framework for analysing everyday managerial work in the modern organization.

Overall, our analysis can be summarized in terms of three key points. First, in modern work organizations personal morality tends to be squeezed out by instrumental rationality. This was illustrated by the exclusive preoccupation with material self-interest in the exchange between Vic Wilcox and his boss. However, it may also occur in the domestic sphere, as indicated by Sherman McCoy's struggles to suspend his personal morality in *The Bonfire of the Vanities* when devising an elaborate strategy for leaving the apartment in order to phone his mistress. Second, culture prescriptions extend rather than reverse the displacement of personal morality by instrumental rationality. They do so by appealing to, at the same time as exploiting, social identity for organizational purposes. In this process, employees are encouraged to invest their souls in the corporation, much like Stevens did in *The Remains of the Day* when he committed himself wholly to service to his master. The desired effect is to merge personal and corporate identity. Third, despite the domination of instrumental rationality, members of organizations still have personal agendas and values. Relations of power and inequality operate both to impede and to stimulate their development and expression. Certain values (e.g. individualism) and agendas (e.g. career) may be selectively encouraged in so far as they can be exploited for corporate ends, but their manipulation can induce the very resistance that they seek to avoid. In their different ways, Sherman McCoy, Vic Wilcox and Stevens all felt that their ambition, dedication and loyalty had been exploited by their employer and ultimately counted for little. They each had grave misgivings about how they had invested themselves in work. Their employers had exploited their energies and devotion, only to abandon them like expended commodities when they were no longer of use to them.

This was most clearly demonstrated in the case of Sherman McCoy, whose job as a bond salesman typifies the era of advanced capitalism. Sherman worked as a highly rewarded salesman in order to fulfil his fantasy of being, or becoming, 'a Master of the Universe. In this role, he too was a respecter only of performance'.[74] Only later, when he had been dragged through the courts and been a target of media character assassination, did he reflect on his fantasy. No longer striving to 'become someone' who would be admired if not loved, especially by his father, Sherman acknowledges that his identity as 'Sherman McCoy' had become untenable, assuming that it ever was:

> I'm not Sherman McCoy anymore. I'm somebody else without a proper name. I've been that other person ever since the day I was arrested. . . . At first I thought I was still Sherman McCoy, and Sherman McCoy was going through a period of very bad luck. Over the past couple of days, though, I've begun to face up to the truth. I'm somebody else. I'm a different human being. I exist *down here* now . . . if I think I'm above it, I'm only kidding myself.[75]

Sherman had viewed himself as a Master of the Universe and contrived to emulate a lifestyle and to control others, including his wife and daughter, in ways that would confirm this self-image. It is not simply that his arrest and trial were accompanied by a radical change in his social status. More fundamentally, his sense of identity was no longer invested in the project of being recognized as a Master of the Universe. Sherman compares his experience to training a pampered pet to become a vicious watchdog. His self-deception had, as it were, been beaten out of him in much the same way that a watchdog is trained by being chained up and baited so that it 'is ready for the final fight every time it hears a sound'.[76] The ex-bond salesman formally known as Sherman McCoy re-cognizes himself as a pampered pet that had never previously had to confront with sober senses the conditions of his own existence.[77] At the same time, he appreciates how difficult it is for anyone to abandon the illusions and habits of a previous existence. He acknowledges how our sense of personal history can be a serious impediment to change. In contrast to human beings, when a pampered pet is chained and baited, it:

> doesn't cling to the notion that it's a fabulous house pet in some terrific dog show, the way the man does. . . . The dog knows when it's time to turn into an animal and fight.[78]

Facing up to insecurity and relations of power is often very painful and difficult. Efforts to resist these relations repeatedly come up against the structure of the employment relationship where, in western capitalist economies when push comes to shove, the pursuit of profitable growth overrides employee security – as both Sherman McCoy and Vic Wilcox found to their cost. Likewise, in *The Unbearable Lightness of Being*, when Tomas deviated from the norms of the state socialist Czech regime by critically comparing its operation to the tale of Oedipus, and then refusing to retract it, he had little choice but to resign from his job as a surgeon.

Our intention in this book has not been to conclude that management lives are doomed to suffer the gloomy outcomes experienced by almost all these anti-hero characters in the four novels that have been our inspiration in writing this alternative student text. Novels have a tendency to take an extreme path, if only to retain the reader's interest in a world where diverse and continuous images are competing for what would seem to be an ever-diminishing span of consumer attention. Apart from the desire to render learning about management more meaningful and relevant to students' lives, a major concern in writing this book has been to encourage a self-reflexive relationship to both the theory and practice of management. To this end, we have sought to encourage a pedagogy that is critical in respect of process as well as content, thereby facilitating an approach to learning that is more questioning in inspiration and participatory in design.

Accordingly, we hope that the conceptual framework guiding our analysis of management and organization will be taken as a point of departure for discussion that highlights its limitations as well as its benefits, and provokes efforts to move beyond it. Linking the practice of management to the management of everyday life, and vice versa, has been our vehicle and we trust that the journey has been worth while. If we have succeeded, even partially, in showing how the practice and study of management can be no less interesting and challenging than many other seemingly more exciting or glamorous endeavours, then our efforts will not have been in vain.

Notes

1 Wolfe, T. (1988) *The Bonfire of the Vanities*. London: Picador. p. 692.
2 *The Bonfire of the Vanities*, p. 21, emphasis added.
3 *The Bonfire of the Vanities*, p. 20.
4 *The Bonfire of the Vanities*, p. 20.
5 *The Bonfire of the Vanities*, p. 20, emphasis added.
6 *The Bonfire of the Vanities*, p. 21, emphasis added.
7 *The Bonfire of the Vanities*, p. 21.
8 *The Bonfire of the Vanities*, p. 22.
9 *The Bonfire of the Vanities*, p. 22.
10 *The Bonfire of the Vanities*, p. 22.
11 *The Bonfire of the Vanities*, p. 22.
12 *The Bonfire of the Vanities*, p. 20.
13 *The Bonfire of the Vanities*, p. 19.
14 *The Bonfire of the Vanities*, p. 20.
15 Littler, C. (1982) *The Development of the Labour Process in Capitalist Societies*. London: Heinemann.

16 Weber, M. (1978) *Economy and Society*, eds. G. Roth and C. Wittich, 2 vols. Berkeley, CA: University of California Press.

17 Thompson, E.P. (1967) 'Time, work-discipline and industrial capitalism', *Past and Present*, 38: 56–97.

18 Brittan, A. (1969) *The Privatised Worker*. London: Routledge.

19 *Economy and Society*, p. 225.

20 *The Bonfire of the Vanities*, pp. 74–5.

21 Ishiguro, K. (1989) *The Remains of the Day*. London: Faber and Faber. p. 51.

22 *The Remains of the Day*, p. 51.

23 *Economy and Society*, p. 22.

24 *Economy and Society*, p. 26.

25 *The Bonfire of the Vanities*, p. 474.

26 *Economy and Society*, p. 973, emphasis added.

27 *Economy and Society*, p. 26.

28 Taylor, F. (1911) *The Principles of Scientific Management*. New York: Harper.

29 *Economy and Society*, pp. 261–2. Cited in Clegg, S. and Dunkerley, D. (1980) *Class, Organization and Control*. London: Routledge and Kegan Paul, p. 82.

30 *The Remains of the Day*, p. 5.

31 Lodge, D. (1989) *Nice Work*. Harmondsworth: Penguin. p. 143.

32 *Nice Work*, p. 144.

33 *Nice Work*, p. 144.

34 See Roberts, J. (1984) 'The moral character of management practice', *Journal of Management Studies*, 21 (3): 287–302.

35 *The Remains of the Day*, p. 146.

36 *The Remains of the Day*, p. 148.

37 *The Remains of the Day*, p. 148.

38 *The Remains of the Day*, p. 148.

39 *The Remains of the Day*, p. 148.

40 *The Remains of the Day*, p. 148.

41 *The Remains of the Day*, p. 199.

42 *The Remains of the Day*, p. 149.

43 *The Remains of the Day*, p. 149, emphasis added.

44 *The Remains of the Day*, p. 43.

45 *The Remains of the Day*, p. 173.

46 *The Remains of the Day*, pp. 174, 175.

47 Gouldner, A.W. (1954) *Patterns of Industrial Bureaucracy*. New York: Free Press; Gouldner, A.W. (1955) 'Metaphysical pathos and the theory of bureaucracy', *American Political Science Review*, 49: 496–507; Merton, R.K., Gray, A., Hockey, B. and Selvin, H.C. (eds) (1952), *Reader in Bureaucracy*. Glencoe, IL: Free Press.

48 For example, Peters, T.J. and Waterman, R.H. (1982) *In Search of Excellence: Lessons From America's Best-Run Companies*. New York: Harper and Row; Crosby, P.B. (1979) *Quality is Free*. New York: McGraw-Hill.

49 Barnard, C.I. (1936) *The Functions of the Executive*. Cambridge, MA: Harvard University Press.

50 *The Functions of the Executive*, p. 83.

51 *The Functions of the Executive*, p. 83.

52 *In Search of Excellence*, p. 29.

53 Wright Mills, C. (1956) *White Collar*. New York: Oxford University Press.

54 Ouchi, W.G. (1981) *Theory Z: How American Business Can Meet the Japanese Challenge*. New York: Addison-Wesley.

55 Burns, T. and Stalker, G.M. (1961) *The Management of Innovation*, 2nd edn. London: Tavistock. p. 122.

56 *In Search of Excellence*, p. 11, emphasis added.

57 Zuboff, S. (1988) *In the Age of the Smart Machine*. NY: Basic Books.

58 *In search of Excellence*, p. 395.

59 *Economy and Society*.

60 Rose, N. (1989) *Governing the Soul*. London: Tavistock; Willmott, H. (1993) 'Strength is ignorance, slavery is freedom: managing culture in modern organizations', *Journal of Management Studies*, 30 (4): 515–52.

61 Knights, D. and McCabe, D. (1997) 'How would you measure something like that?' Quality in a retail bank', *Journal of Management Studies*, 34 (3): 371–88; Knights, D. and McCabe, D. (1998) 'What happens when the phone goes wild? Staff, stress and spaces for escape in a BPR regime', *Journal of Management Studies*, 35 (1): 163–94.

62 'The moral character of management practice', p. 288.

63 Emphasis in original.

64 *Economy and Society*, p. 26.

65 Kunda, G. (1992) *Engineering Culture*. Philadelphia, PA: Temple University Press.

66 *Nice Work*, p. 88.

67 *Nice Work*, p. 88.

68 *Nice Work*, p. 89.

69 *Nice Work*, p. 89.

70 *Nice Work*, p. 88.

71 *Nice Work*, p. 37.

72 *Nice Work*, p. 37.

73 *Nice Work*, p. 88.

74 *The Bonfire of the Vanities*, p. 74.

75 *The Bonfire of the Vanities*, p. 692.

76 *The Bonfire of the Vanities*, p. 693.

77 cf. Marx, K. and Engels, F. (1967) *Selected Works in One Volume*. London: Lawrence and Wishart.

78 *The Bonfire of the Vanities*, p. 693.

Recommended further reading

The following offer challenging accounts of the changing meaning and contemporary significance of work.

Anthony, P. (1977) *The Ideology of Work*. London: Tavistock.

Berger, P.L., Berger, B. and Kellner, H. (1973) *The Homeless Mind*. Harmondsworth: Penguin.

Giddens, A. (1973) *Capitalism and Modern Social Theory: an Analysis of the Writings of Marx, Durkheim and Weber*. Cambridge: Cambridge University Press.

Grint, K. (1991) *The Sociology of Work*. Cambridge: Polity Press.

Habermas, J. (1984) *The Theory of Communicative Action, Vol. 1: Reason and the Rationalization of Society*. London: Heinemann.

Habermas, J. (1987) *The Theory of Communicative Action, Vol. 2: Lifeworld and System*. London: Heinemann.

Meahim, D. (1976) *Man and Work: Literature and Culture in Industrial Society*. London: Methuen.

Peters, T. (1989) *Thriving on Chaos*. London: Pan.

Vargish, T. (1994) 'The value of humanities in executive development', in H. Tsoukas (ed.), *New Thinking in Organizational Behaviour*. Oxford: Butterworth-Heinemann.

Industry, academia and society

Studies that illuminate the relationships between industry and society and society and academia respectively are as follows.

Alvesson, M. and Willmott, H. (1996) *Making Sense of Management*. London: Sage.

Bauman, Z. (1990) *Thinking Sociologically*. Oxford: Blackwell.

Crook, S., Pakulski, J. and Waters, M. (1992) *Postmodernization: Change in Advanced Society*. London: Sage.

Deetz, S.A. (1992) *Democracy in an Age of Corporate Colonization*. New York: State University of New York.

Douglas, J. (1971) *Understanding Everyday Life*. London: Routledge.

Fineman, S. and Gabriel, I. (1996) *Experiencing Organizations*. London: Sage.

Grint, K. (1995) *Management: a Sociological Introduction*. Cambridge: Polity Press.

Heckscher, C. and Donnellon, A. (eds) (1995) *The Post-Bureaucratic Organization*. Thousand Oaks, CA: Sage.

Jacques, R. (1996) *Manufacturing the Employee*. London: Sage.

Knights, D. and Murray, F. (1994) *Managers Divided*. London: John Wiley.

Knights, D. and Willmott, H. (1999) *The Reengineering Revolution: Critical Studies of Corporate Change*. London: Sage.

Prichard, C. and Willmott, H. (1997) 'Just how managed is the McUniversity?', *Organization Studies*, 18 (2): 287–316.

Reed, M. (1989) *The Sociology of Management*. Brighton: Wheatsheaf/Harvester Press.

Slaughter, S. and Leslie, L. (1997) *Academic Capitalism*. Baltimore: Johns Hopkins University Press.

Watson, T. (1994) *In Search of Management*. London: Routledge.

Wilkinson, A. and Willmott, H. (1994) *Making Quality Critical*. London: Routledge.

References

Barnard, C.I. (1936) *The Functions of the Executive*. Cambridge, MA: Harvard University Press.

Brittan, A. (1969) *The Privatised Worker*. London: Routledge.

Burns, T. and Stalker, G.M. (1961) *The Management of Innovation*, 2nd edn. London: Tavistock.

Clegg, S. and Dunkerley, D. (1980) *Critical Issues in Organisations*. London: Routledge and Kegan Paul.

Crosby, P.B. (1979) *Quality is Free*. New York: McGraw-Hill.

Gouldner, A.W. (1954) *Patterns of Industrial Bureaucracy*. New York: Free Press.

Gouldner, A.W. (1955) 'Metaphysical pathos and the theory of bureaucracy', *American Political Science Review*, 49: 496–507.

Habermas, J. (1984) *The Theory of Communicative Action, Vol. 1: Reason and the Rationalization of Society*. London: Heinemann.

Habermas, J. (1987) *The Theory of Communicative Action, Vol. 2: Lifeworld and System*. London: Heinemann.

Knights, D. and McCabe, D. (1997) 'How would you measure something like that: quality in a retail bank', *Journal of Management Studies*, 34 (3): 371–88.

Knights, D. and McCabe, D. (1998) 'What happens when the phone goes wild? Staff, stress and spaces for escape in a BPR regime', *Journal of Management Studies*, 35 (1): 163–94.

Kunda, G. (1992) *Engineering Culture*. Philadelphia, PA: Temple University Press.
Littler, C. (1982) *The Development of the Labour Process in Capitalist Societies*. London: Heinemann.
Marx, K. and Engels, F. (1967) *Selected Works in One Volume*. London: Lawrence and Wishart.
Merton, R.K., Gray, A., Hockey, B. and Selvin, H.C. (eds) (1952) *Reader in Bureaucracy*. Glencoe, IL: Free Press.
Ouchi, W.G. (1981) *Theory Z: How American Business Can Meet the Japanese Challenge*. New York: Addison-Wesley.
Peters, T. (1989) *Thriving on Chaos*. London: Pan.
Peters, T.J. and Waterman, R.H. (1982) *In Search of Excellence: Lessons from America's Best-run Companies*. New York: Harper and Row.
Roberts, J. (1984) 'The moral character of management practice', *Journal of Management Studies*, 21 (3): 287–302.
Rose, N. (1989) *Governing the Soul*. London: Tavistock.
Thompson, E.P. (1967) 'Time, work-discipline and industrial capitalism', *Past and Present*, 38: 56–97.
Weber, M. (1978) *Economy and Society*, eds G. Roth and C. Wittich, 2 vols. Berkeley, CA: University of California Press.
Wright Mills, C. (1956) *White Collar*. New York: Oxford University Press.
Zuboff, S. (1988) *In the Age of the Smart Machine*. New York: Basic Books.

Appendix A   Synopses of Novels

1 *Nice Work*

This novel explores the different worlds of work experienced by a middle-aged male managing director of a foundry and an attractive, young female academic, who are brought together through a joint industry–university shadow scheme, instigated by the UK government. Vic, a squat, terrier-like man, is an unwilling participant in the shadow scheme, having had it imposed on him by his immediate boss in Midland Amalgamated. Robyn is a specialist in an esoteric (poststructuralist) form of analysis in the English department of the university. She is on a short-term contract and has reluctantly agreed to participate in the shadow scheme in the hope that it will help her to secure the renewal of her contract. So, in different ways, Vic and Robyn are each beholden to those on a higher rung of their respective organizational hierarchies.

The novel compares and contrasts the financial pressures within the private and public sectors during 1980s Britain. At the foundry, Vic has been recently appointed to return it to profit. Against this background, the novel provides deep insights into management and the organization of work in both the factory and the university. In an effort to beat the competition, Vic is set the challenge of weeding out slow workers and reducing the product range. In doing so, he also seeks to train his staff to become more commercial in their outlook and, where funds allow, to substitute capital for labour. For Vic, the imperative is simple – make a standard, quality product at a price for which there is a demand – but achieving this objective is highly stressful. Despite his strong track record and seemingly assured manner, he worries privately about all the elements that can frustrate its realization and wonders, in the small hours, whether life has more to offer.

These doubts grow as Robyn opens his senses to other interests, both sensual and cerebral. Under her influence, he makes changes in the factory, such as insisting on the removal of soft porn pin-ups from the factory floor, which are eventually used to justify his dismissal when the foundry is sold. Similarly, Vic tests Robyn's unexamined faith in the importance of her academic work. Her passion for poststructuralist analysis, her politically correct feminism and her professional views about university work come under intense scrutiny as Vic 'naively' questions their value and sense.

It is through this mutual exploration of each other's worlds that they become emotionally closer to each other than to their respective partners.

Though he lives with his family and sleeps with his wife, Vic's marriage is dead and he has become estranged from his children. Robyn's partner Charles is also an English academic, but elects to leave academia for a job with better pay and prospects in the City. In contrast to Charles, Vic does not view Robyn as a rival. He is also highly attentive to her sexuality. Vic, whose inexperience of women leads him to bully and patronize her initially, repulses Robyn. When he takes her on a factory visit, Vic's treatment of his staff and the narrowness of his interests appall her. Yet, as they get to know each other, frequently crossing swords over values and principles, Robyn grows to admire Vic's gritty determination and his genuine, though highly sceptical, willingness to appreciate her world. Gradually, she finds herself attracted by his raw energy, his directness and also by his innocence. Even though Vic expresses his desire for her in terms that are incoherent from her poststructuralist perspective and politically incorrect from her feminist standpoint, Robyn finds this flattering which, on reflection, she finds amusing but disconcerting.

Through these two main characters, Lodge is thus able to highlight and challenge the taken-for-granted assumptions underlying their respective professional ideologies and the institutions in which they work. Vic envies Robyn's freedom to pursue her academic interests – 'nice work if you can get it', he says. Robyn, on the other hand, envies the obvious value of Vic's work in producing goods that people want and keeping people in work – unlike her esoteric interests, for which 'ninety-nine point nine percent of the population couldn't give a monkey's'.

2 The Unbearable Lightness of Being

Tomas, the hero of Kundera's novel, is a hospital surgeon who lives in Prague in the late 1960s. This was a turbulent period in Czechoslovakia when the Soviet army intervened directly to suppress the liberal uprising against communism headed by Alexander Dubcek. However, Tomas is too preoccupied with his work and a seemingly insatiable desire for promiscuous sex to become involved, except inadvertently, in the struggle against Soviet domination. Tomas is largely estranged from family and community. Divorced seven years ago, and choosing never to see his son again because of the difficulties of transforming court access into an everyday practical reality, Tomas has also been disowned by his parents:

> In practically no time [Tomas] managed to rid himself of wife, son, mother, and father. The only thing they bequeathed to him was a fear of women. Tomas desired but feared them. Needing to create a compromise between fear and desire, he devised what he called 'erotic friendship'.

Tomas's fear of the power of women (e.g. a mother's power to deny love to her child) leads him to favour relations with women in which there are no mutual obligations other than the requirement to fulfil the desire for sexual pleasure. However, a series of coincidences leads Tomas to find himself in a relationship where expectations and obligations extend beyond the bounds of 'erotic friendship' as, despite himself, he becomes drawn into a romantic friendship whose outcome is marriage. However, his compulsive desire for 'erotic friendship' remains. There is then a fundamental conflict between the 'lightness' of (adulterous) promiscuity and the 'weight' of marital obligations. This, and much else in the novel, suggests that Tomas is trapped in a life of sexual conquests; a life that temporarily makes him feel 'free' from the demands of emotional commitment, the weight of responsibility of marriage and the unending duties of the professional.

At first, Tomas rationalizes his infidelities to his wife, Teresa, by telling himself that sex and love need not be synonymous – the implication being that his promiscuity in no way diminishes his love for Teresa. Later, he develops a more sophisticated explanation, or rationalization. The uniqueness of each person, he contends, is accessible only through knowledge of their most intimate expressions where social conventions are momentarily suspended. Tomas understands and justifies sexual intercourse as a search for the unique 'I', that one-millionth 'part dissimilarity' which 'only in sexuality . . . becomes precious because not accessible in public'. It is the small part in another human being that is unimaginable – 'that is, what cannot be guessed at or calculated, what must be unveiled, uncovered, *conquered*' (our emphasis).

While much of Tomas's life is absorbed with fulfilling his sexual desires, as is the case with at least two of the other main characters in the novel, Sabina and Franz, there is a section where moral indignation and political authenticity play a central part. Tomas finds himself under suspicion by the secret police for subversive activity. Rather than cooperate with them and save his professional position as a surgeon with 'good' career prospects, Tomas resigns to take on a job as a window cleaner. This provided him with even greater opportunities for illicit sex with those of his customers who were married women staying at home while their husbands were at work. Kundera draws out the sharp contrast between the deep moral integrity of Tomas's refusal to be complicit with the secret police and his continuous adultery. This and much else in the novel provides us with ideal material to discuss issues of identity and insecurity in Chapter 3.

3   The Remains of the Day

Especially in its Merchant and Ivory film version, *The Remains of the Day* can be seen primarily as a story of romance never consummated. However, the historical, political and social terrain on which the story unfolds contains many insights into issues that are central to our interests in this book. The novel records the historical reminiscences in 1956 of Stevens, who has spent the best part of his life as head butler to Lord Darlington. Stevens narrates the story in the first person as he takes a motoring trip some time after Darlington's death. Rationalized as a well-deserved holiday, the ostensible purpose of Stevens's journey to the West Country was to see whether it might be possible to persuade Miss Kenton to return to Darlington Hall where she had been a housemaid in the 1930s. While this concern to re-employ Miss Kenton could be, and was, justified to his new American master at Darlington Hall on the grounds of a depleted staff, a more fundamental motive for Stevens was to repair a part of his past.

Stevens had several regrets in his life as he reached his twilight years or what might be seen as the 'remains of the day'. One was his sheer devotion and unquestioning loyalty to his master Lord Darlington, who had been vulnerable and naive in accepting much Nazi propaganda and had used his influence in political circles to persuade the British to appease Germany in the interwar years. While regretting his minor part in this unfolding of political events, perhaps Stevens's greatest regret was more personal, in that he had failed to recognize and, more to the point, to reciprocate Miss Kenton's feelings towards him when they had worked together 20 years previously. Both regrets had come about because of a devotion to duty and the insistence that he led by example in refusing to allow personal matters to intervene in the conduct of service work. At the time, of course, he believed that his sacrifice was justified because he was serving a master who was engaged in such noble causes as the affairs of state about which he could not possibly have an understanding. In the event of his master having made the grossest errors of judgement in supporting a fascist Germany, the justification for a life of personal sacrifice no longer existed.

The novel illustrates in graphic detail not only how this domination of work over life can smother the tiniest shoots of human sensuality, but also how the legacy of an aristocratic tradition continued to play an intricate part in British politics long after the rise of democracy. It depicts in great detail the dedicated professionalism of Stevens to a life of service, against the rank amateurism of the aristocratic tradition that continues to seek its influence on world affairs and, in this particular case, at some cost in appeasing fascist leaders in Germany. The insights of the novel into the British aristocracy and the hierarchical relations of status distinction and deference that prevail both between and within the master and servant class are invaluable for our study of power and inequality in Chapter 4.

4 The Bonfire of the Vanities

Set in 1980s New York, this novel explores the fast-living, quick-money, dog-eat-dog world of city slickers, petty criminals, big-time hustlers and a crumbling infrastructure that struggles to stem the tide of decadence and corruption. Published just before the Wall Street crash of 1987, it charts the rise and fall of Sherman McCoy, from highly paid bond salesman living in a lavishly furnished apartment on Park Avenue to 'professional defendant' accused of a hit-and-run, racist killing.

Sherman comes from a modest background but is determined to prove himself – to become a Master of the Universe. He marries well, but he also wants, and feels he deserves, a mistress 'to allow his rogue hormones out for a romp'. Married to an aged Jewish millionaire, who had made his second fortune flying Arabs to Mecca, his mistress Maria is street-wise. It is she who uses and manipulates Sherman, preying on his insecurity and vanity. When collecting her from the airport, Sherman takes a wrong turn off the freeway and winds up in the Bronx, a black ghetto. Driving his Mercedes through its unfamiliar darkened streets, both he and Maria feel intensely threatened. Seeking a way back on to the freeway, they find themselves blocked by an obstruction. Getting out to remove it, Sherman is approached by two black youths who ask him if he needs help. He panics and runs back to the car. Maria takes the wheel and hits one of the youths as they race away.

Police detectives Martin and Goldberg trace the car to Sherman. A dead-beat journalist, eager to revive a flagging career, is given the story. He is happy to sensationalize the incident as a racist attack on a harmless, law-abiding black youth with a promising academic career ahead of him. Black activists capitalize on the story for their own propaganda purposes, as does the district attorney, Weiss, a man with political ambitions. Sherman becomes a political football as this is turned into a racist issue that is intended to mobilize the black vote. When the news breaks, Sherman fails to close a big financial deal as he loses his nerve and his concentration. The other youth at the scene of the accident, a hood, identifies *Sherman* as the driver in order to avoid having to explain away why Sherman had stopped at the barricade with the result that Maria had taken the wheel. When Sherman tells his employer about his position, he is immediately fired in order to protect the name of the firm. The Master of the Universe is shown to be instantly dispensable.

Not only does Sherman lose his job and his family, but his becomes a 'show trial', with orchestrated mass demonstrations outside his apartment. Despite hiring the best lawyer (Killian), Sherman is powerless to stop a campaign that portrays him as the white hit-and-run driver. An attempt to confirm Maria's involvement by taping a meeting with her ends in farce and humiliation when she discovers the bug. But an illegal recording made by the landlord of an apartment rented by Maria, which includes a conversation in which she reveals her involvement, is presented to the court as if Sherman taped it. The prosecution lawyers, Kramer and Fitzgibbon, are flabbergasted by this evidence and the case is adjourned by the judge.

The Bonfire of the Vanities provides dramatic and highly humorous material to illustrate our views about power and inequality in Chapter 4 and our broader concerns in Chapter 5.

Appendix B The Conceptual Framework

The theoretical framework for analysing management and organization in this book has been informed by four major concepts: *identity*, *insecurity*, *power* and *inequality*. In our view, the ideas expressed in our use of these concepts offer a means of making sense of the complexity of social relations without involving excessive simplification on the one hand, or student disorientation because of obscure and esoteric language on the other.

Identity

As a concept, identity draws attention to the importance of our distinctive self-consciousness in producing, understanding and transforming the social and natural world. Although we can never be entirely sure whether other animals (e.g. dolphins) share our 'freedom' to attribute to ourselves and others a socially constructed identity, only if the (aquatic) circus roles were completely reversed would the uniqueness of self-consciousness in human beings be directly challenged.

It is through our self-consciousness that we identify ourselves and are identified by others. Our actions are mediated by this knowledge of ourselves. We are conscious of our-selves as cultural, historical beings, not only as 'natural' beings. Virtually all human processes, even physiological ones, are mediated through our social relations with others. Individual identity is not natural but social: it is a medium as well as an outcome of human history. Identity is, in this sense, always changing despite our best endeavours to render it *stable* and *secure*.

This simple observation has the most profound consequences for understanding almost every aspect of human life. For although our self-conscious, reflexive freedom is the source of creative self- and social development, it is also what makes for possible psychotic or neurotic self- and social destruction. The big issues of world politics (e.g. the threat of a nuclear holocaust, biological or conventional warfare, energy crises, ecological disasters, third world poverty, Aids etc.) reflect this tension between the positive and negative potential of human existence, as does the thin line between genius and madness. The attribution of freedom to human nature may be seen as a pre-scientific, metaphysical assumption.

Individual freedom, and the responsibility associated with it, are more plausibly understood as a 'social fact' created by modern civilizations as a condition of citizenship. In this context, the freedom of the individual is not just a condition and consequence of self-consciousness; it is also, and more significantly, a key articulation as well as a source of legitimization of historically specific, liberal-democratic capitalist regimes.

Regardless of the differential capacities of individuals to purchase goods (market freedom) caused by massive inequalities of wealth, the ideology of individual freedom is elevated to a position of great sanctity in contemporary society. It could be argued that most attributions of freedom are rooted in a metaphysical belief, but some are more sophisticated than others. So, for example, as noted in Chapter 3, behaviourism refuses to explore the 'mind' but remains convinced that individuals can always choose between pleasant and painful stimuli on the basis of their past experience. Underlying the theory is a crude and unquestioned metaphysics of freedom. Symbolic interactionism and phenomenology are more sophisticated in identifying freedom as residing in self-consciousness and the ability for human beings to see themselves as both subjects and objects of their own activities. Only minors, the mentally ill and, to a partial extent, prisoners are absolved from this historical 'fact' of human existence – which is merely another, less contentious, way of saying that 'normal' human beings are free.

This humanistic 'knowledge' of the identity of human beings as free, autonomous agents exerts some powerful effects. As individuals, we are responsible not only for what we become (i.e. our own identity and behaviour) but also for others, in so far as our actions always affect the actions of those with whom we interact. In this sense, human freedom imposes a very considerable burden – experienced as insecurity, anxiety and guilt – from which it is difficult to resist the desire to escape.[a] Our self-conscious freedom can be used positively to expand meaningful relationships, but it can also have the exact opposite effect.

Insecurity

Because identity is a social phenomenon dependent on the evaluations and judgements of large numbers of people, its formation and confirmation cannot readily be controlled. As a consequence, it is frequently a major source of anxiety and insecurity. Indeed, we are all prone to being incapacitated by insecurity and defensiveness, which render us impotent to relate meaningfully to anything except our own neurosis.

---

a   This burden of freedom was an explicit assumption behind most existentialist writings, either in the form of philosophy (Sartre, *Being and Nothingness*), theology (Kierkegaard, *Either/Or*), social philosophy (Fromm, *The Fear of Freedom*) or novels (Sartre, *Nausea*, *The Roads to Freedom*; Camus, *The Outsider* and many others).

In seeking to escape the burden of freedom, individuals are highly vulnerable to mechanisms of power, especially hierarchical and other judgements (e.g. examinations) that separate out the successful from the unsuccessful, and the competent from the incompetent. Consequently, we are all routinely directed towards attempting to secure a position that is less vulnerable to charges of incompetence or to experiences of failure. Yet the paradox is that in order to secure what we think are comparatively secure positions, we are drawn into the lion's den where our competence and success are on the line. Of course, these institutional positions can provide limited degrees of protection, as they give access to material and symbolic resources that others seek. Such control can encourage compliance and even consent from subordinates. But, of course, this is a fragile basis for security, since the cooperation of subordinates may be motivated more by their own ambitions and/or insecurities than by any more than a fleeting and instrumental sense of solidarity or community. There are, of course, numerous ways of becoming 'successful' and 'competent'. But, by definition, the 'success' of the minority is contingent on degrees of 'failure' for the majority. There are numerous ways of becoming successful and competent but, also by definition, a large minority if not majority must fail.

Many find the competition and struggle too much and respond to the burden of freedom by subordinating themselves (i.e. their identities) almost entirely to the expectations of a significant other (e.g. deferential worker, henpecked husband or 'groupie'). An alternative response to failure is to seek to protect oneself from the reality of a lack of success and the indignity of subordination. This can be done through mentally distancing oneself from, or acting indifferently towards, the situations of everyday life, pretending that an inner identity, a private self through which we 'really' live our lives, is thereby preserved. To a large degree, the latter is something of an illusion (albeit perhaps important for maintaining one's sanity in the face of material and symbolic deprivation), since even the most reclusive of hermits cannot ultimately escape the expectations and judgements of others. This is because judgement is an implicit, if not explicit, feature of all human relations, social practices and institutions. There are few occasions when we are not judging or evaluating ourselves and/or being judged by others. Indeed, it is an attempt to escape from being adversely judged that prompts people either to dominate or to subordinate themselves to others.

Domination and subordination are associated with some of the most horrific examples of terror and destruction. The death camps of Nazi Germany and the Gulags of Stalinist USSR are cases in point. Psychologically, the appeal of subordinating the self completely to an other is that it seems to offer the least risky way of gaining confirmation of one's social existence and thereby avoiding the anxiety and insecurity of isolation. Uncritical and unselfconscious investments of identity in institutions and routines are not confined to totalitarian regimes! Insecurities provide a strong motivation for individuals to invest themselves in established and socially legitimized institutions – for example, in the institution of marriage. But, equally, security may be sought in conspicuous, fashionable forms of counterconformity most evident in, for example, youth and other counter-cultures where identity is founded on the negation of conformists as 'straights', 'sheep', 'proles' etc.

Power

In contrast to how the conventional literature often describes it, we argue that power should not be seen as a 'thing' that is possessed by individuals, groups or classes. Nor is power necessarily negative and constraining. Rather, we suggest that power is a relation in which the actions of some people have an effect on the actions of others. The possession of material resources or access to specific knowledge (see the section on inequality below) may facilitate the exercise of power, but only if those over whom power is exercised are tempted by the material rewards offered or have considerable respect for the knowledge surrounding the exercise of power.

As can be seen from the previous section, power and freedom go hand in hand in contemporary society. That is to say, power involves social actions that, often unconsciously, direct the freedom of others towards practices that develop their abilities to exercise power. One example is the examination. As an institutional practice, this consists of a set of norms or expectations and obligations that direct, or exercise power over, students to use their freedom to read, revise, memorize, question spot, and possibly even develop their intellect. Such self-discipline is sustained in the belief/hope that they will advance their own sense of freedom and thereby enhance their ability to exercise power. In a majority of cases, this hope is fulfilled. Yet in the immediacy of student life, forms of assessment such as the examination are frequently seen as a negative constraint on the freedom to pursue more pleasurable activities.

In exercising power, further knowledge is generally produced – such as knowledge of the effects of its exercise. It is this that leads us to say that knowledge is both a medium and an outcome of relations of power – whether this is between the state and the populace, between employers and employees or between men and women. This does not mean that power operates exclusively in one direction. For example, the populace can overthrow its rulers either through a popular uprising or the ballot box, by voting them out of office. Employees often use their practical knowledge of production to exercise power over employers by restricting their output or withholding their full cooperation; and women have developed diverse individual and group strategies for circumventing and deflating male domination. However, it is relevant to note how the exercise of power by subordinates can have the countereffective consequence of reinforcing subordination. This occurs, for example, where employees challenge managerial prerogative, only to find themselves being made redundant. Also, when women challenge the 'head of household' or 'breadwinner' status of men, it often happens that they acquire two full-time jobs – a career in addition to the lioness's share of domestic and child-rearing responsibilities. Moreover, the feminist privileging of a commodified labour model of economic citizenship diminishes the value of domestic labour, thus further eroding the identity of those who choose not to seek paid employment.

Despite almost a century of the women's movement, the exercise of power in contemporary society continues to be gendered and to be patriarchal in character. A limited reflection on our use of language reveals how words can express and institutionalize patriarchal relations of power; the obvious example is the (common-sense) use of the term 'mankind' or 'man' when 'humanity' provides a ready alternative. In using language to describe the world, we actually reflect or reinforce, construct or reconstruct that world – in this example, a world that is male-centric and provides differential resources and privileges for the sexes. The very existence of the feminist movement is at once indicative of – as it seeks to expose, challenge and diminish – patriarchal relations of power in modern society. Moreover, despite legislation (such as the Sex Discrimination Act and the Equal Pay Act in the UK) that provides some support and redress, feminists have secured only comparatively small gains and have precipitated a backlash for their troubles. What most men do not recognize, however, is that their domination is also oppressive to them/ourselves. Very often, men are unable to relate to themselves and others except in a 'cold', disembodied and rational manner. Given that all human beings are emotional and embodied subjects, this overemphasis on 'rationality' impoverishes the 'richness' of human experience.

Inequality

The concept of inequality underscores the importance of differences in possession of, and access to, valued material and symbolic goods (e.g. wealth and expertise) for understanding the organization and management of work. In the absence of reflection on structured inequalities, there is a danger of understanding the behaviour of subordinates in a hierarchy, for example, as an expression of their irrationality, ignorance or incompetence, rather than of their limited access to scarce material and symbolic (e.g. educational) goods. In turn, an attentiveness to structured inequality can prompt reflection on the economic and political principles that underpin reproduction in work organizations and society more broadly. The behaviour of people in organizations is then understood socially and historically, as an articulation of the wider context that is reproduced through their actions.

In capitalist workplaces, for example, inequalities are the product of a range of mechanisms of power (e.g. legal or hierarchical judgements) that express a fundamental (class) antagonism between the demands of capital and the supply of (productive) labour. Reflecting the identity preoccupations of individuals, this antagonism has the effect of reproducing a diverse range of struggles that reflect and reinforce everyday insecurities and tensions. In particular, there are struggles to achieve and maintain a socially acceptable (i.e. materially or symbolically successful), or merely dignified, identity.

Organizations, whether of a national or international character, mirror as well as sustain inequalities, for example of gender, class and race, that are a part of the broader society. Rarely are women, blacks[b] and the children of manual workers represented in the higher echelons of an organization in equal proportions to their membership as a whole, or to general population distributions of these categories of people. Even if they were, this would not in itself indicate the absence of inequality, but rather the presence of a meritocracy of equal opportunity where sex, class and racial discrimination are more or less eradicated; and where, in principle, social inequalities simply reflect and reproduce differential social competencies as judged ordinarily by those who have already been successful against such criteria. However, while meritocratic inequality might secure a greater degree of social legitimacy – since there is a greater acceptance, or common-sense faith, in its fairness within western cultures – there remains the issue of which group determines the skills that are to be most highly prized and rewarded within these societies. This issue cannot be resolved on the basis of merit, only on the exercise of value judgements and/or by political clout.

While there are degrees of meritocracy in our society, inequalities are overlaid by class and compounded by ethnic and other minority inequalities and anxieties, insecurities and tensions associated with sexual relations and gender identities. As indicated earlier, patriarchy embodies a range of power mechanisms and strategies (e.g. the view that men are naturally more capable of undertaking supervisory and managerial roles) that sustain inequalities between men and women. In relation to ethnicity, colonial legacies continue to reinforce mechanisms of power that impede opportunities of ethnic minorities to have an equal chance in defining and securing the nature of scarce material and symbolic goods and values, and these inequalities further encourage the prejudice and discrimination that sustain them.

---

b We are aware that while the term 'black' seemed quite acceptable a decade ago, recently there has been objection to such an all-encompassing category and, for example, the more complex nomenclature 'Asian, black and other minority ethnic' is advocated (Cole, 1993: 672). For reasons of brevity, however, we continue to use the currently less politically correct term.

An illustration

There is a tendency to treat 'racial' inequality and 'discrimination' as if it were a discrete entity unrelated to other issues explored in the study of organization and work. However, it is relevant to link prejudice about different social *identities* (i.e. 'whites' define themselves as different from and as better than 'blacks' or vice versa) to discrimination that is institutionalized as social *inequality* between different 'races' or ethnic groups. This institutionalized inequality denies those on whom it is forced any sense of a dignified *identity* and thereby generates a *symbolic insecurity* that *reinforces material insecurity*. By institutionalized racism is meant the inequality of access experienced by blacks in the labour markets, the housing markets, in healthcare, education etc. In contemporary western societies, most blacks find themselves near the bottom of the heap, and it is the (institutionally racist) actions of the gatekeepers of resources that keep them there. In turn, the actions of these gatekeepers (some of which, as agents of the powerful, may themselves be black) are motivated and certainly legitimized by a concern to avoid a backlash from white employees/customers/houseowners/tenants/parents. Of course, the latter may identify blacks as competitors for scarce resources – a concern that reproduces the inequalities that are a condition and consequence of prejudice and discrimination.

The more privileged members of society bear a considerable burden of responsibility for the presence of institutionalized racism. Historically, the view of blacks as 'primitive' and 'subhuman' was a convenient ideology for their exploitation as slave labour as well as a means of confirming the superiority of European civilization. Currently, a degree of assimilation and solidarity has occurred between 'working-class' people irrespective of their colour. However, major inequalities and forms of social distance continue. Underprivileged white males, in particular, tend to be more (overtly) prejudiced against blacks (and women) than are members of the more affluent middle class. Lacking institutional power, they are more prepared to use the weapons of prejudice and violence to undermine the claim of ethnic minorities to material (e.g. housing) and symbolic (e.g. community membership) resources. They strive to privilege their own identity (as 'true Brits') against others whose skin colour bars them from assuming this identity. Partly in an effort to reduce these social tensions (e.g. on the shopfloor), the gatekeepers develop mechanisms of power that appease the white majority (e.g. discriminatory recruitment and promotion policies) – and thereby compound the grievances felt by ethnic minorities. In response to this unequal treatment, ethnic minorities have developed a variety of more or less 'separatist' counterstrategies, involving a range of political and cultural movements whose concern is to challenge institutionalized racism and protect the heritage and identity of black culture (e.g. Rastafarianism).

Although we have dwelt on the issue of 'race', a similar form of analysis could be applied to 'class', 'gender' and 'disability'. In each case, an attribute of human beings (e.g. their labour, sex or a physical impediment) is selected out for special attention. It is then productive of social divisions that go way beyond any 'natural' endowment such as work competence, the capacity to bear children or the ability to perform physical actions like the majority. These divisions are neither irrelevant nor even marginal for understanding management, work and organization. Even so, as in the case of Vic in *Nice Work*, people are inclined to compartmentalize these issues so that they are viewed as problems for the state, politicians or social workers rather than responsibility of employers, managers or us all.

References

Camus, A. (1976) *The Outsider*. Harmondsworth: Penguin.
Cole, M. (1993) '"Black and ethnic minority" or "Asian, black and other minority ethnic": a further note on nomenclature', *Sociology*, 27 (4): 671–3.
Fromm, E. (1970) *The Fear of Freedom*. London: Routledge Kegan Paul.
Kierkegaard, S. (1949) *Either/Or*. Harmondsworth: Penguin.
Sartre, J.P. (1966) *Being and Nothingness*. New York: Washington Square Books.
Sartre, J.P. (1938) *Nausea*. Harmondsworth: Penguin.
Sartre, J.P. (1945–1949) *The Roads to Freedom*. Harmondsworth: Penguin.

Index